FIELDS

FIELDS

Richard and Nina Muir

MACMILLAN LONDON

Books by Richard Muir

The English Village

Riddles in the British Landscape

The Shell Guide to Reading the Landscape

The Lost Villages of Britain

History from the Air

Visions of the Past (*with Christopher Taylor*)

The National Trust Guide to Prehistoric and Roman Britain (*with Humphrey Welfare*)

A Traveller's History of Britain and Ireland

The Shell Countryside Book (*with Eric Duffey*)

The Shell Guide to Reading the Celtic Landscapes

The National Trust Guide to Dark Age and Medieval Britain

The National Trust Guide to Rivers of Britain (*with Nina Muir*)

Landscape and Nature Photography

Hedgerows (*with Nina Muir*)

Old Yorkshire

The Countryside Encyclopaedia

First published 1989 by
MACMILLAN LONDON LIMITED,
4 Little Essex Street, London WC2R 3LF
and Basingstoke

Associated companies in Auckland, Delhi, Dublin, Gaborone, Hamburg, Harare, Hong Kong, Johannesburg, Kuala Lumpur, Lagos, Manzini, Melbourne, Mexico City, Nairobi, New York, Singapore and Tokyo.

ISBN 0-333-43622-9

A CIP catalogue record for this book is available from the British Library.

Design by Behram Kapadia

Typeset by Bookworm Typesetting
Printed in Hong Kong

CONTENTS

INTRODUCTION

In this book we explore both the history and the wildlife of fields. This is an unusual approach but one which seems rational since the field is a man-made habitat and its animal and plant life is very sensitive to any changes in its cultivation. We have tried to provide a guide to understanding the fieldscape in both its historical and natural contexts. Given that most country rambles partly or entirely take the walker through fields, it is rather surprising that much more popular literature has been devoted to woodland or coastal settings.

Consequently many readers will not appreciate that each period in the

human colonisation of the countryside produced its own field-types, each type adjusted to the agriculture of the times. As a result it is, more often than not, possible to recognise the general age of a particular field-pattern, whether it exists in a living or a fossilised form.

During the last four decades field habitats which were rich in plant and animal life have, so frequently, been replaced by relatively sterile monocultures. The traditional hay meadow, water meadow or cornfield spangled with cornflower, poppy and field marigold is now a rare sight. Increasingly, country-lovers are missing the richness and vitality of the old countrysides, so that when a noted fritillary meadow is open to the public literally hundreds of visitors can be expected, all clamouring to see a scene which their forebears may have regarded as commonplace.

With the wealth of material available, we have stayed true to our title and largely confined our attention to fields, that is, enclosures. We have resisted the temptation to describe the wildlife of unenclosed upland and mountain areas, although open commons were a vital component of medieval and earlier farming systems and so we explore commons in the historical chapters.

Thanks are due to the county record offices of Essex and Nottinghamshire for providing the materials which formed the basis for diagrams, and to those who kindly allowed us to reproduce diagrams and tables.

The hedged landscape of lowland Shropshire as seen from the vantage-point of Nordie Bank hillfort

Field-walls of different types and ages ascending the steep sides of the Ure valley in Wensleydale

CHAPTER 1

THE HUNT FOR ANCIENT FIELDS

Most of the countrysides of Britain are composed of fields. Many of our finest panoramic views are fieldscapes, but how often does one look really closely at a particular field or group of fields? Most of us are shocked and angry when a well-loved scene is suddenly rendered bland and featureless by the grubbing-up of hedgerows or dismantling of walls, but otherwise fields tend to be taken for granted. Even so, each 'living' field has its own history and its ancestors. On any particular piece of land a dozen different fields may have existed successively since the infancy of farming, and sometimes the current or living field may display the shadowy imprints of its forebears. The living field may often be a youngster, less than a couple of centuries old, but evidence is emerging that some still-cultivated fields were created in Roman or Iron Age times, while in some upland areas fossilised fields of the Bronze Age are plainly traced by earthworks of tumbledown walls. Archaeological excavation has exhumed fields of Neolithic age, while each new attempt to expose the secrets of the past adds a little more to our perceptions of former landscapes and helps us to recognise the evidence preserved in the visible countryside.

We will never discover the first field or the first farming family in Britain, and the nature of pioneer farming practice is still a matter for debate. We can be quite sure that farming was not a native invention, for archaeology can demonstrate the inexorable advance of agriculture across Europe from its Middle Eastern homeland to the Channel shores. By about 8000 BC a well-developed system of agriculture, exploiting domesticated strains of wheat and barley, was established on the eastern seaboard of the Mediterranean, in Syria and in Palestine. By 6000 BC the spread of agriculture had spanned the Balkans, while by 5000 BC the farming way of life had advanced to the Low Countries.

At this time Britain supported a Middle Stone Age or Mesolithic population which lived by hunting, fishing and gathering the varied fruit and vegetable resources of the forest. Already man had left his mark on the landscape by deliberately creating clearings in the wildwood and also more extensive hunting ranges on the open upland. These areas supported richer and more varied grazings than did the natural environment, and their open nature also facilitated organised hunting operations. Not all the animals exploited may have been wild, for it is likely that the origins of pastoral farming had already been established with, for example, the systematic culling of herds of semi-domesticated red deer.

Our native fauna and flora contained some of the animals associated with farming – swine, horses and dogs or domesticated wolves; and there were two surviving forms of deer – the red and the roe – and a third, the reindeer, which may have endured in Scotland until the dawn of historical times. There were plenty of edible wild nuts, fruits, shoots and roots to sustain life at the Mesolithic level, but several of the most important products of farming had to be introduced from abroad: sheep, goats and cereals. Wild cattle were present here in the formidable shape of the aurochs, but domesticated cattle must have been another important introduction.

The essential adjuncts to farming must have been brought to Britain around 5000 BC in seaworthy boats, for Britain had been an island for about 2,500 years. As yet we do not know whether the agricultural settlers who brought with them the ideas and means of farming arrived in large numbers and dislodged the indigenous hunters and gatherers from many of the most promising agricultural settings, or whether the newcomers were few and it was the idea of farming that was introduced and then adopted and imitated by the native population. Whatever the truth may be, it is plain that between about 5000 BC and 4500 BC the Mesolithic culture was being replaced by one that was Neolithic: the key characteristic of the Neolithic or New Stone Age culture being the cultivation of the land. Even so, the transition from one manner of living to the other may not have been as abrupt as one might imagine; hunting still played an important rôle in the Neolithic economy, and vast stands of uninterrupted wildwood remained for some time in most regions. All the excavated Neolithic sites in the vicinity of the great stone circle at Avebury in Wiltshire reveal the continuing importance of hunting and gathering, and yield the remains of wild boar, roe and red deer and aurochs as well as the traces of crab apples, hazelnuts and sloes which have been found at several sites. Settlement sites dating from between about 4400 and 4000 BC which have yielded fragments of pottery of the Grimstone/Lyles Hill type, which is thought to be associated with early farming communities, have been found at places as far apart as Shippea Hill in Cambridgeshire and Fochabers in Grampian, yet a typical Mesolithic hunting camp dating from about 4100 BC has been found at Wawcott in Berkshire.

The pioneer farmers must have commenced their labours by creating clearings within the wildwood. Whether such clearings could be regarded as the first fields is debatable. The browsing of growing crops by wild herbivores must have been a constant threat – and even today wild deer cause havoc in some rose gardens. Were the clearings protected by some kind of barrier – like a dead hedge of woven thorns and branches – then they could be thought of as being the first British fields. In fact we know very little about the earliest pioneering phases. It has been argued that the initial stages involved no more than the gathering of leaves as fodder for domesticated animals. It is very probable that the early farmers used trees as indicators of the quality of forest soils. The then widespread but fastidious lime may have been one such tree, while it has been suggested that in Ireland the pioneers sought out pure stands of elm.

The methods of land clearance are also debated. Were large trees 'ringbarked' (by removing a complete ring of bark around the base of the tree) and then left to die? More probably the areas selected for farming were felled and

The clearance of the wildwood to create farmland was made possible by the perfection of the craft of creating axes of polished flint or stone. After agriculture, axe-making was the principal industry of Neolithic Britain. This specimen, found in central Wales, of beautifully speckled stone, was surely a prestige item and would not have been used for mundane tasks

the trunks and branches burned to release a supply of fertilising wood ash. Experimental reconstruction of the practice of felling using Neolithic-type stone axes has shown that the 'primitive' tools were not greatly inferior to modern steel axes and that a Neolithic man might clear a hectare of forest in five weeks. It is possible that the earliest phase of woodland clearance was of the 'slash and burn' type, with clearings being hacked out, the timber burned, the land worked to exhaustion and then abandoned to be recolonised by weeds, shrubs and trees.

If such methods were used, they soon gave way to a more permanent clearance of woodland. The best of the evidence available relating to early farming operations has resulted from the careful analysis of ancient pollen grains, which have tough protective coats and can be preserved for thousands of years in waterlogged conditions. The pollen evidence has revealed a very widespread decline in the elm, which took place about 3700 BC. It is clear that by this time farmers had gained many footholds in Britain, but the significance of the 'Elm Decline' is still much debated. Does it represent an ancient outbreak of Dutch elm disease, the wholesale stripping of leafy branches or bark for fodder, or a very vigorous episode of woodland clearance? The issue is still to be resolved, though it is clear that by this time considerable amounts of land had already been permanently cleared for farming.

Looking backwards from our own troubled standpoint in time, it might seem that the distant days of the Neolithic farmer were a time of innocence, a golden age untroubled by the ecological blights of life today. However, evidence marshalled by the archaeologist A. Whittle paints a rather different picture. By around 3400 BC the Neolithic farmers may have fallen victim to their own success, with overpopulation and an overtaxing of the fragile land resources. In many places it appears that farmland was abandoned and recolonised by woodland, while much cultivated land became permanent pasture. This would reflect a switch in emphasis from cereal cultivation to livestock farming.

Pasture with livestock farming supports far fewer people per unit of area than does land growing cereals, but the grassland is far more productive of humus than is woodland. Consequently it would have seemed rational for the ancient farmers to have adopted a system like the 'up-and-down husbandry' which was popular at the time of the Agricultural Revolution and survives in some places today – growing cereal crops and then allowing the land to recover its fertility as grazed fallow. But any Neolithic farmers attempting to develop such a system may have been frustrated by weaknesses in their technology, for the plough that was generally employed was of the 'ard' type, consisting essentially of a pointed branch – and such a crude implement would not have been able to break up well-established pasture. However, there is also evidence that a more purposeful 'rip ard' was developed, which could rip through the sward. Many of the flint and stone 'axes' that were produced may well have been used not as conventional axes but as ploughshares and mattocks; but, even so, the sod-busting or the stripping of turf could have been a time-consuming operation.

In Britain the Neolithic period lasted for almost 3,000 years, and so it is not surprising that the countrysides passed through several stages of evolution during this time. The evidence for the region around Avebury in Wiltshire has been studied by the archaeologist R. W. Smith. Here the earliest evidence of cereal cultivation so far discovered dates to about 4000 BC, when the clearance of valley woodland was already advanced. The parcels of cleared land were ploughed and then grazed as fallow; rip ards were in use, and stones gathered from the ploughland were dumped at the field-margins. Gradually weed infestation became a problem, and the spread of bracken made it more practical to abandon the bracken-infested lands and break in new ground.

Cultivation expanded outwards from the valleys initially favoured by the farmers, while in the older areas of farming weed growth may have been more of a threat than soil exhaustion, for the development of farming had spelled success for weeds which had not flourished in the shady conditions of the forest. In the

latter part of the Neolithic period there seems to have been a great expansion in pig-keeping, while the raising of sheep declined in importance. Pigs, with their rapid rates of reproduction, may have been needed for periodic feasts associated with the stupendous ritual monuments of the area; but the pig, with its vigorous rooting habit, may have been the only animal capable of countering the spread of bracken.

Normally the evidence of Neolithic cultivation was destroyed by later episodes of ploughing, but it was preserved beneath some of the long-barrow tombs of the Neolithic period. At South Street long barrow, near Avebury, excavators discovered from the buried land-surface that the mound of the tomb was built on bracken-infested pasture, while beneath the pasture an earlier agricultural phase was represented by 'ard marks' – grooves in the bedrock caused by ploughing. Criss-crossing ard marks have also been found beneath the banks of the massive 'henge' monument at Avebury, showing that the land here was farmed prior to the building of the great temple around 2600 BC.

The expansion of agriculture created an enormous demand for stone axes. A small proportion of those produced were splendid prestigious ceremonial objects of unusual size, immaculate finish, or strangely coloured stone, but most were used as felling tools, hoes, mattocks or ploughshares. Flint mines were developed at various south-eastern and East Anglian sites, most notably Grimes

Opposite: The infestation of farmland by bracken appears to have become a major problem for the early farmers and may have been countered by the keeping of pigs to grub up the plants

Below: The land around the remarkable complex of Neolithic monuments at Avebury in Wiltshire was farmed from about 1,500 years before the great stone circles were built

Graves in Norfolk, while tough but workable stones were exploited at a variety of places in the west and north. It has recently been estimated (from an evaluation of waste debris) that just one of the scores of 'axe factory' sites in Cumbria's Langdale Pikes produced between 45,000 and 75,000 stone axes.

It is easier to sketch the outlines of Neolithic farming than it is to discover the fields. We have seen that the balance between pastoral and arable farming fluctuated during the course of the period but, even so, the farming was essentially of the mixed variety, with hunting often still playing a significant rôle. In any well-developed system of mixed farming there must be fields or enclosures to prevent the horn from devouring the corn. Also, with the increase in population, territorial and property boundaries will have become important. Yet the evidence of Neolithic fields is not easily obtained. Air photographs reveal ancient field-patterns discerned as belonging to the age of Iron, Bronze or Stone. Moreover, the older a field-relic is, the greater the likelihood that it would be destroyed by subsequent farming operations or obliterated by natural erosion and deposition.

The survival and discovery of a pattern of Neolithic fields would obviously require a remarkably favourable juxtaposition of circumstances, but occasionally in archaeology features survive in a much better state of preservation than anyone is entitled to expect. Such is the case with the ancient fields revealed at several locations in County Mayo, where the stone-walled enclosures were later sealed beneath a thick accumulation of peat. Local farmers digging the peat near Behy discovered a hollow which was in fact part of a Neolithic tomb – and decided that the hole was an excellent situation in which to set up an illicit whiskey-still. Eventually archaeologists heard of the site, and in 1962–3 they excavated what proved to be a most unusual monument which combined elements of both English and Irish features of megalithic tomb design and was dated to about 3000 BC. More interestingly, it was realised that stone field-walls ran out from the tomb beneath the man-high accumulation of peat and appeared to be contemporary with the tomb. It was also realised that several other groups of ancient walled fields were entombed by peat at other locations in County Mayo.

The walled fields tend to be fairly small, around 3–4 acres (1.5 hectares) in extent, and roughly rectangular in shape, though the enclosures around the Behy tomb were about 6 acres (2.4 hectares) in area. Excavations in a Neolithic field at Belberg, a few miles to the west of Behy, revealed an episode of criss-cross ploughing using an ard which had been followed by a later phase of spade cultivation that had produced cultivation ridges which corrugated the field-surface to produce 'lazy beds'. At Carrownaglogh, also in County Mayo, lazy beds arranged in 'fishbone' patterns were discovered.

In Britain various excavations have revealed traces of field-boundaries of Neolithic date in the form of possible fence-lines or ditches (which may quite probably have been accompanied by hedgerows). However, nothing as spectacular as the ancient fields of County Mayo has been discovered. Nevertheless, the British legacy of Bronze Age field-relics is remarkable. The most extensive and complete network of field and territorial boundaries is displayed across vast expanses of Dartmoor, where many of the old field-boundary walls or 'reaves' are plainly visible to the discerning rambler. Their current name comes from the Old English raew, meaning 'a row'.

In recent years the Dartmoor reaves have been subjected to expert scrutiny, although it was only in the late 1960s that the nature of the reaves was recognised and the archaeologists were able to claim that Dartmoor displays one of the most complete prehistoric landscapes and the most extensive system of ancient field and territorial boundaries in Europe. According to the archaeologist Andrew Fleming, most of the boundaries on Dartmoor were laid out in response to a single decision taken around 1700–1600 BC. Various communities were established around the margins of the moor, each community occupying a territory which was about 2–2½ miles (3–4 kilometres) in breadth and sometimes covering over 2,500 acres (1,000 hectares) in area. The largest unit, around Rippon Tor, measured about 4 miles by 4 miles (6 kilometres by 6 kilometres) and covered 8,150 acres (3,300 hectares), while on Dartmoor as a whole over 125 miles (200 kilometres) of reaves have been recognised. The effect of the partitioning of the moor was to create about ten units, each including valley and slope terrain as well as an expanse of open moorland, which seems to have been grazed as a common.

The reaves seem to be of two main types: first, those which run for long distances across country, often following ridges or marking the upper limits of

Ancient field-walls of great slabs of moorstone pattern the countryside like dragon's teeth at Kestor on Dartmoor

17

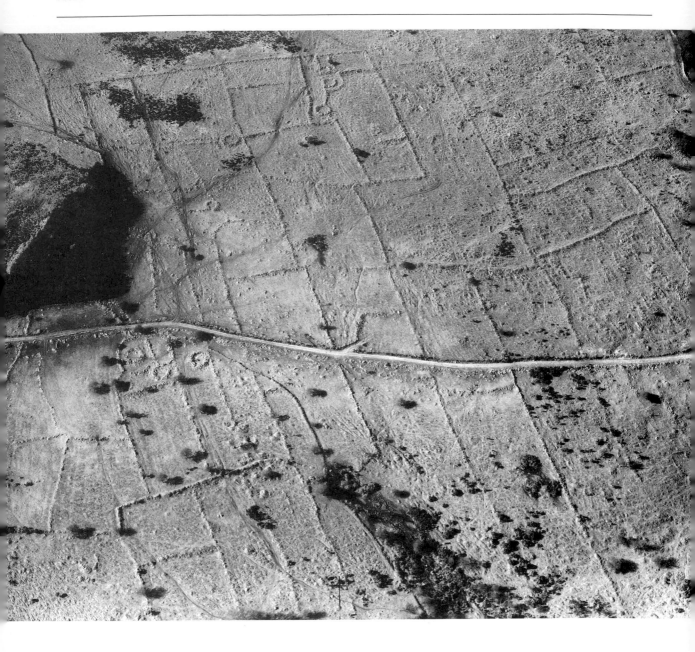

Fossilised Bronze Age fields defined by reaves at Ilsington, Devon

cultivable land, with this type of reave seeming to have the function of dividing Dartmoor into territories; second, running down more or less at right angles from the 'cross country reaves', are systems of 'parallel reaves' which subdivide the territories into long ribbons of land. Individual fields are created by short lengths of wall which run between adjacent parallel reaves to create roughly rectangular enclosures.

Although a few cross-ridge reaves may be earlier, the main period of reave-building seems to have spanned only two or three centuries and much of the system seems to have been built by gangs or teams of workers. This work, it is argued, seems to have resulted from a single decision, the effect of which was to divide the moor into territorial packages subdivided by the parallel reaves and short linking walls into fields, while the upland area above the reaves seems to have served as common grazing land shared by the bordering communities.

Today the reaves are very conspicuous when seen from the air but are most visible from the ground under conditions of low sunlight and light snow-cover. Good views of parallel systems can be seen on either side of the River Dart, below Dartmeet. While today the reaves appear as low tumbled banks of earth and stone, during the Bronze Age it is probable that they existed as hedgebanks and may have looked very much like the splendid living hedgebanks seen in many of the countrysides which border the Dartmoor National Park. Later in the Bronze Age a deterioration in climate led to waterlogging of the ground and the spread of peat, causing the abandonment of Dartmoor and consequently the preservation of a remarkable Bronze Age landscape of fields, boundaries, dwellings and small settlements (the numerous impressive round barrows and stone rows of the moor belonging to a phase of Bronze Age occupation which preceded the reorganisation of the countryside by the reave-builders).

While the Bronze Age field systems on Dartmoor are often masked by the moorland, systems of Bronze Age fields and dwellings are very obvious in the closely grazed pastures on the flanks of Rough Tor in Cornwall. On the north-western flanks of Little Rough Tor are 'clearance cairns' composed of piles of granite or 'moorstone' boulders or of surface stones collected during the initial clearance of the pasture, and these cairns are linked by stretches of drystone walls to create enclosures. Also present are small rings of stone, which are the ruined walls of circular Bronze Age dwellings. These are plainly displayed on the south-western slopes of Rough Tor, and the 'hut circles' are often surrounded by small oval enclosures which are linked by field-walls punctuated by clearance cairns. The Rough Tor community were pastoralists, but tin-working may have played a part in their economy as tin gravels occur close to their settlement.

Both the Dartmoor and the Rough Tor communities were eventually evicted by the effects of the decaying climate, which affected the south-western moors very severely. Conditions were different on the other side of Britain, where excavations at the Fen-edge site at Fengate, near Peterborough, have revealed evidence of Bronze Age fields and farming. Here, during a phase of expansion which ran from just before 2000 BC to about 1000 BC, the land was partitioned by field-ditches into long strips or ribbons of territory which were about 55–165 yards (50–150 metres) in width and which were usually separated by droveways. These ribbons were orientated to run inland from the Fens in a north-west–south-east direction and were subdivided by less impressive ditches to create fields and paddocks of various sizes. The excavator, Francis Pryor, reports that: 'It seems probable that the main northwest–southeast elements were laid out first and that the strips were subdivided later, according to local need. We may suppose that the strips formed the basic unit of land tenure and the pattern of development represented by the subdivisions might indicate the slightly different practices of, for example, different families.'

Although the physical environments were quite different, it is difficult to overlook the similarities between the long ditch-girt strips of Fengate and the areas of land defined by parallel reaves on Dartmoor. In fact this form of land-division occurs again and again in explorations of Bronze Age and later field-patterns. It does not accord with any vision of isolated pioneering farming families clearing patches of wilderness in isolation but, rather, it gives the impression of the organised allocation or reallocation of land on a grand scale. Powerful decision-makers and far-reaching planning of the countryside are implied; in fact at first the Fengate experts, seeing air photographs of the area to be excavated, thought that the straightness and regular spacing of the long field-ditches favoured a Roman rather than a Bronze Age interpretation. In due course enormous lengths of field-ditches were excavated, producing materials giving radiocarbon dates which ranged from 2000 to 1000 BC. In three places human burials were found, the corpses being placed in crouched positions in the bottom of the open ditches. It has long been realised that barrow burial was reserved for a special élite in Bronze Age society, and these discoveries suggest how the common folk of the time may have been laid to rest. In Britain today most field-ditches run beside hedgerows, and in the Fengate excavations it was found that a short section of Bronze Age ditch had been protected from later destruction by ploughing beneath the protection provided by a Roman road known as the Fen Causeway. Here the remains of the ditch-side bank, which was presumably a hedgebank, were preserved. Along with the current interpretation of the Dartmoor reaves as hedgebanks, here was further evidence that much of the agricultural landscape of Bronze Age Britain was partitioned by hedgerows.

Around 1000 BC the increased wetness of the climate, which had already caused a depopulation of the south-western moors, resulted in the demise of the Fengate field system, with periodic flooding, the breakdown of the land's natural drainage system and, consequently, the loss of reliable summer grazings in the nearby Fen.

The chalk downs of East Sussex present an environment which is quite different from those of Dartmoor and Fengate, and at the Black Patch site archaeologists have explored a Bronze Age settlement dating from about 1300 to 900 BC. Here the circular thatched huts with low walls of flints were set within a system of rectangular fields and were overlooked by old round barrows. A careful examination of the evidence allowed the archaeologist Peter Drewett to postulate a calendar of the economic activities and food consumption at similar downland settlements of the period (see p. 22).

Prehistoric fields can be detected in a variety of ways: by excavation, by aerial photography, or from surviving walls or earthworks which are visible to the non-specialist rambler. The term 'Celtic' fields has unfortunately been applied to systems of smallish, square or rectangular fields which were associated with arable farming. The label is unfortunate because several of the systems are known to be much older than the settlement in Britain of any Iron Age Celts, and such settlement could in any event have been relatively light and localised. It is rather like calling all chariots 'Roman chariots' even though Romans were not their main or original users. To survive as visible earthworks the 'Celtic' fields have had to escape any subsequent episodes of ploughing, for such ploughing would soon level the boundary banks and scarps. Consequently they have only survived in areas like the chalk downlands of Wessex and the

Opposite: The ruins of Bronze Age dwellings and field-walls pattern the slopes of Rough Tor on Bodmin Moor in Cornwall

Calendar of Economic Activities and Food Eaten at Downland Settlements

Months	Activities	Foods eaten
March	Plant crops – barley, wheat Feed animals on stored hay	Stored grains
April–May	Weed crops, plant more crops Trips into Weald to collect resources and provide woodland forage for pigs	Stored grains Wild plants and animals
June–July	Haymaking, weed crops Animals to lowland pasture Shear sheep	Stored grains Wild plants and shellfish
August	Harvest crops, thresh crops, dry crops for storage	Grain for bread, porridge, etc. Wild plants
September	Collect nuts, berries Animals grazing over fields Local and regional exchange Build new huts	Grain for bread, porridge, etc. Blackberries, hazel nuts
October	Break up soil for next year's crops, lay out new fields, repair fences	Stored grains, hazel nuts Mutton, beef
November– February	Collect shellfish Feed animals on stored hay Extensive movement of animals around all available pasture Main period of craft activities: weaving, potting, leather and woodworking.	Stored grains, shellfish Wild animals Mutton, beef

Source: Peter Drewett, 'Later Bronze Age Downland Economy and Excavations at Black Patch, East Sussex', *Proceedings of the Prehistoric Society*, vol. 48 (1982), p. 397.

limestone uplands of northern England – terrain considered too marginal to be cultivated in later ages.

'Celtic' fields were the creation of ploughing using a single crook ard or a more advanced beam ard, which had an arrow-shaped ploughshare. Such ploughing involved tilling the land twice, the second ploughing being at right angles to the first, with such a technique favouring the adoption of a square or rectangular field-shape. The small size of 'Celtic' fields, which are usually between ½ and 1 acre (0.2 and 0.4 hectare) in area, is probably explained by the limitations of the ploughing technology. It is estimated that a typical Celtic field of 1 acre (0.4 hectare) in area would have been cross-ploughed in about eight hours by a plough team drawing an ard, so that the typical field would roughly represent the amount of land that could be tilled in a day. 'Celtic' fields

have survived on upland slopes, where they tend to give the slopes a somewhat stepped appearance. At the uppermost end of a field the plough would bite into the slope, eventually creating a step or 'negative lynchet'. Rain would gradually wash ploughsoil down where it would accumulate as a 'positive lynchet' at the lower margin of the field, so that each lynchet bank at the upper and lower edges of the field combined a negative and positive component. Such lynchets can survive as scarcely perceptible steps or massive earthworks much higher than a man. The sides of the fields are also marked by lynchets, though these are normally much less pronounced than those at the upper and lower limits. Tethered animals might have grazed on the lynchet banks.

The age of a particular set of 'Celtic' fields can be difficult to deduce, and some systems will have been in use for hundreds or even thousands of years. Some evidence can be gained from analysing pottery which accumulated in the ploughsoil when the fields were in use. Dung from animals folded beside the farmstead would be collected for use in manuring the arable fields, while broken household pots would be dumped on the dung-heap and spread on the land in the course of manuring. Examination of pottery fragments and the relationships between field and ancient monuments, like Bronze Age round barrows, suggests that some systems of 'Celtic' fields were introduced in the early Bronze Age, before 2000 BC, while some were still being used at the time of the retreat of Roman power from Britain in AD 410

Many of the 'Celtic' field systems in Wessex have been destroyed by recent ploughing. Some fragments survive, as here near Littlebredy in Dorset

23

Above One of the finest expanses of 'Celtic' fields lies above Grassington in Wharfdale
Left: Some of the Grassington ancient fields survive as lynchet bound enclosures; the outlines of others are traced by tumbled limestone walls

Below: On the slopes high above Grassington, Iron Age and Romano-British peasants farmed land which sometimes now exists as impoverished limestone pavement

Excavations of lynchets suggest that in some cases low stone walls were originally used to define the outlines of 'Celtic' fields. On Fyfield Down, in Wiltshire, for example, slabs of sarsen stone were smashed up to provide walling materials, and such walls could be engulfed by soil as lynchets developed, though on Overton Down nearby it appears that some similar walls were constructed yet the plots which they defined were never developed as arable fields. Fyfield Down has also produced evidence of fencing being used to demarcate the field-boundaries, though in some other cases there is no evidence of any original field-boundaries buried beneath the lynchet banks. The Dartmoor reaves were probably hedgebanks, and it would seem reasonable to guess that some 'Celtic' field systems were also hedged. Hedgerows would certainly have helped to stabilise the downslope drift of ploughsoil, and this would lead eventually to the accumulation of massive positive lynchets of soil around the foot of the hedges.

Because 'Celtic' fields have only been able to survive on land which was deemed too marginal to merit arable cultivation in all later ages, they do not necessarily provide us with a picture of the types of field favoured on lower, flatter and more productive ground, where archaeologists have identified much evidence of ditch-girt enclosures (which are likely to have been hedged as well as ditched). One final feature of 'Celtic' fields, which often emerges clearly in air-photograph evidence, is the fact that, although some small groupings occurred, most of the fields were components of extensive systems of land allocation which appear to result from important decisions about the organisation of farming over an extensive area. One network in Dorset has been recognised as extending across some 900 acres (about 364 hectares) of land and was probably larger still; a system on Nutwood Down in Berkshire has been traced over an area of 1,050 acres (425 hectares); and that on Fyfield Down covered at least 280 acres (113 hectares).

Until quite recently 'Celtic' fields were an important and fascinating feature of the visible landscape of the Wessex downs. Sadly, during the postwar period British and Common Agricultural Policy (CAP) farming subsidies have encouraged the ploughing-up of old downland pastures, so that the taxpayers have underwritten the wholesale destruction of rich and beautiful plant communities and extensive systems of ancient fields. Isolated groups of 'Celtic' fields survive in a few localities like the Valley of Stones, near the Hardy monument in Dorset, though now the best surviving system of these fields is seen far away to the north on the upland limestone pastures above Grassington in Wharfedale. Back in Wessex, vandalised 'Celtic' field systems can be recognised not as earthworks but as soil marks in newly ploughed fields.

'Celtic' fields were the product of arable farming – or, rather, a mixed farming system in which the arable fields would presumably have been fallowed with livestock being folded on the fallow grazings. Some of the areas associated with 'Celtic' fields have also presented evidence of a different and, it is assumed, more pastoral bias in farming in the form of great blocks of land defined by banks and ditches or 'ranch boundaries'. The ranch boundaries are thought to date from the middle or later part of the Bronze Age, from the centuries around 1500 BC. In some cases they sliced across existing systems of 'Celtic' fields, indicating a forceful reorganisation of farming. On Martin Down in Hampshire, for example, a long ranch boundary dating from the closing centuries of the second millennium BC was driven across a set of arable fields. Where ranch boundaries have been recognised, they are presumed to indicate an enforced switch from mixed farming to livestock ranching. The boundaries seem to have defined the extent of vast ranching territories which might be around 4 square miles (10 square kilometres) in area, and a ranch territory of about 8 square miles (40 square kilometres) existed on the Dorset–Hampshire border. It has been estimated that in Hampshire alone some 500 miles (800 kilometres) of ranch boundaries were constructed, and individual examples could be up to 5 miles (8 kilometres) in length. It seems quite likely that the ranch boundaries were hedged to enhance their stock-proof qualities, although their original dimensions were quite impressive, the ditches being up to 10 feet (3 metres) in depth and up to 20 feet (6 metres) in width, with the upcast material from the ditch being used to build the adjacent bank.

Although most ranch boundaries seem to pre-date hillforts of the late Bronze and Iron Ages, a system of ranch boundaries radiates outwards from Segsbury hillfort in Berkshire, and it has been suggested that this citadel commanded the ranch territories below. The boundaries can only represent a forceful reorganisation of land-use imposed by powerful authorities – presumably chieftains. The confrontation between humble communities of sod-busters and powerful ranchers is a favourite theme in Western movies, while in historical times peasant communities have been uprooted to make way for sheep-ranges by Norman monastic interests, Tudor landowners and, most recently, by the eighteenth- and nineteenth-century owners of estates in the Scottish Highlands. In Bronze Age Wessex, and possibly elsewhere, the switch from mixed farming to ranching must have imposed severe disruption and, perhaps, hardship on the farming communities concerned, but we cannot yet discover the causes and details of the changes.

Even so, it would be wrong to see the farmers (peasant tenants?) who worked the 'Celtic' fields as pioneer farmers and individualists in the sod-buster mould. It is clear that most of the 'Celtic' field systems were themselves usually the products of a centralised and far-reaching reorganisation of the countryside. Indeed, when we look at the evidence relating to the field systems of the ages of Bronze and Iron (the Neolithic evidence being too skimpy to support generalisations) we do not seem to be encountering evidence of disorganised pioneer farming activity accomplished by individual families. Instead we encounter convincing evidence of the wholesale organisation of extensive farming territories, and it is not unreasonable to presume that powerful chieftains and their agents were responsible for planning the outlines of farming and superimposing their decisions upon the landscape. This is certainly the impression gained from the study of the Dartmoor reaves, the Fengate excavations and most 'Celtic' field systems, and it is also the impression suggested by the partially surviving (Iron Age?) field-networks introduced later in this chapter.

Where all visible surface relics of ancient farming patterns have been obliterated, aerial photography may often be able to reveal the long-lost fields. The evidence comes in the form of 'crop marks'. These are frequently produced when plants growing above buried field-ditches flourish and grow a little taller than the adjacent crop. As a result they cast shadows upon their neighbours,

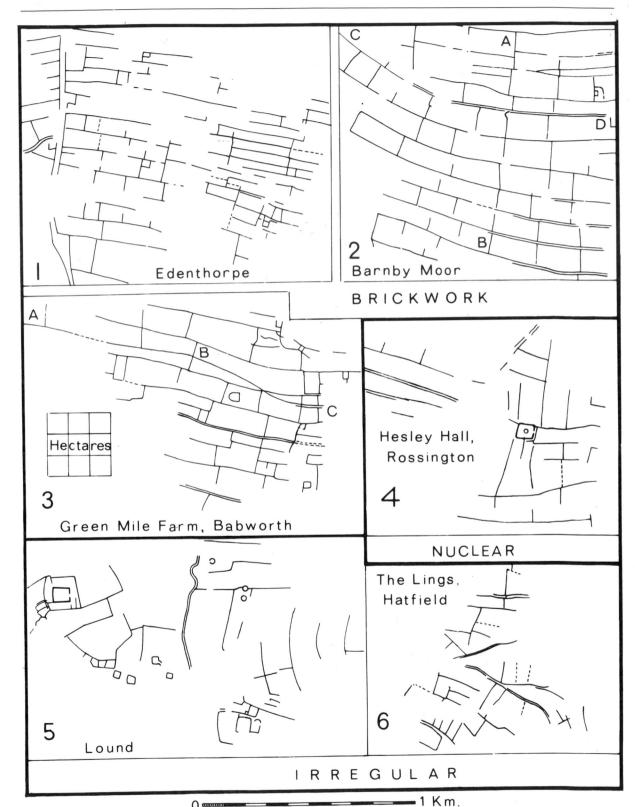

1 Edenthorpe

2 Barnby Moor

C A

D

B

BRICKWORK

A

B

C

Hectares

3

Green Mile Farm, Babworth

4

Hesley Hall, Rossington

NUCLEAR

5

Lound

6

The Lings, Hatfield

IRREGULAR

0 —————— 1 Km.

Examples of brickwork, nuclear and irregular plan fields

and the shadows are longest and clearest when the sun is low in the sky. When viewed from the air such crop marks may reveal the outlines of a fossil field system very plainly, though they do not necessarily indicate its age. Soils developed upon the Bunter sandstone of south Yorkshire and north Nottinghamshire are sandy and are associated with particularly fine crop marks, and this area has been photographed assiduously by the aerial archaeologist D. N. Riley. He has recognised three different types of fossil field-pattern, which he terms 'nuclear', 'irregular' and 'brickwork'.

The nuclear fields are uncommon and are in each case associated with a central nucleus. The nucleus would almost certainly be a farmstead, with its surrounding fields forming a patchwork pattern. Irregular field-patterns were also uncommon and localised, and occurred upon pockets of low and riverside land. In contrast, the brickwork pattern, with the field-ditches resembling the joints in a brick wall, is extremely widespread. The brickwork-pattern fields are, like the others that we have described, the results of planning on an extensive scale. The networks were formed by creating long parallel ditches which were dug about 165–325 feet (50–100 metres) apart and frequently orientated at right angles to the rivers. The long ribbons of land between the parallel ditches were then divided into fields which ranged in size from 1 to 7 acres (0.5 to 3 hectares) by numerous cross-ditches which ran directly between the parallel ditches. The date of these field-patterns is uncertain, but is certainly pre-Roman since the Roman road from Lincoln to Doncaster was superimposed upon the existing field-networks, while Romano-British pottery which has been discovered in some of the old field-ditches shows that the fields were still in use during the third century AD.

So far we have only explored the evidence of fossilised fields, long-abandoned relics of prehistoric farming which exist as crop marks, as eroded walls and hedgebanks, as earthworks, or as buried features which can only be observed during archaeological excavations. Until quite recently nobody would have imagined that Iron Age or Roman fields could actually survive as living entities into the nineteenth or twentieth century. In fact the simple technique which could be applied to explore this question was described a century ago by the famous pioneering archaeologist Flinders Petrie. He realised that if a road slices across a pattern of fields without regard for the integrity of the pattern, so that fields along the routeway are sliced in two and awkward little triangular enclosures are left stranded and separated from their parent fields by the thoroughfare, then the road can only be younger than the field that it has been superimposed upon. The logic of the argument is quite clear, but readers can check its validity by looking at the relationships between field-patterns and younger railways or new main roads or motorways. On the other hand, if a road conforms to the outlines of the fields through which it passes, it must be older than or contemporaneous with the fields which border it.

In Britain most important Roman roads were built during an early stage of the occupation. They were intended primarily to serve military purposes, allowing troops to move quickly to suppress insurrections and facilitating the provision of supplies and reinforcements to legions engaged in the conquest and pacification of frontier zones. And so it follows that any system of fields which is cut across by a Roman road that does not respect the field-shapes and

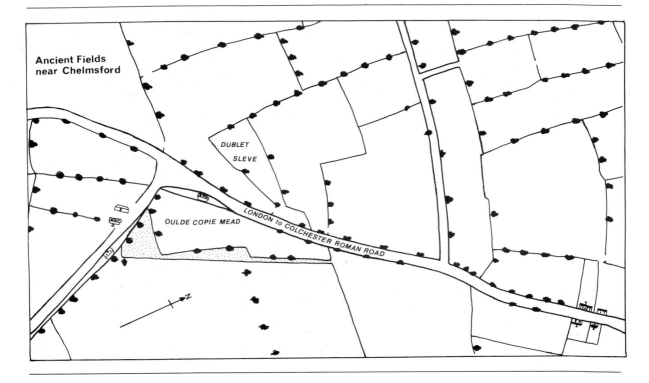

ANCIENT FIELDS NEAR CHELMSFORD

When this map of the Moulsham locality, near Chelmsford in Essex, was drawn in 1591 the fields shown were already at least 1,500 years old, possibly far older still. The archaeologists P. J. Drury and Warwick Rodwell noted that here the London-to-Colchester Roman road appeared to have been superimposed upon an ancient network of fields. The network of small fields is orientated roughly north to south, and the building of the Roman road orientated south-west to north-east cut across the corner of several fields. Our investigations show how the fields called Doublet Sleave and Ould Copie Mead have awkward irregular shapes and contain parts of older fields which were bisected when the road was introduced. When the map was drawn an attempt had recently been made to make Ould Copie Mead more regular, and the 'new enlargement' (stippled) had been added. 'Doublet Sleave' is an imaginative field-name which described the unusual shape of this field. These fields are now overwhelmed by the expansion of Chelmsford.

boundaries must almost certainly pre-date the Roman landings in Britain in AD 43 – and so be prehistoric. The simple road-and-field concept has recently been enhanced by the development of a concept of 'topographical analysis'. This generally involves taking an oldish but reliable and detailed map – like the tithe-apportionment maps of the 1830s and 1840s – and progressively removing all datable features. Thus turnpike roads, Parliamentary Enclosure field-patterns and enclosure roads of the eighteenth and nineteenth centuries would be removed, and then medieval features like open-field systems, deer parks and moated homesteads would be eliminated, leaving a residue of old but undatable features. By applying such techniques, several modern landscape historians have been able to recognise elements in the fieldscapes of the nineteenth and twentieth centuries which pre-date the construction of Roman roads and which must belong to an earlier, prehistoric age of farming.

0   m   200

Much of the most fascinating research has been accomplished in East Anglia and Essex, agricultural regions in eastern England where the survival of ancient countryside features might not have been expected. In 1978, P. J. Drury and Warwick Rodwell described how in the Chelmer valley at Little Waltham the Roman road to Braintree cuts diagonally across a system of fields, some of these still of the 'living' type, with a similar system surviving around Braintree.

In the mid-1980s Tom Williamson applied topographical analysis to a large block of territory in the Scole–Dickleburgh area of southern Norfolk, an area crossed by a Roman road known as the Pye Road. It emerged that this road had been superimposed upon a vast system of older fields. These fields shared a common orientation and were divided into blocks by parallel lanes which were aligned slightly to the west of north. Dr Williamson had in fact rediscovered a prehistoric 'coaxial' field system quite comparable to the coaxial systems of commonly orientated fields described in County Mayo, Dartmoor, Fengate, north Nottinghamshire and southern Yorkshire. Of course, the difference between the Scole–Dickleburgh fields and the remainder is that fragments of the prehistoric fieldscape of Norfolk still survived in living field-boundaries. Before the modern blight of hedgerow removal and the creation of prairie fields, more substantial components of the ancient system survived and they were portrayed on the nineteenth-century tithe maps. It is estimated that originally the field system extended across an area of at least 14 square miles (35 square kilometres), making it larger than the Bronze Age system recognised in the

Dr Williamson's maps showing a Roman road, the Pye Road, superimposed on an older network of fields at Yaxley in Suffolk. The fields are drawn from the Tythe map of 1839 when they were still largely intact

Rippon Tor area of Dartmoor and consequently the largest network of prehistoric coaxial fields so far recognised in Britain. The actual date of the system is still uncertain, but it mainly covers areas of sticky boulder clay soils which may not have been colonised effectively until the Iron Age. As work on the patterns proceeds, a clearer picture of Iron Age Norfolk is beginning to emerge. It is one of vast open hedge-girt commons hemmed around by extensive networks of coaxial fields and with parallel drove-roads following the grain of the field-patterns to give access to the commons.

Dr Williamson has recognised several prehistoric and later coaxial field systems in East Anglia, and meanwhile Stephen Bassett applied topographical analysis to a study of the area around the deserted medieval village of Goltho in Lincolnshire. Here it was found that a Roman road had similarly been superimposed across a system of coaxial fields. So far very few areas of Britain have been subjected to such an analysis, and much more is still to be learned about the survival of prehistoric patterns of fields. Readers who are interested in local history could compare field-patterns recorded on tithe maps or first editions of the Ordnance Survey Six-Inch Survey maps of the nineteenth century with Roman roads to see if the roads conform to the field-patterns or are 'nonconformist' and therefore later additions to the countryside. We would be keen to learn of any unconformities discovered in this way.

Although much is still to be learned about prehistoric fields, the recent discoveries which we have described do allow us to generalise about their characteristics. From late Neolithic or early Bronze Age times until the end of the prehistoric era most fields created existed as components of extensive and sometimes vast systems of coaxial fields, so that field-boundaries shared common orientations across wide areas of countryside. Frequently the field-networks were produced by constructing great lengths of parallel ditch, bank, wall or hedgebank boundaries and then subdividing the ribbons of land between these boundaries with numerous short lengths of cross-boundaries to produce small or smallish square or rectangular fields. The field systems of this type could not have been created spontaneously and sporadically by individual peasant farmers but can only have been imposed upon the countryside by leaders who had the power and resources to accomplish far-reaching transformations of agricultural life across areas which were often several or many square miles in area. Such visions of the ancient past will certainly surprise all those who imagined that prehistoric communities were small, isolated, parochial and dwarfed by the forces of the natural environment, but the emerging evidence is consistent and open to no other interpretation.

The prehistoric period ended with the conquest of England, Wales and southern Scotland which followed the landing of the legions of Emperor Claudius in AD 43. Political and economic life was transformed, roads, military bases and towns appeared, and the most productive and secure countrysides witnessed the establishment of villa-centred farming. Even so, the Romans do not appear to have attempted to reorganise the field-patterns of Britain as they did in some other parts of their empire, although some new field systems were introduced, perhaps as the result of domestic initiatives. In their Continental empire the Romans introduced 'centuriation', with mathematically surveyed fields being established according to a standard grid within extensive and

The living fields shown on this Luftwaffe photograph of the Dengie peninsula of Essex appear to have been surveyed and established in Roman times

precisely delimited areas. Although evidence of centuriation has been claimed in several areas, like those of Rochester in Kent or West Bletchington in Sussex, no completely convincing cases have been discovered in Britain, and it seems that the conquerors were content to leave the British to farm in their traditional manner. It is often suggested that the Romans introduced a new, heavy plough which was equipped with a mould-board to turn the sod and which would remove the need for cross-ploughing in the traditional manner. The evidence for the introduction of such a plough comes from plough marks excavated at Gwithian in Cornwall, a locality on the margins of the Romanised area, and the marks actually date from the centuries following the Roman withdrawal. Probably more important at the time than the new plough was the creation of roads and the establishment of towns and trading systems, all of which encouraged the indigenous farmers to develop a more productive and commercial form of farming. Systems of fields of Romano-British date have been recognised in several places. Two adjacent systems of fields in the South Elmhams— Ilketshalls area of Norfolk appear to be Roman in date, one of the systems conforming to the orientation of the Stone Street Roman road. Another system

33

around Long Stratton in the same county conforms to Roman Pye Road, and these systems are so neatly set out as to suggest that Roman surveyors were involved in their creation. On the better-drained parts of the Dengie peninsula in Essex there is another extensive set of neatly planned fields, and excavation evidence here argues very strongly for a Roman date. When photographed by Luftwaffe spy-planes during the Second World War this Roman system of rectangular fields still survived virtually intact, and much of it still endures. The living Roman fields are hedged almost entirely in elm, though the elm could have invaded and dominated hedgerows that had a different original composition.

In addition to fields and farmsteads other facets of the ancient countrysides included stock-pens, small paddocks located beside farms and hamlets, and garden plots. One of the most distinctive types of small enclosure was the 'banjo enclosure' of the Iron Age. It is named because of its shape, with ditches (and probably hedges) being used to funnel livestock into a circular pen. Some of the smaller embanked sites identified as hillforts could actually have been livestock-enclosures, while at Danebury hillfort in Hampshire banks and ditches just beyond the defensive rampart represent cattle-enclosures where the livestock of the substantial hillfort community could be safely penned or where beasts rustled from neighbouring territories could be guarded.

Although the prehistoric countrysides contained a few village-sized settlements, most farmers lived in solitary farmsteads or hamlets. Sometimes these settlements were fortified with banks, ditches, walls or palisades, and usually they were associated with a few small pens and paddocks, which might have been used in the lambing season, to fold a milk-cow, to corral a horse, or to accommodate the small oxen of the plough team. Some of the Bronze Age farming settlements on Dartmoor were 'open', while at others groups of circular stone-walled dwellings stood inside stone-walled compounds. The compounds do not seem to have been genuinely defensive constructions, but cattle could have been driven into the compounds if there was a threat of trouble. One of the longest of these enclosures is Ryders Rings, high on the moor in South Brent parish. The tadpole-shaped compound encloses about 6 acres (2.4 hectares) and contains the remains of thirty-six dwellings which were variously free-standing or attached to the compound wall, while numerous roughly rectangular-walled pens or yards were also linked to the inner face of the wall. A fairly typical Iron Age and Romano-British farming settlement is exemplified by a site at Riding Wood in Northumberland. Three circular dwellings stood at the centre of a stone-walled enclosure which was subdivided by internal walls to create a trio of pens which could have accommodated cattle or sheep, while the dwellings are likely to have accommodated the members of an extended family.

An important feature of most excavated farming settlements of the Iron Age is the complex of storage-pits – mistakenly interpreted as the actual dwellings of Iron Age people until just a few decades ago! Experiments at the reconstructed Iron Age farming settlement at Butser Hill in Hampshire suggest that around 1 tonne of harvested grain could be stored in a typical pit, which was then sealed with clay to exclude rainwater and oxygen. The grain directly beneath the clay plug becomes moistened and activated so that it releases carbon dioxide. The gas sinks into the grain below and induces dormancy, so that the grain can be preserved through the winter months without deteriorating. Some

Iron Age settlement sites are known to have hundreds of pits, the average pit being capable of storing the harvest of between three and six small 'Celtic' fields. The experimental archaeologist Peter J. Reynolds has described how the multitudes of storage-pits and the vast numbers of new archaeological sites which were discovered by aerial photography during the scorching summer of 1976 reveal that 'in the Iron Age there was virtually total domination of the landscape and a proportionately large population . . . our problem in the future will be to isolate the areas where prehistoric man was not active'.

Garden plots have been recognised at a number of excavated prehistoric settlement sites at places as far apart as the island of Arran and Cornwall. At the Romano-British settlement at Chysauster in Cornwall there are nine well-preserved dwellings, and gardens enclosed by low stone walls were attached to each house. It is not easy to discover the sorts of crop which would be cultivated in such plots, though herbs for flavouring and medicinal uses are likely candidates. Other possibilities include fat hen, which is today a weed of cultivation

This carefully reconstructed Iron Age farmstead is at Butser Hill near Petersfield. Nearby is the experimental area in which Iron Age cultivation methods are being rediscovered

but which could have provided both leafy cattle-fodder and seeds which can be ground to produce a flour. The Celtic bean (*Vicia faba minor*) might have been grown in gardens, though as a nitrogen-fixing leguminous plant it could also be grown in rotation with cereals in the main fields to restore their fertility. Flax could have been a field or garden crop with its leaves providing fodder, linen thread being produced from its stalks after soaking, crushing and combing, while its seeds contain an oil which could be used in cooking or as a lighting fuel. Plants which might have been cultivated for dyes include madder and woad. At the Bronze Age settlement on Stannon Down on the fringes of Bodwin Moor circular stone-walled dwellings stand amongst a system of fields which include small strip-shaped garden plots where cereals may have been grown and larger irregular enclosures which probably served as livestock-corrals.

While legumes like beans and vetch and specialised crops like flax and woad will also have been grown in arable fields, the main crops were cereals. Forms of wheat and barley were grown in varying proportions at different sites, and the cultivation of forms of oats seems to have been adopted late in the prehistoric era, as was that of rye. Emmer wheat (*Triticum dicoccum*) was the favoured form of wheat in the earlier phases of agriculture, but in the last prehistorical millennium spelt wheat (*Triticum spelta*) seems to have superseded it; while einkorn wheat (*Triticum monococcum*), which is robust and competitive but difficult to mill, seems to have been popular in the Bronze Age. Einkorn was the original cultivated wheat, but by the time that agriculture was established in Britain emmer wheat, resulting from a cross between einkorn and wild goat grass, was the favoured cereal. Nevertheless, experiments at the Butser farm have shown einkorn to be high-yielding, drought-resistant and relatively unpalatable to birds and deer. Interestingly, all three 'primitive' forms of wheat produce about twice the protein value of modern bread wheat. The Butser experiments also showed that emmer and spelt were more easily harvested by hand-picking the ripe ears of corn than by employing the sickle.

By the time of the Roman conquest many parts of Britain had experienced around 5,000 years of cultivation, and the patterns of farming and creation of fields had passed through several cycles of evolution. Although a deterioration of climate had driven cultivation from upland areas like Dartmoor, in the late Bronze Age most of England and extensive lowland areas of Scotland, Wales and Ireland were spanned by a patchwork coverlet of fields, and England may have supported as little woodland as today. Some of the commons which existed in medieval times had already been established, and there will have been many vantage-points from which the entire panorama consisted of an unbroken fieldscape. By the close of the Roman era the unremitting intensity of cultivation, acerbated probably by the exposure of bare land through the winter sowing of spelt, had created problems of soil erosion sufficient to cause the choking of some rivers by silt. It is now clear that the abuse of the environment was a feature of ancient as well as of modern life, but the most remarkable result of recent archaeological research is the revelation that from at least Bronze Age times most prehistoric fields were components in large-scale exercises in rural planning which produced the systems of coaxial fields which could extend across several square miles of territory.

SOME PLACES OF INTEREST

Grimes Graves (TL 8189). An area of 17 acres (7 hectares) in the Norfolk Brecklands near Weeting is pock-marked by the craters of more than 350 mine-shafts. The mines, which were active in the period about 3000–2500 BC, served the flint axe-making industry. Other Neolithic flint-mining sites are known in the south-east of England, but at Grimes Graves visitors can descend a shaft and see the mining galleries which radiate outwards from its base.

Pike o' Stickle (NY 2907). A considerable number of stone-axe factory sites existed amongst the volcanic rocks of the Langdale Pikes area of the Lake District. Pike o' Stickle is the best-known of these factories, and the helmet-like summit of the Pike is a distinctive landmark of Langdale. Visitors would be ill-advised to set foot on the steep slopes of the Pike, but fine views of the site are obtained by following the footpath which ascends the adjacent ridge, marked on maps as 'The Band'. A trail of axe-making debris can be seen on the flanks of the Pike, running downslope for a distance of about 1,475 feet (450 metres). Axes made from the volcanic tuff rocks of the Langdale area were exported to many distant parts of Britain.

Rough Tor (SX 1482). The granite hill of Rough Tor is a landmark of St Breward parish in Cornwall and stands in Bodmin Moor to the south-east of Camelford village. A small hillfort, probably of late Iron Age date, lies between two rock outcrops on the summit of Rough Tor and below, on the south-western flanks of the hill. Bronze Age hut-circles, stone clearance cairns and tumbled stretches of field- and paddock-wall are plainly visible in the closely grazed pasture.

The Dartmoor Reaves (SX 6872). These eroded Bronze Age hedgebanks of earth and boulders are visible on many parts of the moor but are most plainly displayed on both sides of the River Dart below Dartmeet on the south-eastern sections of the moor. The reaves stand out particularly clearly in winter under conditions of light snow-cover and slanting sunlight.

'Celtic' Fields in the Valley of Stones (ST 6085). This surviving 'Celtic' field system lies in Dorset about 1 mile (1 kilometre) to the west of the Hardy monument and two miles (3.2 kilometres) to the south-east of Littlebredy village. Good views can be obtained from the side of the minor road from Portesham to Winterbourne Abbas, just to the north of its intersection with the Abbotsbury-to-Martinstown minor road. Another 'Celtic' field system can be seen from the roadside as one approaches Abbotsbury from the north-east.

The Isles of Scilly. In several places around the coasts of these islands tumbled field-walls can be seen running down to the sea, and their alignments can be traced on the beaches at low tide. The fields are thought to be of the Bronze Age, and field systems were submerged by the sinking of part of the island land-mass.

Chysauster Romano-British Village and Garden Plots (SW 4735). The village, a well-signposted monument in Madron parish to the north of Penzance in Cornwall, was established around 100 BC and was occupied during Roman times. The remains of nine 'courtyard houses', with their chambers around open yards, can be explored, while low stone walls define the garden plots attached to each dwelling.

The Grassington 'Celtic' Fields (SE 0064). Grassington is an attractive village in Wharfedale. A footpath from Town Head in the north-western part of the village to Conistone traverses a well-preserved system of Iron Age and Romano-British 'Celtic' fields. The ancient fields are overlain by later networks of field-walls, while some of the earthworks displayed are the product of medieval farming and later mining operations. The 'Celtic' fields are recognisable under all conditions but most plainly visible under light snow-cover or when the sun is low in the sky. As well as lynchet banks, sections of tumbled wall, ancient droveways and hut circles can also be found. 'Celtic' fields are visible in various other parts of the Yorkshire Dales, notably near the popular tourist centre of Malham, where elongated walled fields flank the footpath from Malham village to Malham Cove.

Ancient but 'Living' Fields in Norfolk (TM 1778). Fragments of pre-Roman field systems endure in the fieldscape of many parts of Norfolk, and perhaps the best area to see hedgerows marking ancient field-boundaries is near Diss, in the Billingford locality.

Butser Ancient Farm Research Project (SU 7118). The experimental project to reconstruct a farm of 300 BC began in 1972. The experimental area itself is not open to the public, though there is public access to the reconstructed Iron Age farmstead and enclosure which is based on evidence from the excavation of an Iron Age site at Pimperne in Dorset. The 'Pimperne House' is reached through the Queen Elizabeth Country Park, the entrance to which lies on the opposite side of the A3 approximately four miles (6 kilometres) to the south-west of Petersfield in Hampshire.

CHAPTER 2

REVOLUTION IN THE DARK AGES

T he discovery of new evidence usually refines and expands understanding of a subject. However, where the field-patterns of Dark Age Britain are concerned the quest for knowledge has overturned the certainties of the past and replaced them with mysteries. Outdated history-books describe how, following the collapse of Roman power, Anglo-Saxon settlers and warriors conquered England, driving the native British into the rocky outposts of the west and north, establishing a new system of 'open-field' farming and hacking thousands of new fields from the virgin wildwood.

Now we know that all this was wrong. The Saxon settlement was sporadic and seems to have involved only modest numbers of immigrants. Gradually Saxon or partly Saxon leaders gained a political ascendancy in the Dark Age kingdoms and, by means which are uncertain, most of England became an English-speaking land. The agriculture of Roman Britain may, it has been argued, have supported a population as large as 6 million – far too large a population to be swept aside by several thousand immigrants. The exploitation of farming resources reached a peak during the Roman occupation, and the scope for further clearance of ancient woodland by new settlers was very limited. In fact most of the agricultural colonisation that took place during the later Dark Ages must have involved land that had been abandoned in the fifth and sixth centuries – the very period when the Saxon agricultural revolution was supposed to have been launched!

Archaeology has produced no evidence of new fields created in the early period of Saxon settlement, and so it is sensible to suppose that where farming persisted it exploited the fields established during preceding periods. Rather than producing evidence of a massive Saxon settlement and colonisation, recent archaeological work has emphasised the remarkable density of Iron Age and Romano-British rural settlement. Accompanying or following the Roman collapse there was certainly a drastic reduction of population and a retreat of the frontiers of farming, so that many areas which supported fields, farmsteads and hamlets were gradually engulfed by the advance of weeds, thorns and woodland. The causes of this decay were various and must have included economic, political and psychological traumas, while massive epidemics of plague are likely to have played a leading rôle. In addition, the over-exploitation of land in Roman times must have resulted in the destruction of the soil structure and fertility in many localities.

The transformation of scores of countrysides by the introduction of open-field farming did not occur in the fifth and sixth centuries, the period of the Saxon settlement, but began, we now believe, in the eighth and ninth centuries. We do not know why it happened, or how. It certainly did not occur in every parish, estate or region; and, as we will describe, the contrast between those places which acquired open fields around a thousand years ago and those which did not is still apparent in the living countryside.

The debate about the origins of open-field farming has dominated the study of subjects like historical geography, economic history and landscape history for many years, so that thousands of students have been obliged to learn and evaluate the conflicting theories. Theory has its rôle to play, but it can never be as credible as sound archaeological or documentary evidence. Many readers will have been taught a simplified model of open-field farming at school, and the details of the system are described in the chapter which follows. In fact the system was complicated and variable, but it involved four basic components: the existence of two, three or four vast open fields which are subdivided into roughly rectangular blocks or 'furlongs' which are in turn divided into parallel ribbons of land known as 'strips', 'lands' or 'selions'; the existence of common grazing on fallowing ploughland; the existence of grazing rights on the common or 'waste'; and the existence of a manor court or village assembly where decisions about the operation of the whole intricate system could be taken.

Outdated theories argued that Anglo-Saxon settlers of the fifth century AD imported open-field farming ready-made from their homelands, but now we know that it did not exist in the Anglo-Saxon motherlands. More recently Dr Joan Thirsk has suggested that Saxon communities in England originally held land not in common but in 'severalty', and that as the population grew during the currency of a custom of 'partible inheritance', under which land was shared out between heirs, so fields were progressively subdivided into strips. This theory, however, would seem not to account for the evidence of planning recognised in some open-field systems which we will soon describe.

The archaeological evidence shows that open-field systems cut across early Saxon settlements but sometimes seem to be related to what has been called 'the middle Saxon shuffle', a phenomenon of the eighth or ninth century when scores of small settlements were deserted and when new and more durable villages were founded to form the foundations of village England. The documentary evidence shows that terminology which can only relate to open-strip fields had been adopted by the tenth century. The laws of Ine, who was king of Wessex in the late seventh century, refer to husbandmen who hire oxen from their neighbours and imply that some sort of co-operative arable farming was then in existence, but unequivocal references to open-field farming came later. Charters from the third quarter of the tenth century for Hendred and Kingston in Oxfordshire and Ardington in Berkshire describe land mixed 'acre under acre' or 'acre between acre', and most refer to open-field strips, while a charter of 956 concerning land at Charlton by Wantage in Berkshire tells that the land was commonly held and not demarcated by clear boundaries 'because to left and right lie acres in combination one with another'. Similarly in 963 the land at Avon in Wiltshire was described as 'mixed in common by single acres dispersed hither and thither'. Other tenth-century charters include the termi-

Snow highlights ancient and current field patterns in the Langdale Valley in the Lake District

nology of open-field farming and describe 'headlands', the banks of earth which accumulated at the end of strips from the soil shed by the plough when it was turned, and 'gores', the tapering strips which occupy awkward gaps between the parcels of parallel strips. From all this it seems clear that open-field farming was well established in parts of England by the tenth century but that until the eighth century the land was mainly farmed from scattered hamlets and farmsteads set in fields of Roman or earlier date.

Could there have been some continuity between the old and new fields? Certainly furlongs often have a rather rectangular field-like shape, and it has been argued that fields existing in Saxon England may have been divided into strips to become furlongs. The archaeologist Christopher Taylor has noted the existence of what appear to be buried field-ditches beneath the banks or headlands at the margins of furlongs. Such ditches have been seen when modern pipeline-trenches have cut through old headlands. This argument has not received great support as a general explanation of furlong origins, one of the problems being that furlongs were considerably larger than most 'Celtic' fields seen as earthworks or in aerial photographs.

Although the date of the introduction of open-field farming is less mysterious than before, the manner of its introduction and the early stages of its evolution pose various problems. If the new system was introduced in the eighth and ninth centuries, then it must have made its début against a turbulent background of strife between the rival kingdoms and the horrific Viking raids and conquests. Some of the early writers on open fields thought that the strip divisions represented a democratic sharing-out of land by members of a free peasant community, or that the new fields were partitioned as cultivation advanced from villages into the woodlands and wastes. It would seem more likely that the revolutionary new system was imposed by landlords or their agents and, since there was no powerful centralised authority in eighth- and ninth-century England, that it spread from one estate to another by some process of imitation. The notion that open-field farming was imposed by estate-owners and their agents is supported by recently discovered evidence that the original field systems were sometimes planned and were also rather different from those which had developed by the thirteenth or fourteenth century.

The typical medieval field-strip was roughly about 200 yards (180 metres) long, though a few could be almost twice this length. An acre strip measuring 220 yards by 22 yards (201 metres by 20 metres) seems to have been regarded as the amount of land which a plough team should plough in a day. However, archaeologists and landscape historians have recognised evidence of early strips that were up to 1,000 yards (c.900 metres) long in the Yorkshire Wolds and Holderness, while at Middleton near Pickering some strips, much later enclosed by hedgerows, survive which were a stupendous 2,000 yards (c.1,800 metres) in length. Further evidence of such 'long strips' has been found in parts of Northamptonshire and the Fens of Cambridgeshire, Lincolnshire and Norfolk, and research in other parts of England may show that long strips were grouped together in 'long furlongs', and at some later stage in the evolution of open-field farming the long furlongs were subdivided to create several more 'conventional' furlongs of the kind which are portrayed in many field-maps of the seventeenth century; which survived in some places as living furlongs into

Opposite above: Ancient countryside fieldscape near Moretonhampstead in Devon

Opposite below: The varied fieldscape of Devon as seen from Hembury hillfort

41

the nineteenth century; and which can be recognised in aerial photographs and field-work today.

And so there is good reason to believe that many open-field systems were originally composed of long strips lying in long furlongs. The reasons for favouring such strips, which could be more than a mile in length, are difficult to imagine. Medieval strips were around 200 yards (183 metres) long, because the attenuated shape reduced time and energy sacrificed in turning a plough which, on heavy ground, might be hauled by a plodding team of six or eight oxen. Yet no plough team would have been able to pull a plough for distances of over a mile without several pauses for rest.

In a study of the township of Preston in Holderness, Mary Harvey revealed a version of open-field farming that differs considerably from the textbook examples. The medieval village had two open fields and, instead of their being divided into furlongs, each field was neatly partitioned into seven 'bydales', units much larger than conventional furlongs. The bydales were in turn divided into long strips, up to almost 2,500 yards (2,300 metres) in length. These strips seem to have been allocated to their tenants in a regular and systematic manner, though it is not known whether the adoption of the system dated to late Saxon or Norman times.

Further evidence that open-field farming was introduced on the various estates in an organised and planned manner derives from the recognition of the adoption of a *solskift* or 'sun division' layout of holdings. This system is known to have operated in Scandinavia, and a number of English examples have now been detected. According to the fully fledged sun-division model, a peasant family would have the same neighbours in the strip fields as they did in the village, so that if a family lived between the dwellings of the Atwood and the Green families, then each of their strips in the open field would have an Atwood strip on one side and a Green strip on the other. As the years rolled by, the extinction or migration of some families and the inheritance and purchase of land would gradually blur an original sun-division allocation of strips, but in some cases medieval or later records of the holders of strips reveal the enduring fragments of the original pattern. For example, glebe strips (which were reserved for the incumbent village priests) tended to be more permanent than other lands and sometimes they can be recognised to have occurred in a set position within each furlong. In Scandinavia the *solskift* village was approached by four roads at right angles to each other, which thus divided the village lands into four quarters, and the order of rotation of strips followed the direction of the sun, beginning from the side of the furlong that was nearest to the rising sun (that is, moving from east to west if strips were aligned north to south). It is not clear whether such well-developed sun-division patterns were adopted in Dark Age or early medieval England, though a charter of the reign of Henry II granted the nuns of Ormsby land in 'four quarters in the field of . . . Spaldington'. Also, medieval descriptions of strip-patterns frequently include phrases like 'towards the sun', 'against the shade', 'on the sunny side' and so on. The sun-division system may have been introduced by Danish settlers, although it also seems to have existed in the West Midlands as well as in the Danish-settled east.

We have mentioned that most schoolchildren are taught a simplified model of the open-field system of medieval England. As a result they are likely to assume that strip farming in communal open fields was found throughout the medieval realm. This was far from being the case. Where the system existed there were considerable regional and local variations in manorial customs; in the relative numbers of free and bond tenants; in the details of field layout; in the customs of inheritance; in the ratio of arable land to pasture, meadow, woodland and common; and in the terminology used to describe land-holdings and field-divisions. Even more important was the fact that, while open-field farming was fairly typical of the English Midlands, in other regions it could be less frequently encountered or completely absent. Where countrysides have not yet been defaced and defiled by the barley barons, contrasts between different scenic areas are still greatly influenced by the fact of whether or not they experienced the introduction of open-field farming round about a thousand years ago.

The resultant differences in the local landscapes do not seem to be greatly influenced by topography or soils and seem to be largely the products of historical accidents. We can only begin to speculate upon the nature of the accidents involved. Open-field farming depended upon the unified control of not only an expanse of open-field arable land, but also common grazing, hay meadows and access to timber supplies, each of which made an invaluable contribution of resources to the village economy. Estates that were sufficiently large to embrace a broad spectrum of resources seem to have existed in Roman times and are often referred to as 'multiple estates'. Many were large enough to cover areas now partitioned between a clutch of parishes, while the size of the estates permitted the component townships to produce their own subsistence crops as well as specialising in the production of certain commodities – such as grain, horses, poultry or honey and so on – which would be rendered to headquarters of the estate.

However, in the course of the Dark Ages the old estates became fragmented, perhaps as a result of the disruption of the old order, or the abandonment of land as population declined, or through particular patterns of inheritance. As the old estates declined, so each local community would concentrate on producing subsistence crops alone. In many places the fragmentation of old estates must have proceeded beyond the point where the manorial fragments were large enough to accommodate a village and its fields, common and meadows, and on such small estates the old field-patterns which were inherited from Roman and earlier times would survive. (They might also survive on estates still much larger than normal parishes or manors.) The implosion of settlement to create nucleated villages would not take place, and so the settlement pattern would continue to be dominated by scattered farmsteads and hamlets. Instead of the dispersion of land-holdings in strips scattered far and wide amongst the furlongs of the open fields, land would continue to be held 'in severalty' rather than in common, and the character and many of the details of the traditional landscape would survive.

The distinction between what some authorities now call 'ancient countryside' and the 'planned countryside' of open-field areas has been noticed and described for several centuries. In Elizabethan times it was recognised by William Harrison, who wrote that 'It is so, that our soile is divided into champaine ground [champion or planned countryside] and woodland [ancient countryside]'. William Marshall described the ancient countryside of eastern Norfolk

in the 1790s, recognising it as 'very old-inclosed country' where the eye seemed 'ever on the verge of a forest'. The woodland or 'arden' countryside was so named not because of the presence of many little woods but because of the close networks of hedgerows which yielded a wealth of useful woodland products – timber, firewood, fruit and nuts. Ancient or woodland countryside was not regarded as being primitive or backward, and in 1794 Messrs Griggs described Essex in the following way:

The inclosures, which from time immemorial have almost universally prevailed, make Essex greatly preferable to some of the neighbouring counties; here every man enjoys his own the year around. . . . His ditches carry off the water from his land, and the thick hedges of white thorn, which grow upon the banks raised by what is thrown out of them [silt from the ditches], serve to shelter his stock from the storms of winter, as well as to protect his corn from the intrusion of cattle; and by dividing his land into distinct parcels, enable him to support twice the quantity of stock he could otherwise do; advantages an open [champion] country can never enjoy.

Ancient countryside, with its small, richly hedged fields, patches of woodland and scattered farmsteads and hamlets, is epitomised by this panorama near Luppitt in Devon

45

Ancient countryside near
Llanddewi Brefi in Dyfed

Ancient countryside, as found in parts of Essex, Norfolk and the Chilterns
and much of Devon, is a land of hollowed twisting lanes, scenes that are dotted
with small woods and screened by rich winding hedgerows, a place where large
villages are few and farmsteads and hamlets are many. Open fields were not entirely absent from the regions of ancient countryside, but where they occurred
they tended to be small, divided between just a handful of peasants and likely to
be more ephemeral than the big strip fields of the Midlands.

Planned champion or 'fielden' countryside was the product of wide-ranging
decisions about the reorganisation of the farmland. The features and character
of ancient countryside would be removed when open-field farming was introduced; while in the eighteenth and nineteenth centuries, when the countryside
was again reorganised by the Parliamentary Enclosure of common lands and
strip fields, the straight hedgerows, walls and local roads of the Enclosure era
would remodel the landscape according to the planned geometry of surveyors
(as described in Chapter 6).

Several modern authorities have emphasised the contrasts between the history and fieldscapes of ancient or woodland countryside on the one hand and
planned or champion countryside on the other. Yet there is a third type of
countryside which can still be encountered and which might be termed 'early
enclosure countryside'. Here the enclosure and privatisation of open-field land
was achieved by piecemeal agreements and was largely accomplished before
the period of Parliamentary Enclosure. Rather than superimposing a geometrical fieldscape upon unenclosed parishes through one traumatic episode of

change, strips were gradually bought, sold and swapped around to produce more consolidated holdings. Thus the hedgerows and walls which bound the various enclosures tend to follow the curving margins of the old field-strips, so that enclosure was achieved gradually and without the rectangular field-geometry associated with Parliamentary Enclosure.

To summarise, the period of the Dark Ages did witness a revolutionary re-organisation of fields, farming and settlement patterns, though this did not occur at the time or in the manner described in the outdated history-books. Around the eighth, ninth and tenth centuries land and tenancies were being reorganised on estate after estate. Simultaneously local populations were abandoning their dispersed farmsteads and hamlets and coming to live – voluntarily or otherwise – in villages located at the centre of new open-field systems. Meanwhile landowners were establishing churches in the new centres or at focal

Ancient countryside on the fringes of Dartmoor near Moretonhampstead

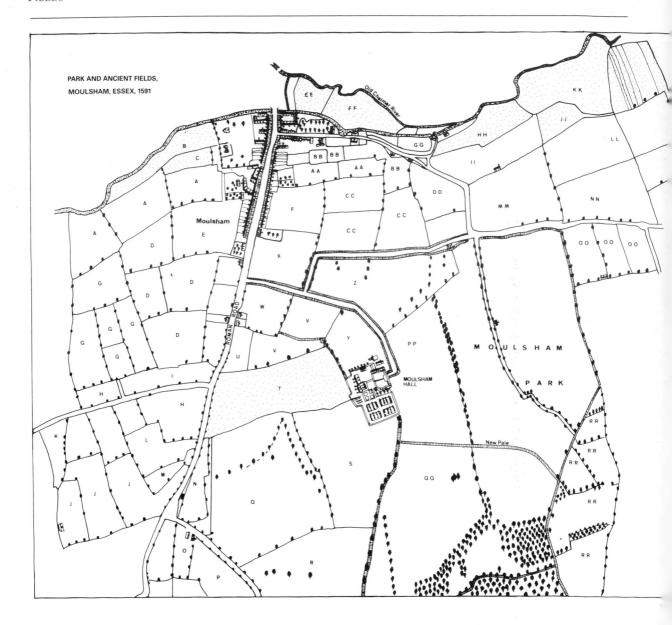

PARK AND ANCIENT FIELDS,
MOULSHAM, ESSEX, 1591

points which were destined to become permanent villages. The introduction of
open fields was apparently the result of deliberate planning by the landlords
and their agents, and sometimes this planning was sufficiently detailed as to
produce an intricate English version of the *solskift* allocation of strips which
existed in Scandinavia.

Initially the patterns introduced were sometimes or often significantly different from those which would evolve during the medieval period, with long
strips grouped within long furlongs. Subsequently almost all the long furlongs
would be subdivided to produce shorter, more compact furlongs containing
strips which were not a mile or even two miles in length but which ranged
around the 200-yard (180-metre) norm.

PARK AND ANCIENT FIELDS, MOULSHAM, ESSEX, 1591

The park of Moulsham Hall has been superimposed upon a network of fields which is older than the Roman road from London to Colchester. The ancient fields lie to the west of the road and emerge beyond the park pale in the lower right corner of the map. Meadows are lightly stippled, hedges and fences are shown as on the original map, and field-names are as follows:

A   Ground Land
B   Friars Mead (near friary)
C   Mead
D   Parcel of West Field
E   Ground West Field ('ground' far from manor)
F   Shoprows (close to the rows of shops)
G   Larks Leaze
H   Saffron Land (where saffron crocus was grown)
I   Wannells alias Great Brownes Croft
J   Cross Field
K   Pickend Land (picked or pointed)
L   George Land
M   Doublet Sleeve (shaped like one)
N   Old Copy Mead (copyhold)
O   Little Wannells
P   Stock Land (assart)
Q   Lower Stumps (assart)
R   Upper Stumps (assart)
S   Perry Field (pear-shaped)
T   Great Wannells (perhaps 'Wandels' = share in common field)
U   Little Wannells
V   Brickell Field (brick-kiln)
W   Moulsham Butt Field

X   The Upper Hop Ground
Y   Banton (probably Barton, meaning demesne or farmyard)
Z   Prick Field
AA Low Crofts
BB Horseshoe Land (shaped like one)
CC Low Leaze
DD Mill Croft
EE Bell Meade (shaped like one)
FF Boarshead Mead (shaped like one)
GG Mill Mead
HH Mill Leaze
II Nicholls Land
JJ Corpes Mead (coppice or corpse?)
KK Moulsham Mead
LL Lower Corpes in Baddow Magna
NN Upper Corpes in Baddow aforesaid
OO Warren Crofts (near the warren)
PP Shooting Launde (parkland or wood pasture)
QQ Chapel Lane
RR Parcel of Tiled House

It is interesting that in several cases neighbouring fields share the same name. It is possible that they went through a phase of strip cultivation, though without losing their hedgerows, so that the four Larks Leaze fields may have operated as a small subdivided plough-field. The field-name 'Wannells' could be 'Wandels', i.e. field divided into strips or shares and the name Moulsham Butt probably indicates strip cultivation rather than tree-stumps. The Moulsham area is now engulfed by the suburbs of Chelmsford.

This, then, is an outline of current thinking about the early stages in the development of open-field farming, and much remains to be debated and many details are still unknown; for, while it is one thing to reject a faulty model of the Dark Age farming revolution, it is a greater challenge to perfect a new model to replace the outmoded beliefs.

Although the field-pattern of prehistoric Britain displayed remarkable similarities, open-field farming represented a dramatic change, and we must ask why the peasants and their masters were prepared to accept such a wholesale disruption of life and landscape. What did the new system have to offer? One suggestion is that the adoption of more efficiently and productively worked arable fields released more land for use as valuable pasture. Even if this interpretation is correct, it still does not explain why the open fields were divided into strips with each tenant household having their strips widely scattered throughout the numerous furlongs. Certainly this resulted in much time being wasted in journeys to all the outposts of the arable lands, and it is also true that medieval tenants were often keen to sell or swap strips in order to reverse the pattern and obtain more consolidated holdings. It is generally argued that the dispersal of strips resulted in each family sharing equally in the better and

50   This long-strip group at Middleton near Pickering was fossilised when enclosed by hedgerows

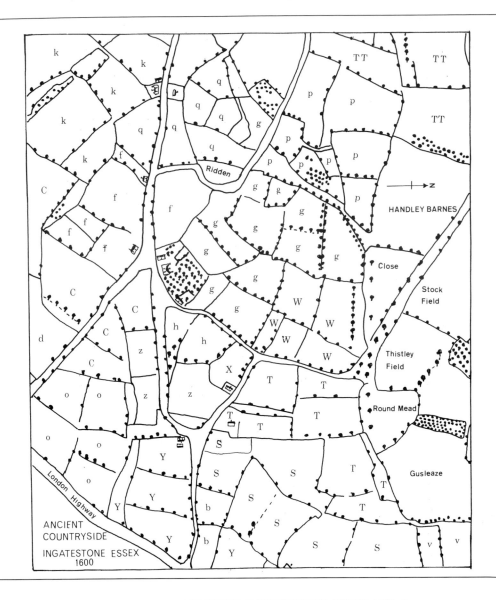

ANCIENT COUNTRYSIDE, INGATESTONE, ESSEX, 1600–1

This area of Essex, as mapped in 1600–1, reveals the characteristics of ancient countryside. Fields are quite small and irregular, and bounded by hedgerows or double hedges. Old winding lanes run through the countryside, and the settlement-pattern consists of dispersed farmsteads and hamlets. There was a village in the vicinity, Ingatestone, off the map to the south, owing its importance to its position beside the London highway. Land is held 'in severalty' rather than in common fields. Code-letters for the original map reveal the tenancy-patten (all the fields marked 'S', for example, having the same copyholding tenant). It is seen that the typical holding consists of around half a dozen adjacent fields. Fields are mainly identified by owners' names, but on the right of the map the named fields are part of the demesne of Handley Barnes Manor. They may be part of an enclosed former common. The name 'Stock Field' refers to land with standing tree-stumps and identifies an assart. 'Gus leaze' probably means 'Goose Pasture'. Away from the demesne we have identified as 'Ridden' is a field called 'Little Phillips alias Ridden', and this must be another medieval assart. The symbols used to portray woods, hedgerows and dwellings are copied from the original map.

poorer grounds, though this explanation is also unproven. One advantage of the scattering of strips is that it prevented any household from becoming temporarily deprived of ploughland through having all its land concentrated in the open field which was temporarily under fallow. Finally there is the possibility that the different features of open-field farming appeared at different times, so that mature open-field systems evolved gradually. Field-strips could have appeared in the late seventh century, but the development of intricate arrangements for synchronising crop rotations and organising common grazing on the fallowing field may not have developed until the twelfth century. While our understanding of open-field farming has increased, there is still much to be learned, debated and discovered.

Some Places of Interest

Long Strips at Middleton (SE 7885). Middleton in Yorkshire is a fascinating village which stands astride the A170 about 1 mile (1.6 kilometres) to the north-west of Pickering. The open-field lands appear to have been set out in two great blocks divided into long strips up to 2,200 yards (2,000 metres) in length. Much later strips and adjacent groups of strips were enclosed by hedgerows, and the fossilised long strip-patterns survived into the postwar era and should have been designated as a national monument. In recent years many of the hedgerows have been removed, but some still survive, so that in places one can gain an impression of the remarkable long strip-patterns of early open-field farming.

West Stow (TL 8170). The village of West Stow in Suffolk lies about 5 miles (8 kilometres) north-west of Bury St Edmunds, and a minor road running westwards from the village leads to a country park where a pagan Saxon village has been excavated and reconstructed. The village was occupied from a little before the Roman collapse of AD 410 until about 650, when the site was abandoned, and the reconstruction provides an impression of the hamlets or small villages which existed just before the open-field and village revolution.

Bleadon (ST 3456). In the lands around Bleadon village, which is in Avon, about 3 miles (5 kilometres) south-east of Weston-super-Mare, the earthwork evidence reveals how open-field strips were superimposed upon the pre-existing patterns of 'Celtic' fields with the overploughing of the cross-banks of the older fields to create elongated strip fields.

CHAPTER 3

FIELDS IN THE MIDDLE AGES

The field-patterns of the Middle Ages had their roots in the partly mysterious revolutions of the Dark Ages or, where ancient countryside endured, in still older patterns of division and enclosure. Although the origins of open-field farming remain controversial, the more mature patterns and practices of later medieval times are relatively well documented. In some cases the parish or manorial field systems which were mapped in the sixteenth, seventeenth and eighteenth centuries seem to have changed little since the time of Chaucer. Isolated and modified fragments of medieval strip cultivation still survive in a handful of places, while most regions contain some earthworks of ridge and furrow preserved beneath a protective blanket of undisturbed pasture. Nevertheless, farming patterns did not remain static, and if we choose to date the medieval period from the Norman Conquest in 1066 to the Dissolution of the Monasteries in 1536–9, then it is not surprising that many countrysides would experience complete or substantial transformations during almost five centuries of agricultural use.

Yet throughout the period the distinction between ancient or woodland countryside on the one hand and planned or champion countryside on the other remained obvious. It was still obvious in the eighteenth century and is easily recognised in many places today. In 1748 the Swedish naturalist Peter Kalm departed as a member of an official mission to assess the natural resources of America, but he was delayed for six months in Britain while awaiting a vessel for the transatlantic crossing. He therefore turned his attention to English farming and recorded that 'Around Little Gaddesden and on all Chiltern land every farmer more or less had his own severalties which he afterwards divided into small enclosures by hedges. There was one enclosure sown with wheat, another with barley, turnips, peas, oats, sainfoin, clover, trifolium, tares, potatoes or whatever he wished.' This contrasted with the open champion countryside which he saw in the flat vale just beyond the Chilterns:

On the other hand, here about Ivinghoe, where the common fields are everywhere in use, no hedges are seen. Nor are there here any peas or kinds of grass sown as fodder. . . . Nor had they any turnip land to feed sheep upon. Therefore they were deprived of the advantage of getting to sell any fat sheep or other cattle, etc. The reason they gave for all this was that their arable was common field and thus came to lie every other year fallow, when one commoner had always to accommodate his crops to the others.

From the wording of his account it seems that in the Little Gaddesden and Chiltern areas Kalm had seen two types of countryside: both the ancient countryside, which can still be recognised in parts of the Chilterns, and hedged countryside with small, privately owned enclosures which was not a living fossil of ancient field-patterns but which had resulted from the enclosure of land previously in open fields. Meanwhile, around Ivinghoe, he saw unenclosed champion countryside which retained much of its medieval appearance. In many places open fields were gradually dismantled even before reaching the time of their maturity, though in others they expanded, perhaps with additional fields being added to the system at the expense of woodland or common. By the thirteenth century most open-field systems had reached maturity, even though there were still considerable variations from manor to manor and from region to region. In some cases the open fields virtually filled the territory of their estate, but this could result in imbalances in the mixed farming system, with little grazing being available apart from that found on whichever of the open fields was being fallowed. In most cases the 'waste', which could exist as woodland, wood pasture or common pasture, was a vital component of the system, offering grazing and other useful resources like thatch, clay, stone, timber, turf and bedding to the peasants of the feudal village.

Commons may have very long histories indeed. As we have mentioned, on Bronze Age Dartmoor the fields enclosed by reaves met the open upland grazings of the moor at a terminal reave, and each land unit appears to have enjoyed access to such an expanse of the common grazings. Very recently Tom Williamson's research into the Iron Age fields of East Anglia has resulted in the

Old commons were exploited for fuel, quarrying and mining as well as for grazing. The humps and bumps on the common at Brill in Buckinghamshire result from the digging of clay for the local pottery industry

recognition of vast commons, and in one place the terminal reave has its equivalent in a double hedge which still marks the ancient junction of enclosed and common land. The old multiple estates included commons, and where later parishes in an area shared access to a common by 'intercommoning' rights it is likely that they all represent fragments of a formerly unified multiple estate. Normally the folk who enjoyed rights on a common lived just beyond its margins, but in a few cases this was not so. For example, all villagers who lived within the old hunting territory of Clee forest in the Welsh Marches enjoyed certain commoning rights on Brown Clee Hill, and these 'outcommoners' drove their stock up and down from the grazings along ways known as 'straker routes'. In Oxfordshire the peasant farmers of the Cherwell valley had common rights on the heaths and woods of Wychwood in the south of the county, while farmers in the valley of the Avon between Evesham and Warwick shared commons in woods lying a few miles to the north.

At the start of the Middle Ages a considerable proportion of common land existed as wood pasture, with animals grazing beneath a light cover of pollarded trees. However, the delicate balance between woodland and grazing was difficult to maintain, and most wood pasture gradually became open pasture. Where the members of a village community had unrestricted rights of access to the grazings of a common, then severe overgrazing could result. In the thirteenth century some attempts were made to avoid the deterioration of the pasture through overgrazing with the introduction of 'stinting' arrangements which regulated the number of animals that each household could pasture on the common, and in the course of the centuries which followed stinted commons became numerous. The ancient Port Meadow at Oxford has lacked an effective stinting arrangement and has been severely overgrazed. It has become infested with ragwort but has few other flowering plants. Nearby, the Yarnton and Pixey meadows are closed to grazing until after the hay harvest, wild flowers have time to disperse their seed, and the meadows are ablaze with flowers. When a system of stinting was not adopted attempts might be made to end any exploitation of the grazings by animals brought in furtively from outside the community by preventing a householder from keeping more animals on the summer grazings of the common than he or she would support during the winter.

Normally the common comprised the poorer terrain of the manor which was least amenable to arable cultivation, like the steep dry chalk slopes of the southern downs or the thin, damp and often acidic soils of the northern fells, but in flat low-lying areas of East Anglia and elsewhere it often existed as fenland. The misleadingly named 'waste' also included woodland, and manors could embrace woods which were exclusively reserved for the lord, like Grass Wood at Grassington, and others where tenants enjoyed common rights, such as rights of grazing in the lightly wooded pasture, pannage on fallen acorns or beech mast and the taking of timber for house- or plough-making, fuel and hedges and fences. Given the multitude of uses for timber in the village economy of the Middle Ages, access to timber resources was a vital consideration.

Most medieval commons have been enclosed so that now only 4 per cent of the area of England and Wales is still common land. There are about 8,500 commons covering around 1½ million acres (c.607,000 hectares), though only

Opposite: An old heathland common on a gravel capping which gives way to enclosed farmland where the chalk is exposed on the lower ground. Bronze Age round barrows, like the pair in the centre of the photograph, were commonly built on marginal land at the edge of the cultivated area

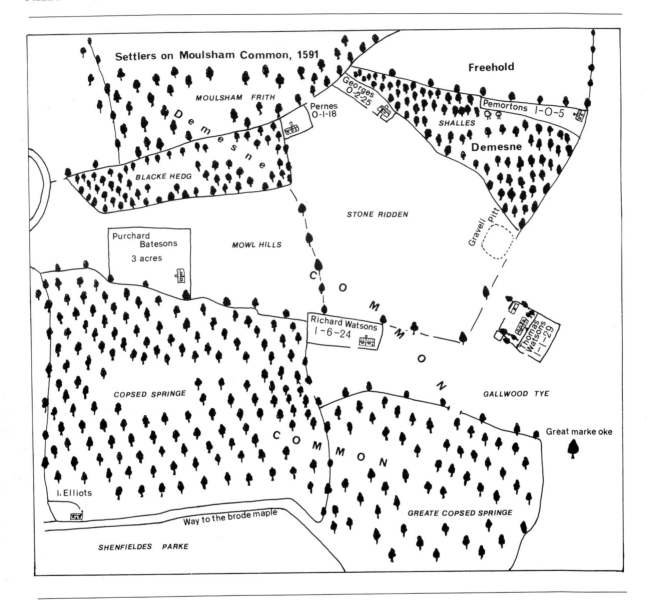

The map shows the following labels:

Settlers on Moulsham Common, 1591

Freehold

MOULSHAM FRITH

Georges 0·2·25

Pernes 0·1·18

Pemortons 1·0·5

SHALLES

Demesne

BLACKE HEDG

STONE RIDDEN

Gravell Pitt

Purchard Batesons 3 acres

MOWL HILLS

C O M M O N

Richard Watsons 1·6·24

Thomas Watsons 1·1·29

COPSED SPRINGE

GALLWOOD TYE

Great marke oke

C O M M O N

I. Elliots

Way to the brode maple

GREATE COPSED SPRINGE

SHENFIELDES PARKE

SETTLERS ON MOULSHAM COMMON, 1591

The map of Moulsham Common, near Chelmsford in Essex, shows that in 1591 a number of families were settled on the common. They had probably arrived as squatters and had in due course been accepted as members of the manorial community, for the map lists them as copyholders. The size of each enclosure is given in acres, roods (quarter-acres) and perches, so that Thomas Watson had 1 acre, 1 rood and 29 perches.

The large common is named Gallwood Tye. 'Gall' may mean wet and barren, and 'Tye' is a southern word for a large common. 'Copsed Springe Wood' is the coppice by the spring, and 'Frith' was a word meaning woodland. 'Shalles Wood' may mean shovel wood and has a vaguely shovel-like shape. The 'Stone Ridden' section of the common may have been rid of stones or trees, and 'Mowl Hills' probably means molehills. The great mark oak could have stood on an old boundary. A gravel-pit is marked, and stone-pits, quarries, marl-pits and mines were often encountered on commons.

one-fifth of the common land has rights of access for the public in general. Those ancient common rights which still survive are registered with the various county councils and include the rights of commoners to 'herbage', or grazing; pannage; 'estovers', or rights to gather firewood; 'turbary', or the right to cut peat; and 'piscary', or fishing rights. At the time of writing there is still no comprehensive law to give the surviving commons suitable protection and management control, and registers of common land are often outdated. An 18-acre (7-hectare) area of Black Mountain, Dyfed, is registered as grazing for 4,071 sheep, 261 cattle, 118 ponies and 24 geese, while a housing estate in Cornwall is still registered as sheep pasture!

In winter the village herd needed to have the food-resources of the fallowing field supplemented by hay, and after the grass had ceased to grow stock were kept under shelter or fed in open stock-pens or 'crew yards'. In medieval times grass was not sown as a crop, but hay was obtained from permanent meadows which normally occupied low moist ground beside a river or which might be obtained by the reclamation of marsh and fen. Meadowland could be worth twice as much as ploughland, and the peasant who held around 30 acres (12 hectares) in arable strips might hold about 2 acres (1 hectare) in the meadow. Meadows were normally divided into 'doles' or strips like the ploughlands, but with the absence of ridge-and-furrow ploughing to define the component strips

Since the introduction of silage-making the sight of hay drying in the meadow in summer is becoming quite uncommon. Medieval meadows often differed from this privately owned example in being divided into strips or 'doles'

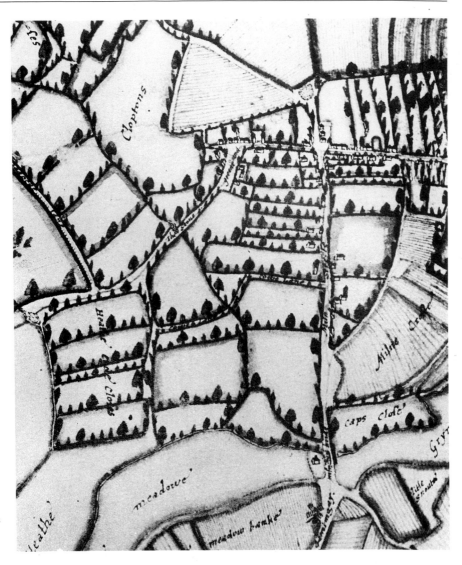

Closes at Gamlingay in Cambridgeshire as mapped in 1601. Elongated little closes run back from the roadside village house-sites and more compact privately owned closes lie between the village and the common meadows and ploughlands

other markers, like stones, were used to mark out the holdings. On some manors the doles were permanent, but in 'lot meadows' the holdings were regularly redistributed by drawing lots. From Candlemas (2 February) the grass was free to grow, and by Lammas (1 August) the hay harvest was completed. After the harvest the meadow was grazed and manured by the village livestock until being again 'put in defence' at Candlemas.

The fine summer weather of hay-time seems to have found the lords in good humour, and it was widely the custom for largess to be dispensed to the mowers. At Wilburton in Cambridgeshire in the thirteenth century the more substantial tenants were rewarded in the following manner: 'He shall mow for one whole day, and shall scatter for one work until the meadow shall be cut and at this he and the whole township shall have one mutton, or 12d and one cheese, or 2d. And he shall have, on the day that he mows, as much grass as he can lift with his scythe, that is, in the evening and if, in lifting the grass he shall break of his scythe, then he shall have no grass.'

The substantial, compact or 'nucleated' village was a feature of champion countryside, and most villages were surrounded by small paddocks and other privately owned enclosures. If the village had developed in a gradual organic manner, then the neighbouring closes might be somewhat square, some of them containing the village homesteads and serving as gardens and places where small livestock could be kept. If the village was the result of medieval planning, then (particularly in the north of England) the enclosures were likely to exist as long narrow 'tofts' with the house occupying the roadside frontage and the enclosed land of the toft running back to terminate at a back lane or at the junction with open ploughland or meadowland.

The arable land of the champion village lay in open fields, these enormous fields sometimes being known as 'seasons'. These were often three in number, sometimes just two; while the village could have more than three open fields, even as many as nine if it had taken over land formerly farmed by failed neighbouring villages or hamlets. In areas of ancient countryside the open fields were different, being small and scattered – and the parish of Ashdon in Essex contained no less than twenty! No Essex parish had as few as three open fields. The fields were generally unhedged within, though some boundaries, particularly those at the roadside, would be hedged. As we have described, the fields were divided into furlongs, which consisted of blocks of parallel strips, the strips being also known as 'parcels', 'lands' or 'selions'. Generally the strips consisted of several adjacent plough-ridges, so that it is usually wrong to equate one plough-ridge with a strip. Ridge-and-furrow ploughland is commonly seen where the corrugations have been preserved under a blanket of pasture, but in such places one sees ridges though the earthworks do not, as is frequently presumed, reveal the dimensions of strips.

Ridge and furrow was not confined to medieval open-field farming. Land was ridged, probably to improve drainage, in various prehistoric fields; and plough-ridges, normally of a more sinuous form than the medieval type, were deliberately produced in various post-medieval privately owned fields. Neither was it the case that all open-field ploughland lay in ridge and furrow, for on the light well-drained soils of parts of East Anglia ridging does not seem to have been practised. In 1598 it was recorded that great strips with high ridges and deep furrows were found throughout the north and in some parts of southern England; that flat unridged ploughland was found in most parts of Cambridgeshire; and that little strips containing no more than two or three (ridges and) furrows were found in Middlesex, Essex and Hertfordshire. Plough-ridges may possibly have been first constructed with spades, but they were maintained by a system of ploughing working around each ridge in a clockwise manner so that the plough's mould-board turned the soil inwards. In this way the crown of the ridge stood between 1 and 3 feet (about 0.3 to 1 metre) higher than the furrows between the ridges. The ridges tended to be orientated in the direction of the slope, so as to facilitate drainage, and if there was severe flooding at least the crops growing on the crests of the ridges might survive.

Plough-ridges are not straight, and if one looks along a pattern of ridges it is usually seen that each ridge has the shape of a reversed 'S' or a 'C'. The curves, it is said, were produced by the need to swing the plough team into the turn before the end of the ridge was reached. This explanation for the curving ridges and furrows has been accepted for many years. However, Philip Brooks, who is both an accomplished local historian in Surrey and a retired farmer, tells us that 'there is not the slightest difficulty in making a square turn with a span of oxen. Ploughing with oxen was done until quite recently and no one needed to make turns like the (supposed) medieval ones'. He points out that lead animals should not be allowed to turn before reaching the end of the furrow as this would produce 'awful headlands' rather than a reversed S. He argues that the last yoke in the plough team should be kept straight until the plough is freed from the ground. Meanwhile the lead beasts swing into their turn and the last beasts are strong enough to pull the plough from the soil. In this way narrow headlands can be produced. With this criticism in mind, the explanation of reversed-S ridge and furrow becomes controversial.

Medieval plough teams, like those of preceding periods, were generally composed of oxen, and as many as eight beasts might draw the plough if the soil was a heavy clay. Ox ploughing could still be seen in some places at the end of the nineteenth century. Occasionally horses were harnessed to the plough, and in 1292 the manor court at Polstead in Suffolk heard how Philip Denelind had misused a horse lent to him by Robert le Coc. Robert complained that 'Philip

Medieval ridge and furrow outlined by melting snow near Appletreewick in Wharfedale. The fossil fields outlined in the upper-left corner above the houses might be 'Celtic' fields or the closes attached to former dwellings

received a certain horse from him in a certain covenant, namely, that the aforesaid Philip should keep the aforesaid horse and pasture it and harness it in the plough. Moreover . . . Philip beat the aforesaid horse and bound a stone onto the ear of this horse.' (Why Philip did this is not explained, but Cossack horsemen would put pebbles in the ear of a fractious horse, reasoning that horses were too stupid to think of more than one thing at a time, so that a horse with pebbles in its ear would think of pebbles rather than of misbehaving.) Mixed plough teams were sometimes used, and on Cottenham Manor in Cambridgeshire teams composed of four oxen and two horses are recorded in 1430. Subsequently the employment of horses in plough teams steadily increased, the main advantage of oxen remaining in the fact that they could be eaten when their working days were over. Special ploughing arrangements were made where the soil was clayey and clinging. An eighteenth- century painting which was found in a barn in Eskdale, Cumbria, depicts a very heavy plough controlled by three ploughmen drawn by two oxen yoked together and preceded by two heavy horses harnessed in tandem.

As the ploughshare moved through the earth a small amount of soil would be pushed ahead of it, while at the end of a furrow the ploughman might wipe clinging earth from the plough. Gradually substantial banks of such soil would accumulate at the end of each parcel of strips to exist as 'heads' or 'butts'.

Ridge and furrow could also be found in ancient countryside areas. This example, highlighted by frost, lies on elevated sloping ground in Nidderdale

'Headlands' formed in this way where a pair of adjacent furlongs had their ridges running at right angles to each other; while when the ridges in adjacent furlongs ran in the same direction a 'joint' developed from earth accumulating at either side of the headland boundary. The nature of the local terrain often made it impossible for the furlong to be divided into a neat pattern of parallel strips and ridges; and tapering strips or ridges, which were known as 'gores', occupied the gaps in the conventional pattern. Access through the open fields was improved when narrow strips or ridges were uncultivated and allowed to become grass-covered trackways, which were known as 'balks'. Following the outbreaks of the pestilence, or Black Death, which arrived in 1348 and recurred at various intervals until the mid-seventeenth century, shortages of peasant labour could result in strips going out of arable cultivation and becoming ribbons of grazing known as 'leys'. In some places, as at Laxton in Nottinghamshire, stretches of common meadow existed inside the open fields, often on difficult or badly drained ground and beside streams. Such little meadows were known as 'sykes' (pronounced 'siks'). Frequently strips were separated by very narrow ribbons of grass, also known as 'balks'.

Wherever expanses of open-field ploughland have been converted into permanent pasture or parkland the reader will be able to recognise the earthworks of ridge and furrow, gores, headlands, joints, furlong divisions and possibly the flatter areas about the size of a tennis-court or cricket-square which existed as 'rick places' which accommodated the stacks. The width of plough-ridges varied, but in general medieval ridges tended to be relatively broad. 'Narrow rigg', ridges about 16 feet (5 metres) wide and thus around half the typical medieval width, generally belong to a later period – being created, for example, when new arable land was broken in to increase grain production during the

This sketch shows the components of medieval ridge-and-furrow ploughland

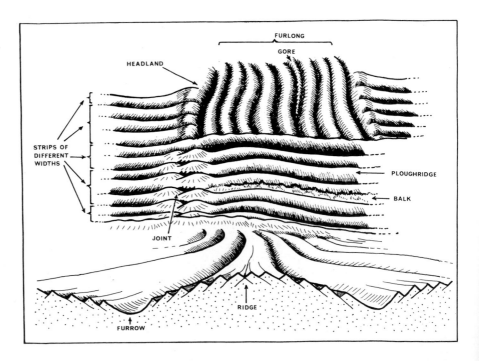

Napoleonic Wars. Finally, in a few places one may see very broad plough-ridges which are straight rather than curving and which were produced by steam ploughing in the nineteenth and twentieth centuries.

Experts disagree as to whether crop rotations operated on a field or a furlong basis. In different places and at different times both fields and furlongs may have served as the units on which rotations were practised, though the furlong rather than the field seems to have been the most common unit of rotation. At the same time it seems to have been universally the case that at any time all the furlongs in one of the great fields was rested as fallow. Frequently some of the other furlongs would be growing a winter-sown crop of wheat or rye and others a spring-sown crop of barley, oats or legumes, such as peas, beans or vetch. In the first season after the fallowing year a winter-sown crop might be cultivated, in the second a spring-sown crop, followed by a return to fallow.

Under feudalism all land was the property of the Crown. Some estates were royal manors which were operated directly for the King, many were held by the King's tenants-in-chief and then subinfeudated to lesser vassals, and every estate had its manorial lord. A portion of each estate was 'demesne' land, which was farmed by labour services exacted from the peasants of the village. Demesne strips were originally scattered throughout the open fields, though in the course of the medieval period attempts might be made to reorganise the pattern of land-holding to create a compact and consolidated demesne, while the gradual decay of feudal services and their replacement by cash rents resulted in the employment of farm labourers to cultivate the demesne.

Feudal society was above all a hierarchical society. Each member of the village community occupied a precisely defined position in the social pyramid, and although the names attached to each class changed during the course of the

Ridge-and-furrow ploughland surrounds the deserted medieval village, partly destroyed by quarrying, in the centre of the photograph, at West Welpington, Northumberland

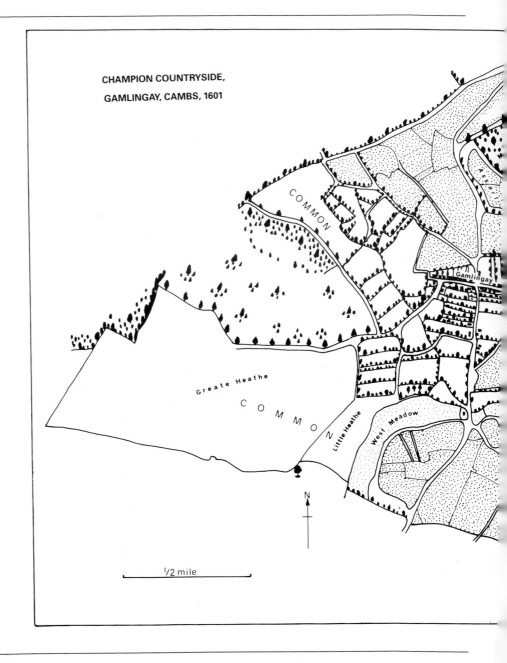

**CHAMPION COUNTRYSIDE,
GAMLINGAY, CAMBS, 1601**

1/2 mile

CHAMPION COUNTRYSIDE, GAMLINGAY, CAMBRIDGESHIRE, 1601

Gamlingay, as it existed in 1601, epitomised champion countryside. Open-field ploughland is shown in heavy stipple, common meadows in light stipple, and hedgerows and woodland are shown in the manner of the original map. The village is surrounded by privately held hedged closes, and beyond are the meadows and three great open fields.

Strips are not shown, but the furlongs and the maze of field-tracks are included. From the general appearance of the map it seems as though both Easte Fielde and Southe Fielde have been extended westwards. This is confirmed by the name 'Stock Inge' applied to the two furlongs just west of Mertonage Wood, which reveals an assart, and the furlong-

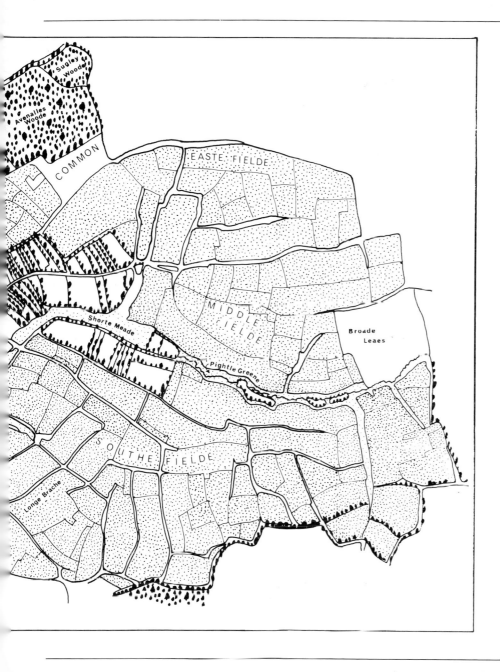

name 'Longe Brache' in South Field, a variation on 'Bratch' or 'Breach', which indicates land newly broken in. Meanwhile areas of common meadow near Pightle Greene have been enclosed, as have field-strips near the village and to the south of Shorte Meade. To the north of the village two furlongs have been enclosed by hedgerows, and their strips are in single ownership in each case. The land shown does not include the whole of the parish but the land of the manors of Mertonage and Avenalles. Woodberry Manor also had land in this parish. The Stock Inge assart is held by Mertonage Manor.

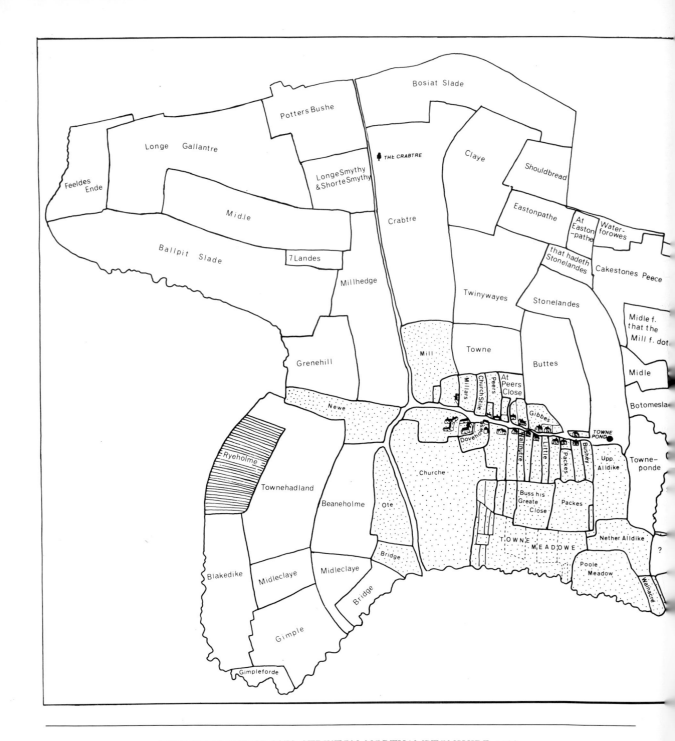

FURLONGS AND CLOSES, STRIXTON, NORTHAMPTONSHIRE, 1583

This shows an intensely arable parish largely covered by the furlongs of the open arable land. Non-arable land is stippled, with a cluster of small closes and meadowland in the vicinity of the village and an outlying cow-pasture. For the sake of simplicity the strip-patterns are drawn only in Ryeholme

Furlong. The furlongs have names which describe their soil or nearby features. Strixton is now a greatly shrunken village. After this map was drawn a great garden was established in Church Close, now only recognisable by the stepped earthworks of its terraces.

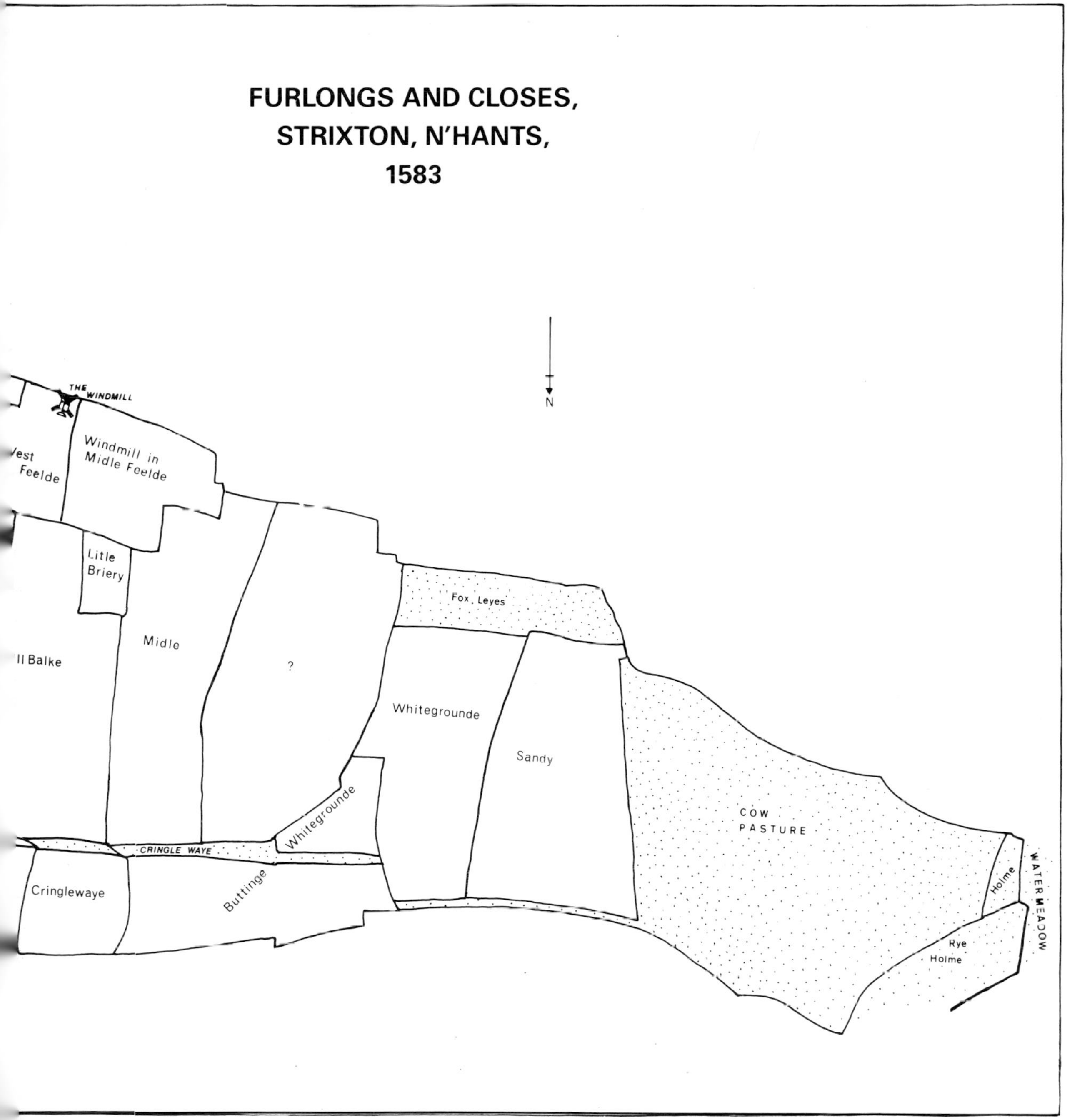

FURLONGS AND CLOSES,
STRIXTON, N'HANTS,
1583

N

THE WINDMILL

West Feelde

Windmill in Midle Foelde

Litle Briery

Midle

Il Balke

?

Fox. Leyes

Whitegrounde

Sandy

COW PASTURE

WATER MEADOW

CRINGLE WAYE

Whitegrounde

Cringlewaye

Buttinge

Holme

Rye Holme

Middle Ages, and members of a lower class might occasionally be more prosperous than their 'betters', each person was aware of his status, rights and obligations and was likely to be enraged if his standing was called into question. After the Norman Conquest efforts were made to simplify the complex social orders of Saxon England by applying the principles of Roman law, which regarded men as either serfs or bondmen on the one hand or free men on the other. The free family might hold less land than their bond neighbours (and could be landless craftsmen or labourers), but their status gave them access to the royal courts, freedom to leave the manor and sell their holdings and, generally, the right to pay rent for land rather than render labour service. On most manors free tenants were a minority within the community, though their numbers varied from region to region and there were proportionally more free people in the eastern lands which had been part of Danelaw.

Within the mass of unfree peasants, 'villeins' were the most numerous class. The offspring of villeins could inherit land, but villeins could not leave the manor of their birth and lacked independence, ten or twelve villeins being grouped together in bands known as 'tithings' or 'frankpledges'. Such groups shared mutual responsibility for the conduct of each individual member. Domesday Book of 1086 also records substantial numbers of 'bordars' and 'cottars', and the distinction between the two low-ranking unfree classes is not clear, both 'bord' and 'cot' being words describing cottages, dwellings which would have been even less attractive than the hovels which the villeins inhabited. Bordars held less land than villeins and consequently had lighter feudal services, and both bordars and the lowly cottars occupied the depths of the social hierarchy which had been populated by slaves in Saxon times.

By the thirteenth century the social order had evolved and the peasant classes were composed of 'franklins' or freemen; 'husbonds' or 'neats', who were the equivalents of the Domesday villeins; while the bordar and cottar classes had merged into one cottar class. Villeins who had managed to substitute the payment of a cash rent or 'mol' for feudal labour services on the demesne were known as 'molmen', while 'undersettles' or 'coterells' held no land directly from the lord of the manor, but were outsiders who were given cottages and small holdings by manorial tenants and served him as farmhands.

The social pyramid was not exactly related to the size of tenancies, and it was possible to be both free and a cottar. Most peasants held between 10 and 40 acres (c.4 and 16 hectares), and the typical holding was a 'virgate' or 'yardland' of around 30 acres (c.12 hectares), though many peasants held half-yardlands. In the north of England, where the terminology and land units were different, the typical holding was of two 'bovates' or 'oxgangs', though single oxgang holdings were frequent. In all cases the holding was composed of strips scattered throughout the open fields with proportional shares in the meadow and rights to grazing on the common. While strips were privately tenanted, much of the work on the land was performed communally and only the most affluent tenant would own sufficient beasts to form a plough team. Open-field farming depended upon a high level of co-operation between the members of the village community. Nevertheless, contemporary records paint a picture not of idyllic co-operation but of people who were individualistic, deeply suspicious of their neighbours, ceaselessly attempting to improve their own situation yet ever ready to believe that other villagers were seeking to cheat them out of bits of land.

Each open-field system was an object of great territorial and administrative complexity, and it is still not clear how, without recourse to maps or the written descriptions known as 'field books' which seem to have appeared in the later medieval centuries, peasants were actually able to identify their respective strips and their doles in the meadow. Bear in mind that a yardland might

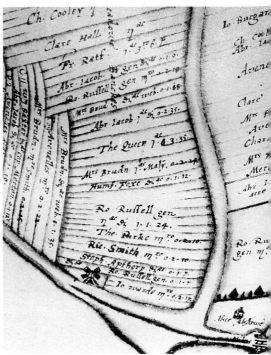

comprise between forty and eighty scattered strips and several times this number of plough-ridges; while where the ploughland was not ridged, as in much of Cambridgeshire, individual holdings would be even more difficult to recognise.

On each estate the major disputes and misdemeanours were respectively resolved and punished by the manorial court. In order to regulate the day-to-day farming operations the courts appointed officers to perform special tasks, like that of the hayward who had charge of the village herd. The bailiff ensured that feudal labour services were performed, and he was assisted by the reeve, who was elected by the villeins. Lesser matters were resolved by informal agreements between villagers, and members of the community arranged contracts concerning matters like the sharing of plough beasts. Every open-field system depended upon a multitude of arrangements, regulations and customs; yet, despite all the complexities, some endured for a thousand years.

As we have described, open-field farming was a feature of the champion countrysides and was most characteristic of the English Midlands. In areas of ancient countryside the system could be absent or unusual, poorly developed and short-lived. It scarcely penetrated Cornwall, where areas of countryside which largely preserve Romano-British or older field-patterns still endure. In Kent peasant land seems to have been held not in scattered strips but in compact 'yokelands' and farmed independently rather than communally. Although the division of yokelands between heirs could cause a fragmentation of the holdings, there was no development of the open-field farming of the champion areas. In East Anglia land could be held in dispersed strips, but without the appearance of communal farming and crop rotations. As a result Roman and prehistoric fields could pass through a medieval phase of strip cultivation yet emerge with their ancient boundaries still intact — so that extensive areas of Norfolk and Suffolk preserved their archaic coaxial field-networks until the modern era of hedgerow destruction.

Above left: Strip-patterns mapped at Gamlingay in Cambridgeshire in 1601. Note how many of the strips display a 'reversed-S' outline. Also, note the 'assart' name 'The Mertonage Stockinge', lower right

Above right: Detail from the Gamlingay map identifying the owners or tenants of some field-strips. The Queen had three strips sandwiched between those of Abraham Jacob and Mrs Brudnell

Open-field farming of the Midlands type appeared in some of the more productive localities of Scotland, Ireland and Wales. In both Ireland and the Englisheries of south Wales it will have been an English feudal introduction, though in some places it may have been developed by indigenous societies. Not all open fields were of the type described, and in the Celtic countries and in the less affluent and more difficult areas of northern England variations on the 'infield–outfield' system were found. With this form of farming the best ploughland was designated as the infield, and this area was never fallowed but kept in constant production by heavy applications of farmyard manure. Meanwhile, different pockets of the surrounding outfield grazing land were ploughed, cropped to exhaustion and then allowed to revert to pasture while fertility gradually recovered. Some experts have argued that infield–outfield farming was very widespread in Dark Age Britain and that the Midlands form of open-field farming developed from the infield–outfield system as the result of population pressure. This, it is claimed, caused the infield ploughland to expand across the outfield pastures, thus creating a need for common pasturing arrangements to be developed for grazing the open-field stubble and fallowing field. A weakness of this interpretation lies in the fact that there seem to be no firm documentary accounts of infield–outfield farming which pre-date the fourteenth century. It is quite possible that it was just a version of medieval

Field-strips survive in Braunton great field, north Devon. The dark-coloured strip in this photograph contains a crop of leeks and is bound by low balks

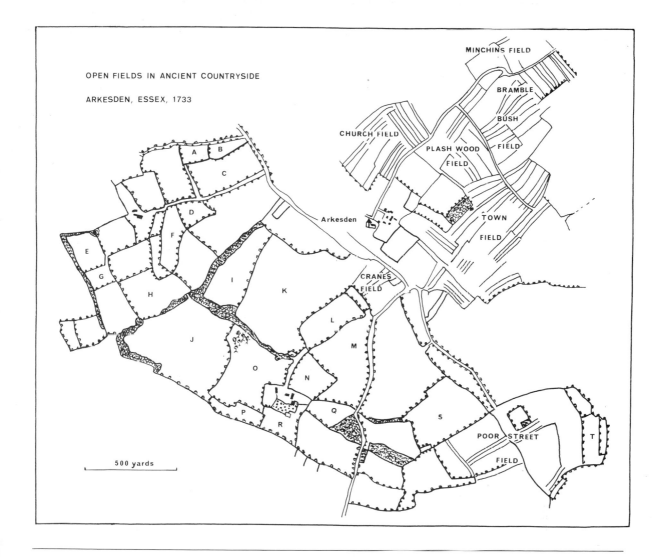

OPEN FIELDS IN ANCIENT COUNTRYSIDE

ARKESDEN, ESSEX, 1733

MINCHINS FIELD

BRAMBLE

BUSH

CHURCH FIELD

PLASH WOOD FIELD

FIELD

TOWN FIELD

Arkesden

CRANES FIELD

POOR STREET

FIELD

500 yards

OPEN FIELDS IN ANCIENT COUNTRYSIDE, ARKESDEN, ESSEX, 1733

Open fields were found in ancient countryside areas, but they were small, relatively short-lived and shared between just a few tenants. The map of Arkesden shows seven little open fields, though not one of them would compare with a large furlong in champion countryside. The open fields are obviously declining; strips have been amalgamated, and some packages of strips enclosed with hedgerows. The name Michin Field reveals a field associated with nuns, and a nunnery existed nearby. With its hedged pastures, winding lanes, irregular pastures and small woods this is typical ancient country. The name 'Stockin' reveals assarts, and Stockin Field (J) is unusually large. There is a medieval record of a strip in this field, and it was probably previously an open field.

Field-names, which are not simply recording owners or areas, are:

A	Upper Horse Pasture	H	Stockin alias 13 Acres	O	The Lawn
B	Lower Horse Pasture	I	West Mead	P	Horse Pasture
C	Further Chardwell	J	Stockin	Q	The Ley
D	Barn Mead	K	Great Darvel	R	Tump Close
E	Mill Field	L	Rush Darvel	S	Mad Ley
F	Wrights Mead	M	Cote Field	T	Dauney Hook
G	The Ley	N	Dovehouse Close		

Tump Close may have contained an ancient burial-mound, and Mad Ley means Meadow Ley.

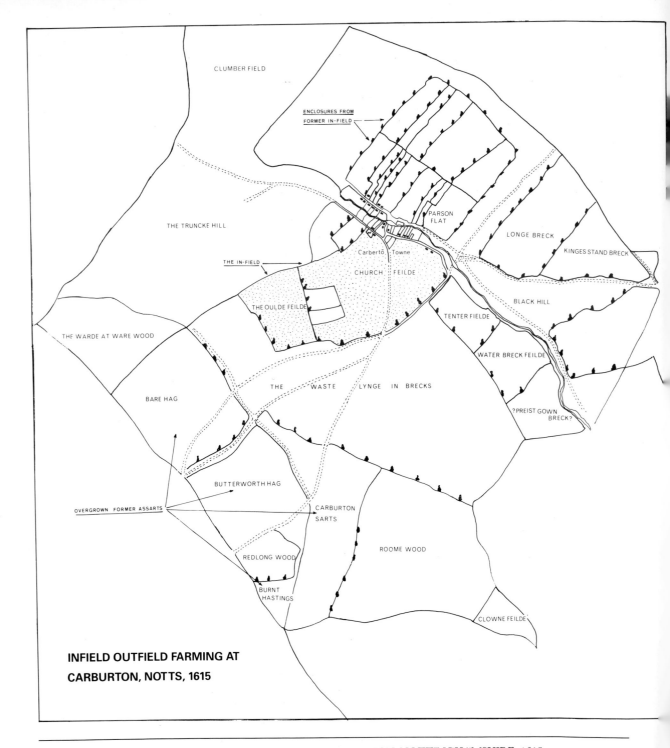

INFIELD OUTFIELD FARMING AT CARBURTON, NOTTS, 1615

(Labels visible on the map:)

CLUMBER FIELD

ENCLOSURES FROM FORMER IN-FIELD

THE TRUNCKE HILL

PARSON FLAT

LONGE BRECK

KINGES STAND BRECK

Carbertō Towne

THE IN-FIELD

CHURCH FEILDE

BLACK HILL

THE OULDE FEILDE

TENTER FIELDE

THE WARDE AT WARE WOOD

WATER BRECK FEILDE

BARE HAG

THE WASTE LYNGE IN BRECKS

?PREIST GOWN BRECK?

OVERGROWN FORMER ASSARTS

BUTTERWORTH HAG

CARBURTON SARTS

ROOME WOOD

REDLONG WOOD

BURNT HASTINGS

CLOWNE FEILDE

INFIELD – OUTFIELD FARMING AT CARBURTON, NOTTINGHAMSHIRE, 1615

The map portrays a declining infield-outfield system with the infield area above the village now enclosed by hedgerows. Below the stippled infield the land is divided between the 'brecks' of the outfield. Several outfield assarts have become overgrown. The name 'hag' denotes an assart, while 'tenter' reveals a field where cloth was stretched on frames, 'flat' reveals an old furlong, and 'lynge' or 'ling' is land where heather grows.

open-field farming that appeared and evolved along with other versions as an adaptation of the system to localities where little good arable land was available.

Infield–outfield farming was characteristic of the poorer parts of Britain where the supply of arable land was restricted. The sandy Brecklands region of the Norfolk–Suffolk border zone takes its name from the temporary 'brecks' or breaks made for cultivation. The Brecklands are often given as an example of an area where infield–outfield farming predominated, but now it is suspected that the region actually supported three field systems of the Midlands type. The infield–outfield system was common in the valleys and hollows of northern England where areas of suitable ploughland existed in pockets or ribbons amongst the fells and moors. Most of the small villages and hamlets of the Lake District had infields nearby. At Threlkeld on the southern flanks of Saddleback, one still existed in the middle of the nineteenth century. It covered only 14 acres (c.6 hectares), and the holders of five adjacent farmsteads tilled the total of just eleven strips. In Ireland an infield–outfield system known as 'rundale' was oper- ated and survived in some remote localities until recent times, though the simi- lar 'runrig' system of the old Gaelic-speaking areas of Scotland which endured into the nineteenth century in many remote localities is more clearly under- stood. The first mention of runrig, which describes the intermixing of tenants' strips across the infield land of a farming township, 'toun', 'fermtoun' or *clachan,* dates from 1428, although the system must have been well established by then and there are strong hints of its existence in a Kelso Abbey charter of the mid-twelfth century. In the Lowlands the land tended to be owned by feudal magnates, while in the Highlands by clan chieftains who were virtually supreme within their respective clan territories. It was then sublet to 'tacksmen', members of the lesser gentry and often relatives of the clan chief. The tacksmen in turn sublet the land to tenants. Sometimes one tenant controlled all the land in a toun or township, but often the land was subdivided between several tenants holding shares of differing sizes. Those who farmed the land generally lived in conditions of considerable hardship and squalor, though the bottom of the rural hierarchy was composed of landless cottars who served as farm labourers and sometimes lived in distinct settlements or 'cottouns'.

Within the infield, runrig produced a landscape of strips and plough-ridges reminiscent of open-field land in the English Midlands. The system whereby strips were allocated may have been different, for it appears that landholders were regarded as having shares in the resources of the township, so that a tenant holding a share of a fifth might sometimes be allocated every fifth strip as the allocation worked its way around the infield. In other cases a form of sun divi- sion may have been involved, with the allocation beginning in the sunny or south-eastern quarter of the township and moving around to the shadow side of the north-west as the allocation progressed. A tenant who had won the sunny portion was allocated strips to the south and east in each round of allocation. The geographer Robert Dogshon has described how land at Haliburton, near Berwick, was divided between Melrose Abbey and Walter of Haliburton in 1428. The interested parties drew lots to decide which would hold the sunny side and which the shadow portion.

The infield usually covered the flatter lower lands of the township and was commonly divided into three 'breaks' where rotations of oats–oats–barley

Rural scene in County Roscommon, Ireland, sketched in 1880, showing Irish peasants at work in a potato field. Note the thatched mud-walled cabins in the background. By the twentieth century famine and emigration had made scenes such as this quite rare

could be practised. After the harvest livestock were turned into the infield to graze the stubble and fertilise the field, while manure which had accumulated in the farmyards of the township was spread on the break where barley had grown. In coastal settings seaweed was also spread on this land. In this way the infield was fertilised but not fallowed, and the break which had grown barley would then be sown with oats without any respite from arable cultivation.

Beyond the infield lay the outfield, which was divided into numerous breaks. Each year a new break would be brought back into cultivation and cropped for three, four or five years until its soils were exhausted. At any particular time around a third of the outfield would be cropped, with the remaining breaks being fallowed as pasture. The outfield arable land was not manured and grew successive crops of oats, but livestock were folded in turf-walled pens on the outfield break which would next be brought into cultivation, with the turf from the pens being spread along with the manure.

In the Highlands infield and outfield land was surrounded by a substantial turf wall known as the 'head dike', and beyond it lay the extensive common grazings of the 'muir' or moor. High on the moor the community of the township had their 'shielings', settlements of flimsy huts which were occupied by a portion of the population when the herds were driven up to the summer mountain grazings at the start of May. In the Lowlands, where arable farming might predominate over the pastoral element, a town might lack muir and shielings or have rights to upland grazings some distance from their farmland.

In the Lowlands the runrig system was eliminated by the agricultural improvements of the eighteenth century, which favoured the creation of fewer but more viable and compact tenant farms. In the Highlands the notorious Clearances of the eighteenth and nineteenth centuries eradicated the fermtouns, shielings, infields and outfields, and replaced them with vast and desolate sheep-ranges.

The evidence seems to show that in the champion countryside of England open-field farming was present and evolving at the start of the Middle Ages. The antiquity of the infield–outfield forms of open-field farming is much less certain. All kinds of open-field farming varied considerably through time and from place to place, while the champion heartland of England was virtually surrounded by areas of countryside where open fields were absent or uncommon and where rural vistas of great antiquity may sometimes still be glimpsed.

Medieval times, like all times before the mechanisation of farming in the closing decades of Victoria's reign, were days of crowded fields. Since most of the people who might be found toiling in the countryside were impoverished and illiterate, we only encounter the medieval countryfolk in official and manorial documents, which recite their obligations and misdemeanours, so we learn little about their feelings, aspirations and tribulations.

The countryside was built from the grinding and unremitting toil of peasants. A member of each villein household was generally required to perform two or three days' work on the lord's demesne. During the harvest the burden of labour services was increased as requirements for additional 'boon works' were announced, and at such times even free men might be required to perform labour services. In addition, the peasants were fined or taxed as every little milestone in their lives of drudgery was reached. Late in the medieval period the burden of obligations on Wrington manor, held by the Abbot of Glastonbury, was recorded on a sort of inventory known as a 'terrier':

Be it noted that each customary tenant, as often as he has brewed one full brew, shall give to my lord abbot 4d under the name of tolcestre [a tax on ale]. *Item* each customary tenant shall give mast money for his pigs . . . [a tax on grazing pigs in the manorial woods]. *Item,* be it noted that the customary tenants are bound to grind their corn at my lord's mill, or to pay a yearly tribute in money, viz. each holder of a yardland 2s 8d [and so on down to the humblest cottar, who paid 4d]. Be it noted also that, when any shall die my lord shall take his heriot, to wit his best beast. And if there be no beast, from the holder of a yardland or half a yardland he shall have one acre of corn; and from any lesser tenant, if he have so much land in cultivation, the lord shall have half an acre of his best corn. And even though the wife die before the man, he shall give no heriot; but if she die in the holding after her husband's death, and shall have given it up to my lord or shall die in her widowhood, my lord shall have the heriot aforesaid. And if there be no corn, then my lord shall have the best chattel found in the tenement on the day of death. . . .Note, that whosoever shall be tenant of the customary mill, which is now held by Edmund Leneregge, is bound to provide mill-stones, so that the burden fall not upon my lord, as was found upon the copy of William Truebody, lately tenant of that house and mill.

In addition to the demands made by the lord of the manor the peasant household bore the heavy burden of tithes which, if not partly evaded, would remove a tenth part of the annual production. And, just as the lord stepped in to claim the heriot, so the death of a tenant was made even more onerous to the dependants when the Church took its mortuary of the second-best beast. When the heir took over the holding of the deceased the lord claimed an 'entry fine', and when the daughter of a tenant married the lord was likely to demand a 'merchet' of cash or kind. The household was also fined if a son sought to leave the manor to enter the priesthood, while if the daughter was unchaste a fine or 'leywrite' was taken. The manor also profited from fines imposed at the manor court, where the peasants were disciplined for their misdeeds – which often involved reluctance, insubordination or incompetence when performing labour services.

Thus, at Wakefield manor court in 1331, Thomas Tallor was fined four shillings because he 'broke the oven of John del Rhodes and stole therefrom ryebread'. At the same court and in the same year Julian le Spicer was fined two pence 'for baking bread for sale in her own oven without licence'. In 1593 the court found that Margaret and Elizabeth Longfellowe were scolds and should be ducked in the ducking-stool three times before Christmas or pay a fine of 6s 8d. In 1315, John de Damyas was fined a shilling for building two fish-weirs on the River Calder which obstructed a path to a ford and reduced the efficiency of the manorial mill. At Foxton in Cambridgeshire in 1326 ten tenants were each fined two pence for making sheaves that were too small – doubtless in an attempt to cheat the rector of his tithes. On the same manor two years earlier Alice Barley was fined the substantial sum of 3s 4d for attempting to prevent the lord's bailiff from seizing a lamb.

SOME PLACES OF INTEREST

In some places open-field farming endured for a thousand years, so it is not surprising that its influence on present countrysides is still considerable. However, it was virtually eradicated by the Parliamentary Enclosure movement in England and Wales and by the Improvements and Clearances in Scotland, all occurring during the eighteenth and nineteenth centuries. The characteristic corduroy patterns of ridge and furrow can be seen as earthworks in most regions, in places where the ploughlands were converted into permanent pastures or parkland. As a result of accidents of history some strip-like holdings escaped consolidation, and in a few cases some of the institutions of medieval farming also survived. Even so, centuries of change separate the surviving relics from the era of medieval farming and no perfectly preserved medieval field system survives.

Laxton (SK 7266). The village is in Nottinghamshire about 4 miles (7 kilometres) to the east of Ollerton. When Laxton was mapped in 1635 it had four open fields – Mill Field, South Field, West Field and East Field – and a simple rotation of winter corn, spring corn and fallow was operated, with the two smaller fields, West Field and East Field, serving as a single unit for the purpose of rotations. There was little unusual about the medieval farming at Laxton, but the village was unusual in that the strip fields were never fully enclosed, while some of the institutions of medieval farming survived. The old patterns are imperfectly fossilised; East Field was enclosed in the present century, there have been many amalgamations of neighbouring strips, and the enclosure of the little riverside meadows has resulted in the existence of twenty-three meadows where previously there were 322 doles which were mown for hay each year before the meadows were thrown open as common grazing. Between 1906 and 1909, Earl Manvers, the Lord of the Manor, instituted a reorganisation of the strip-patterns, and strips were consolidated and redistributed, with typical half-acre (0.2-hectare) strips being combined in packages of eight or ten to produce four- or five-acre (1.6- or 2-hectare) units. The Court Baron of Laxton is summoned by the Bailiff and presided over by the Steward. It appoints a jury and a pinder, an official responsible for placing stray livestock in the village pound or pinfold. The jury is responsible for ditching, the pegging-out of holdings and enforcing the custom of the open fields.

Braunton (SS 4836). This settlement in Devon, five miles (8 kilometres) to the north-west of Barnstaple, claims to be Britain's largest village. More interesting is the fact that it retains parts of its medieval open fields. Some strips were enclosed, singly or in groups, by hedgerows long ago, but much of the Great Field remains open. In 1979 only about twenty proprietors remained, and many field-strips were consolidated, so that most of those seen today are, as at Laxton, much broader than were the original strips. In places one can still see the 1-foot (0.3-metre) grass balks which separate adjacent holdings. The Great Field lies to the south of Braunton village, and can be entered via Greenaway Lane, recorded as 'weste grene waye' in 1324.

The Isle of Portland (SY 6870). The Isle of Portland is connected to the Dorset mainland near Weymouth by a causeway which carries the A354. In 1842 open fields covered about 825 acres (333 hectares) on the island, though by 1970 the piecemeal enclosure of field-strips had reduced this area to about 150 acres (60 hectares). In the areas where the strips have endured they are separated by balks of grass, while repeated episodes of cultivation have resulted in the creation of steps or lynchets between adjacent strips on areas of sloping ground. Those on flatter ground are defined by narrow balks of grass. The strips, known locally as 'lawnsheds', can be over 300 yards (274 metres) long and 10–75 yards (9–69 metres) in width. In the 1970s the surviving strips were given protection under Ancient Monument status.

Soham (TL 5973). This village is in Cambridgeshire, about 5 miles (8 kilometres) to the south-east of Ely. To the north of the village a tongue of medieval ploughland projected into the Fens and constituted the North Field of the village. Soham experienced no formal Act of Enclosure and, although much of the village ploughland was enclosed piecemeal at various times, North Field retained its strip-patterns. The field is not farmed in common, so that the strips are privately owned and not subject to a single rotation, but they are still unenclosed and are not divided by balks, while the old furlong-patterns can still be recognised.

Forrabury (SX 1092). The fields of Forrabury occupy sloping ground to the north of the village and failed medieval town of Boscastle in Cornwall. Forty

surviving open-field strips are rented to six tenant farmers by the National Trust. On the flatter ground the strips are divided by balks of grass, while on the steeper slopes they become terraces, their lynchets being stabilised by low walls of slate. The strips are probably relics of the open field of the medieval borough, although it has been suggested that they may be relics of Iron Age in-field farming. Consolidation of older strips has resulted in the formation of strips which are considerably broader than the original units, although the characteristically curving strip-boundaries are plainly displayed in this, a county in which open-field farming made few advances.

South Zeal (SX 6593). The closes and tofts associated with medieval villages frequently survive, but perhaps the most notable example concerns the tofts at South Zeal on the northern edge of Dartmoor. More properly these tofts should be referred to as 'burgage plots' since South Zeal is a stagnated medieval borough which was founded in 1299. Dwellings were sited along each side of the through-road, and each household had a ribbon of land the width of its roadside frontage running back at right angles to the road to the hedges which traced the boundaries of the town. The plots were hedged and, although there have been some amalgamations, many hedges and several original plots still survive.

Wasdale Head (NY 1808). The hamlet has a magnificent setting below Great Gable and at the head of Wastwater lake in Cumbria. Here the infield covered about 300 acres (120 hectares) and was shared between about eighteen farmers. In preparing the land for ploughing thousands of stones and boulders were gathered together in piles, and these 'clearance cairns' are still prominent. At some stage in the post-medieval period the infield was enclosed and partitioned into irregular private fields by a network of winding walls, some of which incorporate clearance cairns. A track runs through the enclosures, and an overall view of the old infield can be admired from the flanks of Great Gable.

The old infield at Wasdale Head, Cumbria, shared between about eighteen farmers before being partitioned and enclosed by stone walls. The 'clearance cairns' or hummocks within the field are composed of stones gathered from ploughland

CHAPTER 4

CHANGE IN THE MEDIEVAL COUNTRYSIDE

Although some open-field patterns survived almost intact if not unchanged for a thousand years – so that the great-grandfathers or even the grandfathers of some readers will have worked amongst ridges, strips and furlongs which were quite similar to those tilled by Norman villeins – change was a constant feature of medieval and later countrysides. From late Saxon times until the fourteenth century the population grew steadily, and this growth put pressure on the waste of woodland, common pasture, fen and moor. As a result, areas of open land were cleared of trees, stones or heath and enclosed to expand the fieldscape. Meanwhile, the urge to increase and consolidate holdings or to rationalise the working day often led to the gradual dismantling of open-field strip farming and the creation of private fields formed from the gathering-together of blocks of adjacent strips.

The winning of new farmland from the waste was known as 'assarting'. The reclamation of land – much of it wooded land that was farmed in prehistoric and Roman times but which had passed out of cultivation during the decline of the Dark Ages – could be achieved in a variety of ways. Members of a swelling village community which now faced a shortage of ploughland might engage *en masse* in a bout of felling, with the cleared land then being shared out in strips which would add a new furlong or even a new field to their open-field system. One of the open fields at Boarstall in Buckinghamshire was called 'Frith field', and one of the three at Burton Leonard, near Ripon, was called 'Shaw field', both names denoting woodland. Cistercian monks (or more accurately their lay brothers, who did most of the practical farmwork) might clear an area to add new ploughland or sheep-ranges to the monastic estate. Such monastic ploughland might be ridged but would not be divided into strips. Meanwhile, individual peasants might undertake their own little campaigns of assarting, in which case the assart would not be added to the common ground of the open fields, but would be hedged, ditched or walled as a new, privately tenanted field. Lords might also enlarge their personal demesne by assarting – though the Statute of Merton of 1235 obliged the lord to ensure that his tenants still had sufficient pasture. In the Chilterns during the thirteenth century lords shared out newly assarted lands between their tenants, and in a substantial land-reclamation scheme which affected the Lincolnshire Fens between 1230 and 1250 the new land, lying in seven 'hundreds' or districts, was divided between the villages and then between individual village households. At

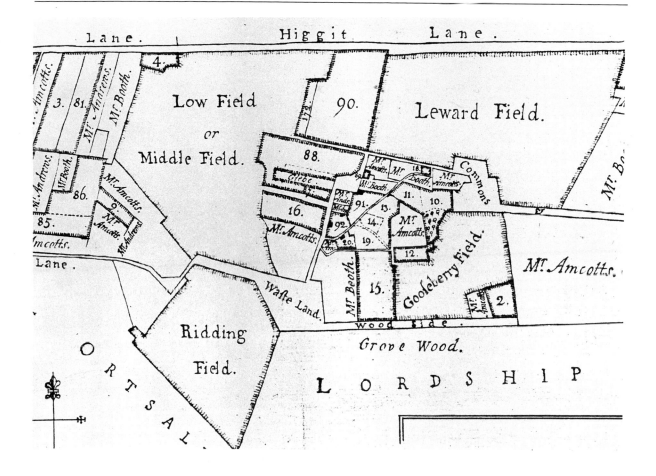

Carburton in Nottinghamshire (see p. 74), an area was described on a map of 1615 as 'Carberton Sarts. The Towne of Carberton free', revealing a block of woodland cleared and incorporated into the common outfield.

Assarts can often be recognised in surviving place-names or on old field-maps, and were known by a variety of names in addition to the obvious 'sart'. 'Stocks', 'stubs' and 'stubbings' refer to the stumps of felled trees. In the north of England names like 'ridding', 'rode' and 'royd' tell of land cleared of trees. In East Anglia 'ridland' and 'ridden' occur. 'Brand', 'brant' and 'brent' names occur in the Midlands and can refer to the burning of woodland – though 'brant' names can also derive from an Old Norse word for sloping ground. Other names, like 'green', 'ley' or 'lees', 'field' and 'bratch', 'breech' or 'bretch' (refer-ring to newly broken ground), will sometimes denote assarts, as do 'hag' names in the Midlands. Where assarted land was taken into the open fields it is unlike-ly to be recognisable today, but many individually cleared and tenanted medieval assarts survive within the present fieldscape, generally as small or very small and rather irregular hedged fields. Where one finds such a field which bears an assart name its origin is scarcely in doubt, and it is also likely that neighbouring fields which have a similar form but may not have tell-tale assart names will also be assarts.

A four-field system surrounding the little village of Gringley in Nottinghamshire, as mapped in 1720. The name 'Ridding Field' plainly implies land assarted in the medieval period

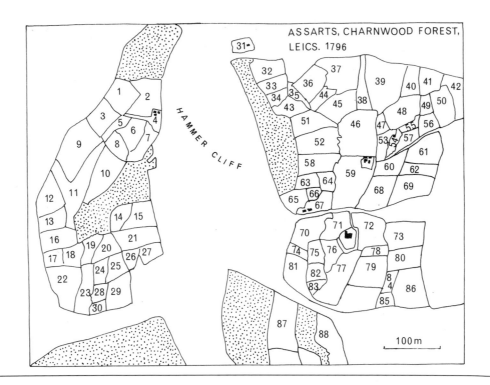

ASSARTS, CHARNWOOD FOREST, LEICESTERSHIRE, 1796

The area of fields shown in this late-eighteenth-century estate-map appears to have been completely assarted by the end of the fourteenth century, with the stippled area of woodland, top left, being bounded by fourteenth-century wood-banks. The rugged ground of Hammer Cliff remained unenclosed. The field-shapes are typical of assarts, though relatively few characteristic assart field-names are seen.

FIELD-NAMES

1 Copt Oak Close	23 Long Close	45 Near Holly Close	67 Homestead
2 Home Close	24 Little Close	46 Corn Close	68 Lower Blackleys
3 Horses Close	25 Old House Close	47 Little Meadow	69 Upper Blackleys
4 Pen Yard	26 Keightleys Yard	48 Hungry Meadow	70 Bastard Leys
5 Top Lane	27 Cooks	49 Faulkners' Close Mead	71 Portals Close
6 Pegg Close	28 Little Close	50 Faulkners' Close Meadow	72 House Close
7 Pegg Close	29 Rough Close	51 Far Conduit Leas	73 Park
8 Garret Meadow	30 Little Close	52 Near Conduit Leas	74 Calf Carts
9 Far Close	31 Collins' Homestead	53 Rough Meadow	75 Three-days works
10 Colbourn Close	32 Rough Close	54 Homestead	76 Ponds Close
11 Rush Close	33 Green Close	55 New Close	77 Rough Meadow
12 White Hills	34 Hill Close	56 Rough Piece	78 Little nook end
13 Corn Close	35 Pingle	57 Close	79 Rushy Close
14 Forge Close	36 Great Gate Piece	58 Conduit Leas	80 Hill Close
15 Far Forge Close	37 Upper Holly Close	59 Home Close	81 Upper Hollys
16 Great Close	38 Long Close	60 Blackley Meadow	82 Lower Hollys
17 House Close	39 Ash Close	61 Corner Blackleys	83 Holly
18 Brook Close	40 Middle Sheep Pen	62 Middle Blackleys	84 Near Wood Croft
19 Cat tails	41 Sheep	63 ⎫	85 Far Wood Croft
20 Broad Meadow	42 Faulkners' Close	64 ⎬ No name	86 Green Close
21 Near Forest Close	43 Johns Close	65 ⎪	87 Near Noels
22 Benty Close	44 Little Gate Piece	66 ⎭	88 Near Noels

Assarting will have gathered momentum in late Saxon and Norman times, to reach a peak of activity in the thirteenth century. Following the onslaughts of the Black Death in the decades after 1348, the activity declined since empty holdings were now readily available on the plague-struck manors, but assarting resumed in many places in the fifteenth century. In royal forests the sale of licences to assart provided a useful source of state revenue. Unsanctioned assarting took place on countless manors but could be legitimised when the lord – unable in any event to stem the tide of clearance – charged the tenants of assarted land an 'entry fine' to take over the new ground. Thus, at the manor court of Wakefield in 1309, William son of Thomas of Hallamshire paid his entry fine of a shilling (5p) and undertook to pay an annual rent of sixpence (2½p) to take over land cleared from the waste at Hepworth which lay 'in front of his door'. Presumably William had already set up house on the waste with every intention of clearing the surrounding land. Plainly the individual could profit from assarting, and some families, like the del Sarte family in the Batley area, were very actively engaged in clearing new land (as the del Sarte name implies). At the same time the newly won lands had not been worthless, but had often supplied the community with timber, woodland grazing and other useful resources. The holders of assarts were obliged to enclose them as fields, often with a ditch to mark the property-boundary and with a hedge just inside the ditch.

The distinction between an assart and an 'intake' is not always precise. The intake could be a piece of land taken in from the margin of the village common or heath and tilled and cropped for a few years before reverting to pasture. However, intakes had a habit of becoming permanently alienated, whether the lord or the community at large liked it or not. Sometimes attempts were made to prevent such permanent alienation of intakes by tolerating temporary 'breaks' or 'brecks' but forbidding the use of compost or manure, so that the decline in soil fertility would quickly deter continuing cultivation. Intakes were known by a variety of names, like 'ofnam', 'innam' and 'inhoc', and were usually a potential source of trouble. As well as encroaching on the common, intakes might also be made in the open field which was fallowing. At Broughton Hackett near Worcester, for example, in the July of 1287 the commoners of Broughton and their neighbours from Upton Snodsbury drove their cattle to Broughton fallow field and found the men of one John Lovet cultivating an intake on the traditionally shared fallow grazings. A brawl ensued in which one of the men was killed.

While assarting was essentially a medieval activity which petered out as the resources of available woodland dwindled, the enclosure of intakes continued into the post-medieval centuries and the attempts by local farmers to enclose 'newtakes' from Dartmoor still poses a problem to the National Park authorities. One of the incentives to the Dartmoor farmer is that on enclosed ground he can select his breeding stock rather than having his sheep or cattle choose their own 'Mr Right' on the open moor – though the roadside newtakes do disfigure the essentially open moorland landscape and impede ramblers walking from roadside to open country.

Intakes, therefore, are of many ages. Some are fossilised enclosures of common land that were originally illegal, some, associated with squatter cottages, were tolerated by the authorities when they were not a severe cause of local

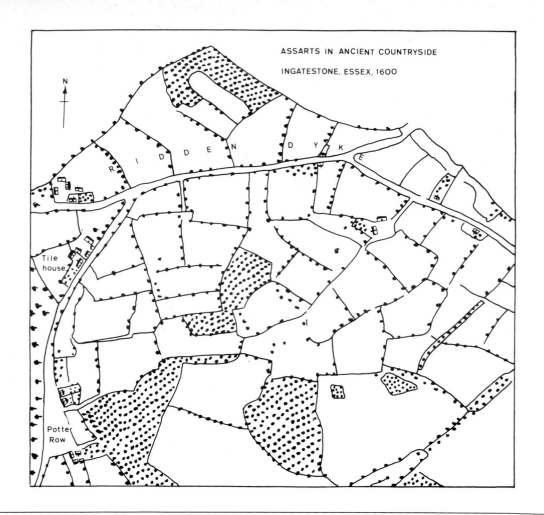

ASSARTS IN ANCIENT COUNTRYSIDE

INGATESTONE, ESSEX, 1600

ASSARTS IN ANCIENT COUNTRYSIDE

While ancient countryside contains many very old features, fields produced by medieval forest clearance can be quite common. In the map of Ingatestone, drawn in 1600–1, almost all the fields lying to the north of the east–west track are labelled 'parcel of Ridden Dyke'. 'Ridden' is one of the commonest assart-names, and the assart must have run from the track to a ditch at the boundary of the lordship. In this case the clearance can be dated, for it is revealed in a charter of John de Geyton, steward of the convent of Barking, dated to around 1225. So the Ridden Dyke clearances relate to the peak period of assarting. The symbols used by the cartographer to represent hedgerows, woods and dwellings have been reproduced. The hamlet of Potter Row, with its little triangular green, and the loose hamlet associated with the tileworks of John Finch, tilemakers, are now gone. Both were probably related to a good local deposit of clay.

contention; while others in old mining and quarrying areas were provided by landlords as small holdings which would supply remote industrial families with an additional source of income and sustenance. Intakes can be seen around the margins of many old upland commons. They are a particularly prominent feature of the countryside in Swaledale, where their irregular stone walls often lie on slopes just below the arrow-straight walls built when Parliamentary Enclosure finally sliced up the moors and the rough pastures of the ancient commons.

Assarting provided a safety-valve for the pressures caused by the medieval population-increase, though by the time that the Black Death arrived to impose a brutal natural remedy the scope for further woodland clearance had been severely reduced. In upland areas of England assarting alone was not the solution to the quest for new land, for in such places ploughland was restricted to pockets of workable soil in the valleys and hollows. As a result, the desperate drive to win new tillage from the thin dry soils of the chalk downlands or the limestone valley slopes of the Pennines produced what is perhaps the most spectacular exhibit in the national portfolio of fieldscapes: the flight of strip lynchets. With agriculture reaching the limits of the more amenable terrain, peasants were obliged to till ground which had not been ploughed since prehistoric times, when the climate was more favourable to upland farming. As open-field farming was extended up the slopes the plough was used to carve a staircase of hillside terraces. Spade and pick might have been used in the initial preparation of the slopes, but by repeatedly ploughing in directions which ran roughly parallel to the contour-line cultivation terraces, which could be between 60 yards (55 metres) and 250 yards (230 metres) in length, were created. Grain could then be grown on the level 'treads' of the hillside staircase, while grazing beasts could be tethered on the steep 'risers'. Earthen ramps provided the plough teams with access from one tread to others above and below.

Old intakes run across this Wensleydale photograph, forming a band above the ribbon of woodland and below the old common, later partitioned by straight Parliamentary Enclosure walls

Overleaf: Stone-walled intakes ascending the hillside near Muker in Swaledale. Note how virtually every field in the photograph contains a field-barn, used for storing hay which was fed to cattle wintering in the barns. Their dung was then spread upon the field

Strip lynchets have frequently been falsely identified as prehistoric fields, though in various places, as in the Malham area of the Yorkshire Dales, it is plain that they are superimposed on the older and really ancient fields. It has also been suggested that they are the terraces of Roman or medieval vineyards – though anyone who has strolled amongst the strip lynchets on the chilly slopes of Wharfedale or Swaledale will know the fallacy of this notion. There can be no doubt that most strip lynchets were carved during a period of land-hunger and population-pressure during the Middle Ages – a period which must pre-date the ravages of the Black Death. In many northern locations the lynchets were abandoned as plough-terraces, and networks of walls were superimposed across the older patterns, though in the south of England some farmers still plough the treads created by their distant forebears.

Strip lynchets are frequently seen on the flanks of the chalk downs in Dorset and Wiltshire and on the valley slopes of the Yorkshire Dales. They can also be recognised in regions like East Anglia, where subsequent ploughings of chalk slopes have, however, often carved away the medieval terraces. Parts of Swaledale, the vicinity of Linton in Wharfedale, and the countrysides near Worth Matravers in Dorset and Coombe Bisset in Wiltshire preserve excellent examples. At Challacombe Down on Dartmoor the flights of strip lynchets probably date from the thirteenth century; here the land on the terraces was ridged and worked from a hamlet now represented only by Challacombe Farm.

Medieval strip lynchets form the horizontal pleating on this hillside in Littondale. They seem to be superimposed on an older pattern of fields running up the slope

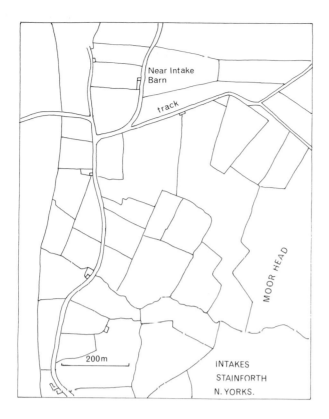

Intakes at Stainforth, North Yorkshire. A typical pattern of intakes representing a series of irregular bites into the moorland edge

Change could also occur within the long-established ploughlands. In Chapter 2 we described how conventional furlongs could result from the division of older long furlongs. Later, the reverse process could sometimes occur, with joints being ploughed over to join up the strips in neighbouring furlongs. Christopher Taylor has suggested that the adoption of horses to replace oxen in plough teams could have encouraged the linking of furlongs to produce new furlongs composed of longer strips.

Where a fully fledged system of open-field farming existed, most or all of the peasant farmsteads would be concentrated in the village that lay at the heart of the little agricultural empire. Here neighbours could easily meet to organise their activities, and the settlement had a conveniently central position in relation to its surrounding fields. However, had an economist been able to mount a work-efficiency study in such a village, he or she would doubtless have been appalled by the amount of time wasted by journeys made in all directions for work on the scattered strips. Not surprisingly, medieval peasants and yeomen would seek to rationalise their efforts and perhaps increase their holdings by swapping or buying strips in order to obtain more consolidated blocks of land. When a group of adjacent strips had been obtained the farmer was likely to hedge or wall around the block, and when the piecemeal process of purchase and exchange had produced a compact holding the fortunate family might even quit the village and set up a new farmstead in the midst of their land.

As these gradual attempts at consolidation proceeded over the centuries the open-field system could be almost completely dismantled, so that in the eighteenth century some open-field patterns were still intact, some had surrendered to piecemeal enclosure, and others were largely intact or largely dismantled.

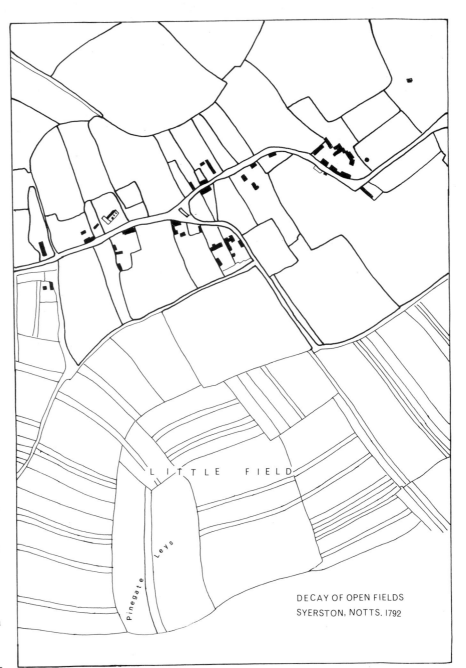

Within the map: LITTLE FIELD, Pinegate Leys

DECAY OF OPEN FIELDS
SYERSTON, NOTTS. 1792

DECAY OF
OPEN FIELDS, SYERSTON,
NOTTINGHAMSHIRE, 1792

By the close of the eighteenth century the open-field system has disintegrated here. The map shows enclosed strips within the old field with an area of former open-field land devoted to grass leys.

The consolidation and enclosure of holdings might seem to be thoroughly practical, for it reduced the time wasted in long journeys between scattered strips and allowed the holder of an enclosed field to opt out of the communal crop rotation. In fact it could be highly controversial, for when the strip field or meadows were thrown open to grazing by the village livestock the animals of the community were deprived of any grazing on land which had been enclosed and 'privatised'.

In some cases the enclosers of arable or meadow strips would acknowledge the traditional rights of the community and open their enclosures as common pasture after the harvest had been completed. The records show that such undertakings were often dishonoured. In 1344, for example, Henry, son of Walter, who had agreed to allow such common grazing in his newly enclosed fields at Killinghall near Harrogate, was accused of excluding his neighbour's livestock and reserving the land for his own sheep and cattle. But by 1545 the Killinghall community bowed to the inevitable and undertook a complete enclosure of their common fields by general agreement 'for the better occupation of the tenants and owners thereof'.

The early enclosure of open-field land (which preceded the Parliamentary Enclosures described in Chapter 6) could be the culmination of a highly complex succession of land purchases and exchanges between individual peasants and farmers, or the result of an agreement between all members of the farming community – or else be effected by the leading lights within such a community at the expense of their less fortunate and acquisitive neighbours. The arrangements could produce results which were a hybrid of private and communal practices; and at Ripon, for example, the open-field land was enclosed piecemeal in the decades around 1700, but farmers there would still open their gates to allow common grazing. Hybrid practices produced all manner of disputes in fieldscapes which experienced the tortuous and sometimes tortured transition from common to private organisation. New hedges and fences barred grazings to the common herds of common men, they cut across traditional field access-tracks and, from time to time, they were uprooted or torn down. When Parliamentary Enclosure virtually obliterated the many surviving village open fields, meadows and commons there was scarcely an unenclosed parish that did not have some evidence of earlier enclosure, while enclosure by exchange and agreement had completely extinguished the old communal arrangement in many parishes, so that there was no scope or call for Parliamentary Enclosure.

Well-preserved early enclosure countryside is extremely attractive and, with its winding hedgerows or walls and scattered farmsteads, it can be mistaken for ancient countryside. But the discerning visitor will not be deceived for very long, for early enclosure countryside is largely cobbled together from fragments of the open-field landscape. Fields which resulted from the gathering-together of bundles of strips will have boundaries which fossilise the characteristic 'reversed-S' outlines of the plough-strips, while if they were not ploughed but converted to permanent pasture, then plough-ridges will also be preserved. If one studies the shapes of fields as mapped on Ordnance Survey maps at the scale of 1:25,000 (or larger), or if one looks along the line of wall or hedgerow boundaries, the presence or absence of gentle reversed-S curves should allow a distinction between ancient countryside and early enclosure fieldscapes.

Enclosure by agreement was often tainted by considerable measures of disagreement of the kinds described, while a few copyholding tenants who did not wish to take part in an enclosure of open-field land could greatly impede the process. Controversy of a much greater magnitude surrounded the attempts by Tudor landlords to evict entire communities from their ancestral lands and convert the ploughlands, commons, meadows and pastures into sheep-ranges. The wholesale extermination of rural populations by the recurrent eruptions of the Black Death resulted in a shortage of peasant labour, while those peasants who had survived exploited the new conditions to the hilt. With landlords

Narrow fields created by the enclosure of medieval field-strips near Tideswell, Derbyshire

anxious to repopulate their stricken estates, peasant households could slip away to take up more attractive tenancies on different manors; workers who had always been servile began to resist the imposition of feudal obligations, and wage rates rose despite all official attempts to hold them down. However, landlords were not at the mercy of their militant tenants: the raising of sheep required just a few shepherds, and the market for wool was buoyant and reliable. On estate after estate villagers were evicted, their houses torn down and their ploughlands converted into pasture.

On Chesterton manor, now largely engulfed by Cambridge, the tenants complained in 1414 that there was 'none housinge left stondinge thereon but it were a shepcote, or a berne, or a swynesty, and a few houses byside to put in beastes'. The evictions and the consequent creation of a class of embittered vagrants reached such a scale as to threaten the stability of the realm. Legislation to prevent the village depopulations or 'pulling down of towns' was introduced in 1489, reaffirmed in 1514 and then revitalised in 1515 with an Act that forbade the conversion of ploughland to pasture, while in 1517 a commission was appointed which attempted to reverse the tide of evictions, which had still continued to rise after 1489. Their evidence shows that churchmen as well as lay landlords had speculated in the sheep and eviction rackets, the Prior of Daventry driving out a hundred peasants who had 'departed in tears and have fallen into unemployment and at length, as it is supposed, have perished in utter poverty and are come thus to their last end'. In the mid-fifteenth century this theme was echoed by the Protestant preacher Thomas Becon, who described how 'whole towns [that is, villages] are become desolate, and like unto a wilderness, no man dwelling there, except it be the shepherd and his dog'.

Hundreds of English villages were emptied and uprooted during the Tudor sheep-clearances, the Midlands and eastern Yorkshire experiencing the most

The solitary church of one of the two villages at Fawsley in Northamptonshire which were destroyed in the early fifteenth century by Richard Knightley. Fawsley became the base for the Knightleys, the most notorious Tudor family of evicting landlords

severe depopulations. However, it was in Norfolk that a popular though abortive uprising took place in 1549, when Robert Kett and his 16,000 insurgents assembled outside Norwich. Here, however, the situation was rather different from that prevailing in the champion countrysides of the Midlands. Sheep had long been of great importance in Norfolk farming, being grazed both on the vast open commons and heaths and upon the fallow and stubble of the open fields, where they helped to fertilise the soil. Kett's principal demand was 'That no lord of no manor shall common upon the commons'. His peasant followers were incensed by the ways in which their lords had enclosed commons for their own exclusive use, overstocked them with demesne flocks, impounded peasant livestock and excluded them from grazing on fallowing demesne land.

The switch from peasant cultivation to sheep-ranges could transform the fieldscape in various ways. In Norfolk it was expressed in the hedges which alienated and privatised the ancient commons, but the best-recorded example is that of Wormleighton in Warwickshire. This was one of the numerous villages depopulated by the Spencer family at the close of the fifteenth century, and the surrounding lands were partitioned by double hedgerows of mixed tree and shrub species which apparently divided the estate into four great blocks of land each accommodating a flock of sheep under the charge of its respective master shepherd. The new boundaries, parts of which survive, were described as 'doble dynched and doble hegged', and oaks were planted in the hedgerows to provide a future supply of timber, which could be quite scarce in the champion countrysides.

In general the fieldscape expanded during the medieval period, with assarting and the enclosure of the waste reducing the area of open countryside. In some places, however, there were local contractions of the fieldscape. About twenty villages and a dozen hamlets with their associated fields were destroyed when William the Conqueror enlarged the hunting preserve of the New Forest, and in the Yorkshire Dales extensive areas of working countryside became desolate hunting forest after the Norman campaign of genocide, the Harrying of the North of 1069–71. By the thirteenth century royal forests covered about one-fifth of the area of England. The designated forests were areas where Forest Law was imposed to protect game and control the expansion of farmland; the protected areas were not continuously wooded, and perhaps only a quarter of forest land was actually covered in trees. After reaching its maximum extent in the thirteenth century the forest area gradually contracted, with successive monarchs obtaining welcome revenue from the sale of licences to assart.

Deer parks were much smaller than the royal forests or the hunting chases of the nobility, existing as areas of around 100–200 acres (40–80 hectares) protected by banks, ditches, hedges and pales or walls from which deer were unable to escape until they were released and then pursued across the surrounding countryside without regard for the peasant crops. The number of parks grew rapidly between 1200 and 1350, the Earls of Lancaster alone holding forty-five deer parks, and the total number of parks was around 2,000. Sometimes a deer park could be accommodated within existing demesne woodland, but in a number of cases the parks were created at the expense of village farmland. The Tudor commissioners heard how the Abbot of Peterborough had:

... enlarged his park at Meldesworth, and keepeth wild beasts now in those tenements; and by what he had taken one plough has been put down and 50 persons who were wont to dwell in the [farmstead] and cottages aforesaid have gone forth and have been compelled to seek their dwelling elsewhere; and, what is sadder still, the aforesaid graveyards wherein the bodies of the faithful were buried and rest is now made into a pasture for wild beasts.

Although the total amount of land devoted to deer parks declined steadily after 1350, the Meldesworth park was not the only controversial late-medieval creation. In 1510 the south Yorkshire hamlets of Stanfield and Whitley were razed by Sir Thomas Wortley in an extension of his chase, while in 1589 his descendant, Sir Richard Wortley, created a new park and extended an old one. George Blount of Moore Hall joined a mob who tore down the pale of Wortley's park – and he underlined their message by hanging a deer's head in the porch of the church. A few decades later a ballad was composed which cast the Wortleys in the guise of a dragon:

> All sorts of cattle this Dragon did eat
> Some say he eat up trees
> And that forest sure he would
> Devour by degrees
> For houses and churches
> Were to him geese and turkies. . . .

Fallow dear in the deer park at Studley Royal near Ripon

Only a very few medieval deer parks still exist, and a high proportion had disappeared before the Middle Ages had ended. But quite frequently traces of an old deer park will endure in the form of a curving sweep of hedge or hedgebank which marks the bounds of the former reserve.

More ink has probably been spilt on theories about the origins of medieval fields than on any other subject in the realm of history, yet still the problem remains unsolved. But, if we do not know just where the fields came from, we do know a good deal about how they evolved. By the close of the Middle Ages field-maps were being produced which provide clear pictures of the layout and appearance of fields in the sixteenth century. In some cases, as with Padbury in Buckinghamshire, the patterns shown on such a map have been directly related to earthworks of plough-ridges and headlands still existing on the ground. Some of the maps depict a reasonably intact system of open fields, strips and furlongs. But in every sixteenth- and seventeenth-century map there are some signs of change. Within the open fields some strips have been amalgamated and hedged around, while on their outer margins little hedged closes may represent old assarts or intakes from the common. The countrysides and fieldscapes existing today may preserve some of the features mapped four or more centuries ago. Often the medieval features have been obliterated completely, and sometimes large fragments of hedgerow patterns survive. One needs only to compare a few countrysides to realise that, whatever may have been achieved in the way of social reform, the old countrysides were far grander than those forged on the anvil of modern materialism.

SOME PLACES OF INTEREST

Chelmorton (SK 1169). This Derbyshire village lies 4 miles (7 kilometres) to the south-east of Buxton on a limestone plateau over 1,000 feet (*c.*300 metres) above sea-level. In such a lofty situation one would expect to find dispersed farmsteads and hamlets rather than a village which had an arable field system. Behind the dwellings, which are ranged along the through-road, are long narrow medieval tofts which have been enclosed by limestone walls. Beyond the tofts are long narrow fields which may result from the early enclosure of the village infield. Further out from the village are the straight rectangular patterns of walls defining fields formed from the enclosure of the village lands after 1809. Derbyshire contains good examples of fields produced for the early enclosure of open-field land, and at *Tideswell* and *Wheston,* not far from Chelmorton and about 6 miles (10 kilometres) to the east of Buxton, the open fields shared between the two parishes were dismantled by early enclosure and curving stone walls preserve the outlines of some of the strips.

Fawsley (SP 5657). The Tudor hall and church stand in a park 4 miles (7 kilometres) to the south of Daventry in Northamptonshire. The manor was bought by Richard Knightley in 1415, and Knightley then proceeded to remove his tenants by raising feudal rents and services to impossible levels. Two villages at Fawsley were removed, and the estate became the base from which the Knightley dynasty, perhaps the most notorious of the Tudor evicters, presided over the depopulation of numerous Midlands villages. In 1547 the depopulated lands at Fawsley are known to have supported a flock of 2,500 sheep.

Garrow Tor (SX 1478). Pressures of a rising rural population in the earlier medieval centuries drove peasant families to attempt to colonise many less inviting settings. Often these attempts failed. After the onslaughts of the Black Death more viable tenancies became available in the agricultural heartlands, while a deterioration in the British climate, which became marked in the fourteenth century, accelerated the retreat from the margins. On the slopes to the south of Garrow Tor in St Breward parish, Cornwall, and to the east of Bodmin Moor are the earthworks of a medieval field system perhaps associated with a solitary farmstead. The rocky slopes have been ridged, with some bundles of ridges grouped within a set of about a dozen parallel earthbanks. The fields were inspected during an excavation of a hamlet of nine dwellings quite nearby, and both sites produced pottery of the thirteenth century. This inhospitable setting may have been abandoned during the transition to wet, cool and blustery conditions in the fourteenth century.

Strip Lynchets in Wharfedale. Flights of medieval strip lynchets can be seen at numerous places: for example, beside the Dorset coast at Worth Matravers to the west of Swanage (SY 9777), on the flanks of the dry valleys or 'combes' to the north-east of Mere to the north of Shaftesbury in Wiltshire (ST 8233), and on the outskirts of Abbotsbury in Dorset (SY 5785). One of the finest panoramas of strip lynchets is viewed from the B625 between Grassington and Hebden in Wharfedale, looking southwards across the river. A closer view of these fields is obtained from the B6160, which runs amongst the lynchets just to the east of Linton. Grassington is a base for exploring the 'Celtic' field-patterns at Lea Green (SE 0065) about 1 mile (1.6 kilometres) to the north of the village, the footpath to Lea Green passing the site of a deserted medieval hamlet.

Studley Royal (SE 2869). The eighteenth-century landscaped park, which lies 2 miles (3.2 kilometres) to the south-west of Ripon, was purchased and restored by the old West Riding County Council and developed as a public park. Its woodland and lawns echo some of the qualities of a medieval deer park, though some of the trees planted were not present in the medieval countryside. There are fine herds of red deer and fallow deer, the fallow type introduced by the Normans being the most popular deer for the stocking of medieval parks. There is also a herd of Sika deer, not released in England until long after the close of the Middle Ages.

Lilla Howe (SE 8898). This 959-foot (292-metre) hill in the North Yorkshire Moors National Park lies between Fylingdales Moor and Goathland Moor. It formed the junction of the boundaries of some eight townships, and as the medieval common of the surrounding villages and hamlets was expanded and defined all the lands below Lilla Howe were partitioned between the neighbouring communities. The villages of Fylingdales, Stainacre and Hawsker shared common grazing rights on Fylingdales Moor.

Manor Farm (SP 3709). While a fascinating history-trail leads the imagination through time via a deserted village and remains of ancient field systems around Cogges in Oxfordshire, one can also see the workings of an Edwardian Oxfordshire farm and local breeds of livestock such as Oxford Down sheep and Oxford Sandy and Black Pigs. Near Witney, off the A40.

CHAPTER 5

SPECIAL CASES

S cattered amongst the more conventional pastures, meadows and ploughlands one may find fields which were developed to play special rôles in the
farming of Britain. Not one of the examples merits a full chapter in its
own right, and all can conveniently be grouped together under the heading of
'special cases'.

WATER MEADOWS

Riverside meadows of the medieval period would often be inundated by winter
floods, and this could have beneficial results. The deposition of silt would re-
fresh the soil, while the river water, though cool, would be warmer than the
ground and grass that it flooded. Consequently an early flush of growth was encouraged. After the close of the Middle Ages systems of dams and leats were
developed which permitted the controlled artificial flooding of riverside lands.
In 1523, Fitzherbert described the advantages of flooding in *The Boke of Surveying and Improvements,* explaining how the waters would 'kylle, drowne and
drive away the moldywarpes [moles] and fyll up the lowe places with sande and
make the grounde evyn and good to mowe'. He specially recommended 'that
water that cometh out of a towne [village] from every mannes mydding [mid-
den] or donghyll'.

By the early years of the seventeenth century, controlled water meadows
were numerous in the valleys of Wessex, and had also appeared in East Anglia
and the Welsh Marches. Flooding early in spring greatly increased the yield of
the hay crop, but water meadows were particularly associated with the production of an early flush of grass for grazing by lambs. Often the flocks were driven
to the water meadows in the morning and taken back to the fallowing ploughland in the evening, where they were folded so that their droppings would revitalise the soils of the Wessex chalklands (see Chapter 10). If the sheep were
removed from the water meadows in April, and the meadows were again
flooded, then a hay crop could be taken around mid-summer. The chalkland
areas had modest rivers but many springs; and, while river water would still be
quite cool in the early months, spring water maintained a temperature of
around 55°F (13°C) and was particularly valuable, being both warmer and rich
in nutrients. The system gained further popularity in the eighteenth and
nineteenth centuries.

Systems of controlled flooding varied in their complexity. 'Flooding up-wards', popular in the Midlands and parts of Wessex, simply involved dam-ming a stream so that the waters could be ponded back to flood the flat valley floor lying upstream of the dam. The more elaborate system of 'flooding down-wards', associated with 'floated meadows', involved damming a stream or river and diverting the waters into a head main. The meadowland was ridged, rather in the manner of ridge and furrow, and water from the head main was taken off to flow into channels or 'carriers' running along the crests of the ridges, it then overflowing into the furrows and eventually returning to the river downstream from the dam. Alternatively, emerging chalk streams could be tapped at their source and the waters diverted into hillside leats running roughly parallel to the contours of the valley slope. As the leats overflowed, so the meadows below would be flooded.

Aerial photograph of water-meadow earthworks at Castle Acre in Norfolk

The elaborate systems of leats and ridges associated with floated meadows required a very precise control of gradients, and so professional 'drowners' were sometimes employed to construct or repair the network of channels. Floated meadows could be privately owned or operated in common meadows, though today very few systems are still operated. Former floated meadows can be recognised from the ridged earthworks of old carriers and the channels of the leats; notches in the leat system may mark the positions of the wooden sluices which were opened or closed to regulate the flow of water.

HILL FARMING

Some aspects of hill farming, such as the history and enclosure of upland commons, are covered in other chapters, and here we focus on the fields in the locality of the farmstead. The Lake District farms can be taken as an example and have some similarities with those of other upland areas. In the medieval period vast expanses of upland fell were monastic sheep-ranges controlled by local abbeys like Furness and Shap, or distant houses like Fountains. Originally monks or lay brothers established in outlying farms or granges organised the farming, but as the monastic movement lost momentum in the closing centuries of the Middle Ages many granges were tenanted by lay families – the hamlet of Grange in Borrowdale has, as its name implies, evolved from a monastic grange. With the Dissolution of the Monasteries between 1536 and 1539 the monastic estates became fragmented. Henry VIII was anxious to sustain a population of yeomen in Cumbria as a bulwark against Scottish invasion, and his encouragement of independent freeholders produced a local class of statesmen' established in farmsteads, some of which were quite humble and unpretentious buildings.

The typical hill farm consists of a farmhouse, barn and byre arranged around two or three sides of a small yard, with a few trees to protect the buildings against the prevailing winds. Sheep-pens stand close to the farm, which is beside or surrounded by meadows which can accommodate the ewes and lambs at lambing time and then produce a hay crop. Beyond the meadow are the walled fields of the 'inbye land', serving as pastures, meadows and as fields where the occasional crop of oats might be grown. Cattle, if they are still kept, may pass most of the year on inbye pastures, being wintered in the byre and fed on hay or silage from the meadows. Sheep are brought into the inbye and meadow for mating in November and for lambing in April. Young and old or weak ewes may spend the whole winter in the security of the inbye. Between the inbye enclosures and the open fell one may expect to find the larger walled fields of the 'intake' containing rough grazing enclosed from the common and so alienated for the private use of the farmer. Normally flocks and farms are sold together, the flock being accustomed and acclimatised to life on the home fell, reluctant to wander too far and thus not needful of walls or fences. The common may be open or enclosed, stinted or unstinted, and where the sheep of several farms run together on an open common a co-operative round-up is needed to separate the sheep of different owners for shearing.

SPADE CULTIVATION

Travellers flying over parts of the Scottish Highlands and Islands may see areas where the artificial corrugations of the land-surface seem to resemble medieval ridge-and-furrow patterns. However, people on the ground below would realise that the terrain was too difficult to have been cultivated by an ox-plough and might deduce that the snaking ridges and furrows were the product of arduous work with the spade. The ridging of the land by spade cultivation would have

A pattern of ridges produced by spade cultivation near Uig, Lewis, Ross and Cromarty

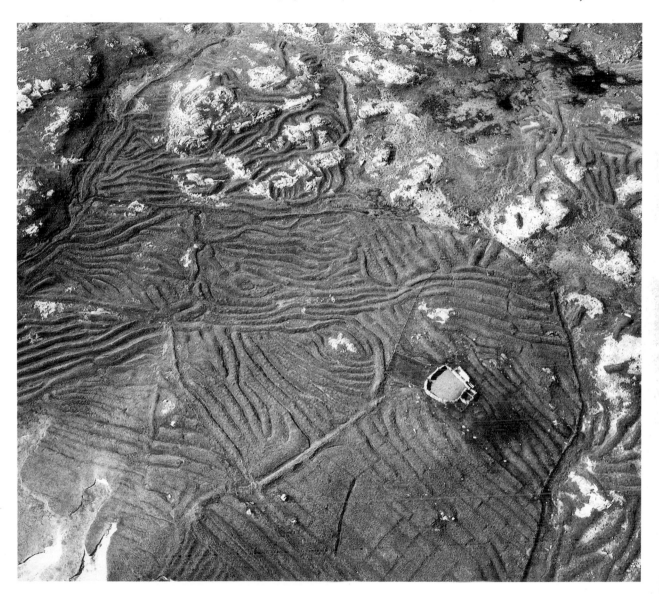

Opposite above: Unspoilt countryside in Wharfedale with field-walls, stone barns and field trees

Opposite: Parliamentary Enclosure countryside near Austwick in the Yorkshire Dales, with medieval strip lynchets pleating the slopes of the distant hillsides

similar advantages to those offered by conventional ridge and furrow, allowing a crop to survive on the crests of the ridges if the land was flooded or endure in the furrows in time of drought. Naturally spade cultivation would not produce other features of ridge-and-furrow ploughland, such as headlands. In the rugged coastal areas of the Highlands and Islands a long spade or foot-plough known as a *caschrom* was employed, and the cultivation of grain crops using such an unsophisticated implement could only occur when labour was plentiful but poverty-stricken, the soil thin and the land barren.

Lazy-bed cultivation was a variation of the spade technique, with the soil being heaped up in ridges to provide a greater depth of root-run. After a lazy bed had been in use for some seasons the soil was turned over, and the beds might be divided down the middle, with the ridge-crests being split to form new furrows. Lazy beds were constructed in the northern and western isles of Scotland and many parts of Ireland. Spade cultivation was probably widespread in prehistoric times and is documented in Scotland from the sixteenth century. Cultivation-ridges dating back at least as far as the early Bronze Age have been excavated from beneath the peat at Carrownaglogh in County Mayo.

Many lazy beds which survive as corrugated earthworks date from the eighteenth and nineteenth centuries and were associated with the growing of potatoes as a subsistence crop for the most impoverished members of rural society. The planting of potatoes in the crests of ridges allowed the crop to be grown on badly-drained or thinly soiled land. Fields composed of lazy beds could be worked in common with individual families owning particular blocks of the field or some of the scattered lazy beds. There were heavy demands for labour, and as many as fifty people might be seen on just one acre of lazy beds at potato-planting time. For a while the potato underwrote a rapid growth in population, with plantings expanding to cover all the arable land. The crop left no stubble grazings after the harvest had been taken, so livestock and the supply of manure diminished, along with the fertility of the land, though in coastal areas seaweed could be spread on the ground. Many of the lazy beds seen in Ireland were abandoned in the Great Famine of 1845–8. The famine was caused by a potato blight which probably resulted in a million deaths through starvation and disease and the emigration of a further million Irish people.

WARRENS

Warrens were not fields in the conventional sense, though their boundaries could be protected and the rabbit-breeding area within the warren could be secured by thick hedges. The rabbit is not a native animal but was introduced by the Normans. They may have come from Spain, and it certainly took the animals a long time to acclimatise. They were known as 'coneys', the word 'rabbit' being reserved for their young. For a few centuries the rabbit existed as a delicacy which only the wealthy could afford. Some early warrens were established by lords on the common pastures of their estates or inside deer parks, and the tunnels and artificial burrows where the animals bred were normally heavily protected by ditches, banks and hedges as safeguards against predators. The warrens or 'coneygarths' were numerous in England and Wales, and in some localities the breeding of rabbits became a specialised industry with the animals being guarded by warreners living in fortified lodges. The islands of Scilly, Farne and Skokholm; the great forests of Essex; Dartmoor, and the heathland grazings of the East Anglian Breckland – all were noted for their rabbit production.

It seems to have been mainly in the post-medieval centuries that artificial mounds, known (from their shape) as 'pillow mounds', were constructed to accommodate breeding-burrows. Such mounds might be built on heaths or commons or in woods – and frequently the defended interiors of ancient hillforts were chosen. A few warrens were still operating at the beginning of the twentieth century, but now the warrens have decayed leaving little obvious contribution to the fieldscape. Field-names like 'Coneygarth', 'Coninger' or 'Clapery' denote areas where rabbits were raised, as do 'warren' place-names and the low earthworks of pillow mounds.

PARKLAND

Some villages or hamlets and their fields were destroyed in the creation of medieval deer parks, while in the post-medieval centuries the long-running fashion for the stately home isolated within its landscaped park resulted in many more assaults on the working fieldscape. Although emparking could be a disaster for the villagers, it also allowed old patterns of cultivation to be fossilised beneath the lawns and spinneys of the park. Some of the finest ridge-and-furrow patterns in Cambridgeshire were preserved in this way at Wimpole Park until an ill-considered campaign of ploughing and reseeding destroyed half the field-earthworks along with old pasture flora and protected deserted village sites. At Studley Royal, near Ripon, some strip lynchets are preserved, while at Ickworth in Suffolk pollard elms from hedgebanks, field-trees and other hedgerow-trees were preserved within the park after the parish was depopulated in 1701, and some of them continue to stand within the park.

Sometimes the landscaping extended beyond the park to prettify the surrounds. In our own village of Birstwith, North Yorkshire, the pastures are graced by many oaks. The Greenwood family arriving here early in the nineteenth century claimed to own all that they could see from their hilltop mansion of Swarcliffe Hall and improved the view accordingly. Now the hall is a school, but visitors and villagers can still enjoy the vistas of mature field-trees.

Both house and park could perish, with the park being replaced by a new fieldscape, but whenever one sees a carefully considered planting of native or exotic field-trees the existence or former existence of a mansion and landscaped park is strongly to be suspected. The disparking of an old park could result in the creation of a new fieldscape. Higham Park, near Higham Ferrers in Northamptonshire, still contained a few deer in 1624, but in 1669 it was referred to as 'the late reputed park'. The historian M. W. Beresford writes: 'The park is now divided into 12 fields, and when it was visited in 1954 only a herd of frisky bullocks provided an element of the chase.'

Overleaf: The ramparts of Dolebury Warren hillfort in the Mendips were commandeered to enclose a post-medieval rabbit-warren (and contain the ruins of the warrener's lodge)

SOME PLACES OF INTEREST

Water Meadows. The shadowy traces of abandoned leats and carriers can be seen in the valleys of many Wessex rivers, like the Itchen, Frome, Salisbury Avon, Stour and Test. A system of floated water meadows on the Avon at Lower Woodford in Wiltshire was probably created in the seventeenth century and is said to be still operative.

Spade Cultivation. Before the potato famine lazy beds could be seen throughout Ireland, and their earthworks can be seen, for example on areas of rough ground close to Belfast. Relics of lazy beds are most commonly seen on the barren slopes of western Ireland and the Scottish Highlands and Islands. On the Aran Islands, County Galway, lazy beds were created by hauling sand and seaweed from the beaches and laying the materials as cultivation-ridges upon the bare limestone surface.

Dolebury Warren (ST 4458). The hillfort and nature reserve are in Avon, about 1 mile (1.6 kilometres) to the south-east of Churchill and just east of the A38. Inside the rubble ramparts of this Iron Age hillfort of the Mendips, the parallel banks that one finds are old pillow mounds, and at the highest point in the enclosure one can see the tumbled walls of the warrener's house.

Legistor Warren (SX 5765). This is one of several Dartmoor warrens and lies in Sheepstor parish. Cigar-shaped and oval 'buries' or pillow mounds can be seen, and these are post-medieval artificial rabbit-warrens, relics of the enthusiasm for breeding rabbits on the moor. The raising of rabbits here lasted from the thirteenth century to the arrival of myxomatosis in the 1950s. Bronze Age hut circles are scattered amongst the mounds, representing the footings of circular stone-walled dwellings, and a small complex of associated walled fields may be contemporaneous with the dwellings.

CHAPTER 6

THE AGE OF ENCLOSURE

In Chapter 4 we described how ambitious peasants sought to combine and enclose packages of arable strips, and how assarting and intakes diminished the communal territory of the waste. The early enclosure, or 'enclosure by agreement', gradually eroded open-field farming in many places, but the Parliamentary Enclosure of the eighteenth and nineteenth centuries could wipe the slate of farming evolution quite bare and completely redraw the map of a parish in very little time at all. Parliamentary Enclosure created fieldscapes based on the logic of surveyors, fieldscapes of uncompromising straight lines and rectangles rather than of the old winding curves which expressed the history and character of the local terrain. Most strongly affected were the areas where open-field farming had been most widespread and robust – and if open-field systems were initially planned, then this new phase of planning was destined to obliterate most traces of what had been superimposed before. In the northern uplands, meanwhile, moors and rough grazings, most of which had probably existed as open commons since the distant dawn of farming, were partitioned and privatised by walls as straight and unyielding as the lines drawn by the surveyor's pen and ruler.

In essence Parliamentary Enclosure was an attempt to privatise common land. In ancient countryside, where, as we have seen, open fields were few, small and ephemeral, the effects were minimal. In areas where enclosure by agreement had spelled a slower and more piecemeal death for open-field farming and where intakes had eroded the common there was much less to catch the encloser's eye. But in the champion parishes where the furlongs were still packed with strips like sardines in a can, and where the ancient common was still open to all the village peasants, Parliamentary Enclosure remained a major and controversial agent of change until the middle of the nineteenth century. But it had become a force that was largely spent long before the last Enclosure Act was passed in 1914, dying on the altar of its own success.

The new enclosure was, as we said, a means of privatising common land – not only the common waste, but also open-field ploughlands, dole meadows and even village greens. By and large, it was favoured by the affluent members of the rural community and loathed by the poorer folk of the parish, particularly by those who had little or no stake in the open ploughlands and survived through their access to the resources of the waste. In terms of social justice it had important points of comparison with current privatisation policies. Those

A gridwork of Parliamentary Enclosure walls of the 1770s in Nidderdale, North Yorkshire

with a substantial stake in the farming assets of the parish were rewarded with consolidated holdings upon which they could, if they wished, experiment with the fashionable improvements offered by the Agricultural Revolution. Their arable fields were unlocked from the rigid fallowing system, and the common was converted into a series of private pastures. The larger landowners could easily absorb the costs of enclosing their new holdings with hedges or walls, and could then invoke the improvements as a pretext for jacking up the rents of their tenant farmers. But since the share-out of common pasture and meadow resources was made proportional to a family's holdings in the arable field the folk with only cottages and access to the common could be left landless and destitute. Meanwhile the smallholder might lack the funds to meet the costs of enclosure, sometimes as high as £5 per acre (0.4 hectare), and have no choice but to sell up to a prosperous neighbour.

Attitudes to enclosure varied greatly. Some who stood to gain from it still opposed enclosure because of its consequences for the poor of the community. Others clearly despised the cottagers, and Robert Stockdale of Knaresborough was one who argued illogically that it gave the poor and small farmer nothing yet at the same time endowed them with lives of indolence: 'This waste . . . afforded their families a little milk, yet they would attempt to keep a horse, and

a flock of sheep. The first enabled them to stroll about the country in idleness, and the second, in the course of every three or four years, were so reduced by the rot, and other disasters, that upon the whole they yielded no profit.' Time and again one sees the unsavoury attitudes which are once again prevalent today mirrored in the prejudices of the comfortable classes of the eighteenth century. It was often argued that if the poor were robbed of their cherished common rights, then they would work harder for their employers. Writing of Somerset in 1795, John Billingsley stated: 'The possession of a cow or two, with

Geometrical patterns of Parliamentary Enclosure hedgerows superimposed on medieval hedge and furrow at Flecknoe in Warwickshire

Surveyors at work using a chain measure, as illustrated in 1617. In the following century Parliamentary Enclosures provided many calls for surveying skills

a hog, and a few geese, naturally exalts the peasant, in his own conception, above his brethren in the same rank of society. . . . Day labour becomes disgusting; the aversion increases by indulgence; and at length the sale of a half-fed calf, or hog, furnishes the means of adding intemperance to idleness.' Reporting on Norfolk a year previously, Nathaniel Kent expressed a more pungent summary of the prejudice: '. . . the larger the common, the greater the number and more miserable are the poor'.

Parliamentary Enclosure operated on a parish-by-parish basis. The leading landowners, having agreed that enclosure was desirable, would petition Parliament to issue the necessary Act. Commissioners would then be appointed to produce the reallocation of common land. Normally they were drawn from the ranks of the lesser rural gentry, middle-class establishment and yeoman classes, so that a typical body of commissioners might comprise a squire-cum-

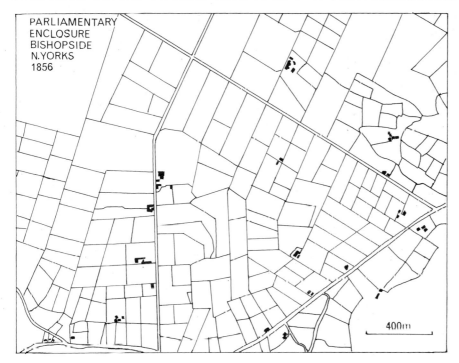

PARLIAMENTARY
ENCLOSURE
BISHOPSIDE
N.YORKS
1856

400m

PARLIAMENTARY
ENCLOSURE, BISHOPSIDE,
NORTH YORKSHIRE, 1856

Here enclosure creates a
surveyor's landscape of
geometrical fields and straight
enclosure roads.

magistrate, a clergyman and a farmer of some substance. A meeting would be
held in the parish, where stormy anti-enclosure meetings might also be con-
vened. The commissioners would obtain the specialist skills needed to draw up
an award by appointing a surveyor, to map the existing and future patterns of
land-holding, and a valuer, who would attempt to produce equivalence between
the old and new worlds of land-holding, within the inbuilt injustices of the system. An Act of 1801 simplified the parliamentary proceedings, while one of
1836 allowed enclosure without recourse to Parliament when the owner of two-
thirds of the land in a parish, by area and value, consented. Such change could
lead to triumphs of wealth over democracy. For example, at Ashdon in Essex
seven landowners controlled 65 per cent of the parish and successfully petitioned for enclosure. One of the seven, Lord Maynard, owned more than half of
the land, but at least thirty-eight other people who were awarded a share in the
award had *not* petitioned for enclosure.

A farmer who had, say, 50 acres (20 hectares) in strips scattered through
three open fields before enclosure would expect to receive a similar amount of
consolidated ploughland after the deliberations. To simplify the calculations
and allocations, the surveyors dealt in straight-line geometry. In a few places, as
at Langley in Essex where the existing furlongs provided the basis for the
award, irregular field-boundaries endured, but in general the award involved
straight-sided rectangular and trapezium-shaped fields. Sometimes the question of access from the fields to village-based farmsteads or a need to share a
water-supply favoured a rather radial pattern of boundaries which focused on
the village, spring or pond. An extreme case of this can be seen at
Grassington, where the Act of 1792 created some elongated fields which both
tapered towards the tracks and droveways leading into the village and

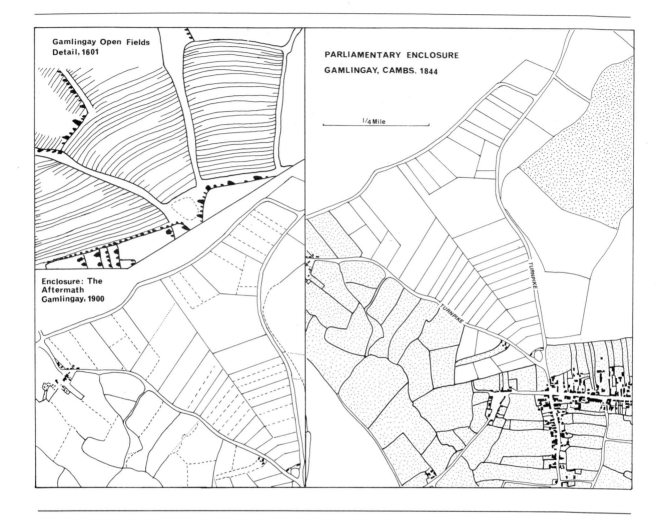

Gamlingay Open Fields
Detail, 1601

PARLIAMENTARY ENCLOSURE
GAMLINGAY, CAMBS. 1844

1/4 Mile

Enclosure: The
Aftermath
Gamlingay, 1900

TURNPIKE

TURNPIKE

PARLIAMENTARY ENCLOSURE, GAMLINGAY, CAMBRIDGESHIRE, 1844

This extract from the enclosure-award map shows how the old enclosed pastures (light stipple) on right hand drawing were unaffected by enclosure, while the open ploughland was transformed. Woodland is shown in heavy stipple. The detail, upper left, shows field-strips and plough-ridges in the area around the junction of the two turnpikes as they existed in 1601 (at a larger scale). Where a strip comprised more than one plough-ridge only the ends of the ridges are indicated. The hedged strip field, upper left in the detail, was worked entirely for Elizabeth I and so existed, in effect, as a single strip. The detail to the lower left shows the field-pattern as mapped in 1900, sixty-six years after Parliamentary Enclosure.

Field-boundaries removed or enclosure boundaries specified but never erected are shown in a pecked line, and new hedges in a dotted line. Many of the fields awarded in 1844 were of little value and offered no real compensation for the loss of rights on the common. We can see how many smallholders sold up to their neighbours, and holdings were amalgamated under the control of the more prosperous farmers. Several recipients of awards probably sold up and quit before the hedges specified in the award were even planted. Some of the medieval pastures have also been amalgamated. For a broader picture of the situation here in 1601, see pp. 66–7.

converged on a spring where stock could drink, Generally the hurried straight-line geometry of the surveyors showed little sensitivity towards the natural contours and curves of the setting, and it tended to produce a rather inflexible 'mass-produced' sort of fieldscape. Often the fields were too large for farming convenience, so that once the awarded fields of around say, 50 acres (20 hectares) had been hedged or walled as specified their owners would then subdivide them into 5- or 10-acre (2- or 4- hectare) fields. Again, a system of straight boundaries would normally be adopted.

The transformation from open-field ploughland or common grazing to enclosed fields was always profound, but Parliamentary Enclosure was less widespread than may be imagined. Ancient countryside areas could be completely unaffected, while in scores of parishes early enclosure, assarting and intaking left little scope for the Parliamentary Enclosure of common land. The estimates by W. E. Tate indicate an affected area of about 7 million acres (2,832,861 hectares). The changes were most striking and comprehensive in the champion countrysides of the Midlands and also in the northern uplands, where the old open commons were partitioned.

In the aftermath of the award each affected parish witnessed a frenzy of activity. Often the local transport system was transformed, with narrow field-lanes being abandoned and new straight enclosure roads being specified. Such roads, frequently 40 feet (12 metres) in width, would have been much more valuable had the revolution not occurred on a parish-by-parish basis. Often a promising little routeway would end abruptly at the parish boundary. The recipients of the award would face the cost of paying a share of the costs incurred in composing it and then the costs of walling or hedging their new fields. (Sometimes the former costs were recouped by auctioning plots of the common.) For the small fish in the parish pond these costs could be crippling.

Nursery businesses expanded as farmers placed bulk orders for hawthorn, though in places not served by convenient nurseries the villagers might resort to the traditional custom of gathering assorted seedlings and saplings from a nearby wood. Fencing was also needed to protect the vulnerable young hedgerows from browsing. In the uplands countless small quarries were opened to obtain stone for the specified walls.

Some farmers regarded enclosure as an opportunity to operate their own versions of 'convertible' or 'up-and-down' husbandry free from the tyranny of the communal rotation. At the start of the nineteenth century a six-course rotation of turnips−swedes−barley−grass−grass−wheat was often favoured in the Midlands. However, the grain shortages and high prices associated with the Napoleonic Wars not only increased pressures to enclose the open commons, but also induced some farmers to grow successive crops of grain until their fields were completely exhausted.

Enclosure eroded the village in at least two ways. First, the fortunate families who had seen their scattered strips consolidated into a compact group of fields would frequently leave the village farmstead and build a new one in isolation in the midst of their new land-holding. A striking feature of Parliamentary Enclosure country is the existence of scattered farmsteads of eighteenth- or nineteenth-century date. Sometimes these farms are easily dated by their names alone, which commemorate an important historical event; Sebastopol

Farm and Waterloo Farm are examples. In areas of pastoral farming, like the Yorkshire Dales, enclosure could also result in the construction of a multitude of field-barns, where hay would be stored to feed wintering livestock, whose manure would next be spread on the surrounding meadow (see Chapter 10). In parts of the Dales, notably upper Swaledale, there is almost a barn to every field. Second, the poorer village homes were abandoned to decay as failed cottagers and smallholders departed. A traveller near Swaffham in the late eighteenth century recorded that 'I was informed that a gentleman of Lynn had bought that township and the next adjoining to it: that he had thrown the one into three, and the other into four farms; which before the enclosure were in about twenty farms: and upon my further enquiring what was becoming of the farmers who were turned out, the answer was that some of them were dead and the rest were become labourers'.

The consequences of Parliamentary Enclosure on the scenery of a champion parish were no less dramatic than the effects on the rural society. Generally the commissioners specified the form of field-boundaries in some detail. The local terrain would influence the choice of hedges or walls: in Norfolk, for example, field-boundaries were often marked by ditches dug around 3 feet (0.9 metre) deep and 4 feet (1.2 metres) wide, with a hawthorn hedge punctuated by oak, elm or holly being planted on the inner edge of the ditch. Burton Leonard, near Ripon, was enclosed in 1790, and the commissioners declared that:

... the several ditches herein awarded to be made to divide the several allotments in Long Mires and Short Mires and in Long Fog Rains and Short Fog Rains shall be four feet Wide at the Top and nine inches Wide at the Bottom and two feet and a half deep perpendicular; and that all other ditches shall be three feet Wide at the Top six inches Wide at the Bottom and of a proportionate depth. AND that the quickwood [hedge] shall be set and planted one foot at least from the edge of the same ditches and shall be guarded from cattle with posts and rails or other sufficient fence two feet from the outside of the said ditches for the space of ten years and the person placing the same shall be at liberty to take them away.

(The weakness of the hedge was always its vulnerability to browsing when newly planted.) On the northern outskirts of Grassington the tall limestone walls of the 1792 enclosure converge towards the village and were built, according to the precise instructions prescribed, within twelve months of the award. Just across the Wharfe at Linton are some enclosure walls of the same date. They had to be built 6 feet (1.8 metres) tall, tapering upwards from a 3-foot (0.9-metre) base, with stones running through both faces of the wall included at specified intervals to bind the wall together. Within the fields the spirit of improvement was often reflected in features like marlpits, common in East Anglia and Kent, or lime-kilns, frequently seen in the Pennines. Meanwhile the enthusiasm for pheasant-shooting and fox-hunting among the landed classes resulted in the planting of small spinneys.

Some people viewed the changes with horror. Although Parliamentary Enclosure would eventually result in the planting of about 200,000 miles (321,869 kilometres) of hedgerow, the poet John Clare (1793–1864) despised the loss of open commons and clearance of old tree-lined lanes and boundaries:

> Oh, words are poor receipts for what time hath stole away,
> The ancient pulpit trees and the play.

In the same poem, 'Remembrances', he wrote that:

> Enclosure like a Buonaparte let not a thing remain,
> It levelled every bush and tree and levelled everyhill. . . .

Others missed the open patchwork of communal arable farming, and even the grit and limestone walls, now so valued and essential as part of the scenery of the Dales, at first seemed an unwelcome intrusion. In the 1780s T. D. Whitaker wrote how the park-like pastures were 'now strapped over with large bandages of stone, and present nothing to the eye but right lined and angular deformity'.

Although only around one-fifth of our countryside in England and Wales was affected by Parliamentary Enclosure, and much of this area has been defiled by the prairie fields of agri-business and the barley barons, few today would complain about the 'right lined and angular deformity' of surviving enclosure hedgerows and walls. The scenery has acquired its own mature personality and provided many niches for wildlife. Where hedgerows are not too severely trimmed and are dotted with fully grown trees the landscapes of Parliamentary Enclosure can be almost as delightful as those of ancient and

Parliamentary Enclosures produced this geometric gridwork of walls between Darley and Dacre in north Yorkshire, following the enclosure of the Forest of Knaresborough in the 1770s

early enclosure countryside. Were John Clare alive today, he would doubtless have become a campaigner for the protection of the trees and hedgerows of the 'right lined' vistas.

While some of the countrysides of England and Wales were undergoing transformations through the formal processes of Parliamentary Enclosure, in Scotland and Ireland individual landlords initiated changes to the fieldscape which were no less drastic in their scenic and social consequences. In both countries the old patterns of infield—outfield cultivation according to the time-honoured traditions of runrig or rundale were swept away. The chaotic hamlets and group farms associated with the old ways – the *clachans* and fermtouns – were removed, many families were displaced, but some fortunate survivors were established in new farmsteads situated amongst consolidated holdings, or else they could be established in purpose-built agricultural villages. New grid-works of rectangular fields were superimposed across the old countrysides. In North-East Scotland boulders removed from the fields were used to build massive field-walls or 'consumption dikes', while in many parts of Ireland field-ditches were dug and hawthorn seedlings were sown in the upcast of soil from the ditches.

The new fields were, like those produced by Parliamentary Enclosure in England, the creation of surveyors and formed geometrical networks. In Scotland and Ireland, however, the countrysides were divided into great estates, there were few independent farmers of the yeoman type and there was less cause to consider the needs of the poor. Consequently the great landlords were free to impose their own designs upon the landscape.

A different type of geometry could be seen in localities where crofting communities (often composed of families evicted during the notorious Clearances) had become established. At Arnol on Lewis, for example, a crofting community migrated from their sea-shore setting to a new site half a mile inland in the years around 1880. A decade or so later roads in the township were improved and Arnol took on a more structured appearance as the crofters built new black-houses along a section of road. The layout of holdings was then reorganised, with long, straight-sided and rather tapering ribbons of land being extended outwards from each dwelling towards the shore, some of the ribbons being half a mile in length. Each long ribbon was then subdivided to provide households with land for potatoes, oats, hay and pasture. In this way crofting could produce a new variation on the theme of planned countryside.

SOME PLACES OF INTEREST

A high proportion of Parliamentary Enclosure scenery was created on the low level lands of the Midlands to replace the old open ploughlands. To appreciate the rectilinear patterns of hedgerows one needs to be in undulating countryside or to have a lofty vantage-point. One of the best such vantage-points is the Iron Age hillfort of *Bratton Castle* (ST 9051) in Wiltshire, which stands on the crest of the chalk scarp above the famous Westbury White Horse and provides magnificent views northwards across the vale towards Trowbridge and Melksham. The 'castle' can be reached on foot or by car from the B3098 a couple of miles to the east of Westbury town. *Dolebury Warren* (ST 4458) in Avon, mentioned at the end of the preceding chapter, offers views northwards across fields enclosed in 1797. The most spectacular expanse of walled enclosures that we know of lies just a couple of miles from our Nidderdale home. *Dacre Pasture* (SE 1960) was enclosed in the 1840s, producing a remarkable rectangular grid-work of walls seen between the villages of Darley and Dacre to the west of the B6165 Harrogate–Pateley Bridge road. In fact this dale abounds in splendid Parliamentary Enclosure fieldscape, and the Yorkshire Dales have many other fine examples on display such as the hedged fields near Masham (SE 2280) in Wensleydale and the common-cutting walls which stripe the plateaux near Pen-y-Ghent.

By 1960, Arnol on Lewis, which had supported forty-five tenant and ten landless households in the 1880s, was reduced to a loose hamlet occupied by only nine families. Ribbon-like crofting holdings can still be seen at places like the hamlets of *Digg* and *Glashvin* (NG 4769) on the north-eastern extremity of the Isle of Skye.

CHAPTER 7

HOW OLD IS THAT FIELD?

The aim of this book is to encourage readers to look more closely at the fieldscape. Faced with a potentially interesting set of fields, the first question to come to mind will surely concern the age of the members of the group. In disproving the theory of hedgerow-dating we have sadly taken away the easy dating option; but many fields, perhaps most, can be assigned, after a little study, to a particular age-category.

Prehistoric fields are often invisible to the man or woman on the ground, but we must remember that most of England and much of Scotland, Ireland and Wales was covered in networks of fields which spanned the horizons from at least 1500 BC onwards. Sometimes networks of ancient fields appear clearly in aerial photographs in places where they would otherwise have been unsuspected. Normally they are seen as 'crop marks', with the grain growing above old field-ditches enjoying a deeper root-run, growing tall and casting tell-tale shadows on their neighbours. The presence or absence of crop marks will depend on a whole range of factors: the depth of subsequent ploughing, the nature of the local geology, the season, and so on. Ancient fields seen in aerial photographs can only be dated by their relationship to other visible features. For example, if a system runs across a Neolithic cursus avenue but is cut by the ditches of an Iron Age hillfort, it must be younger than the cursus but older than the hillfort. Only the excavation of field-ditches detected on aerial photographs can hope to provide a close dating.

Prehistoric fields visible from the ground announce their presence in a variety of ways. The Bronze Age reaves of Dartmoor are seen as low overgrown banks of rubble and earth, while at Kestor, just to the north of the moor, one may see the fragmentary alignments of large stones from the old field-walls. In County Mayo and elsewhere, deeply buried stone field-walls have emerged during peat-cutting.

Most familiar are the lynchets of 'Celtic' fields, and these earthworks will be most prominent when the pasture is closely grazed and a low sun casts long shadows. All that glisters is not gold – and fossilised lynchet-bordered fields may not be prehistoric: hedgerows on hillsides stabilise slopewash from arable fields, and if the hedge dies or is grubbed up, then lynchet-like steps will remain. Just 300 yards (c.275 metres) from our home in Yorkshire there are fossil fields on a hillside pasture which look just like 'Celtic' fields – except for the fact that they contain faint corrugations of medieval ridge and furrow. In a previous

book I published a picture of mine which appeared to show unusual strip lyn-chet running up-slope from a row of 'Celtic' fields. 'Celtic' fields certainly exist nearby in Wharfedale, and a distinguished archaeologist agreed with my inter-pretation. Later an equally distinguished scholar wrote offering the opinion that the 'Celtic' fields were really fossilised medieval closes which had been associated with former roadside dwellings. Only an excavation would provide the right answer.

An aerial photograph of crop marks

123

Medieval fields can be recognised on the ground and in the archives. The oldest surviving plan of a village and its fields depicts Boarstall in Buckinghamshire and dates from 1444. In the course of the next two centuries the standards of cartography improved greatly, and late sixteenth- and seventeenth-century estate maps are quite numerous. Examples are likely to show the shapes, names, extents, uses and owners of fields but, as estate maps, they do not necessarily cover the whole parish. Strip- and furlong-patterns depicted on old estate maps can be matched exactly to earthworks of ridge and furrow, headlands and joints seen in aerial photographs or from ground-level. Such informative earthworks are most clearly visible when conditions are favourable, and we know of several expanses of ridge and furrow which are only discernible from the ground in afternoon sunlight after a light snowfall. Faint ridge and furrow may have been overploughed at a later date, or it may represent a brief expansion of ploughing into unpromising territory at times of population-pressure.

Ridge and furrow will be as old as, and probably much older than, any estate map which depicts open-field farming in the location concerned. In very general terms, broad ridges tend to be medieval and narrow ridges tend to be more

These old walls, near Linton in Wharfedale, are superimposed upon the earthworks of medieval strip lynchets. With patience and a perceptive eye it is possible to work out the history of the fieldscape

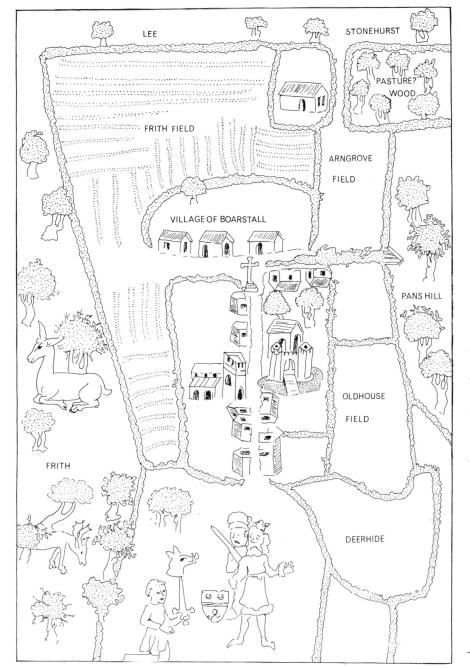

Labels on map: LEE, STONEHURST, PASTURE?, WOOD, FRITH FIELD, ARNGROVE FIELD, VILLAGE OF BOARSTALL, PANS HILL, OLDHOUSE FIELD, FRITH, DEERHIDE

BOARSTALL, BUCKINGHAMSHIRE, 1444

The earliest plan of an English village and its fields we have was found in the Boarstall cartulary. It appears to show ridge-and-furrow ploughland in Frith Field, the name of which suggests land cleared from the 'frith' or woodland. At the bottom of the map a man receives the Fitz Nigel arms from the King. In post-medieval times the village declined, shrank and lost the form portrayed on the map, though a gatehouse tower and moat are still distinctive features of the site.

recent, but there are known to be exceptions to this rule. It is worth remembering that ridge and furrow ploughing continued in some places into the nineteenth century. Straight ridge and furrow was produced by ploughs hauled from one side of a field to the other by steam engines; and, although examples of this sort of ploughing surviving as earthworks are rare, it is as well to be aware of the possibility. Considering the close correspondence between ridge and furrow and open-field strip-patterns shown on old field-maps, it is amazing that until the late 1950s it was argued that most or all ridge and furrow was the product of steam ploughing!

Anyone seeking to explore the medieval fields in a locality should make a detailed study of field-maps preserved in local archives. The county record office should be the first port of call. Sadly, the help that is offered varies – largely depending on the savagery of county spending cuts. The offices of Nottinghamshire, Essex and Northamptonshire proved most helpful to our researches for this book, in contrast to a record office rather closer to home which requires notification some seven weeks in advance before a document will be produced – which is hardly helpful to those who would like help to explore the contents of an unfamiliar archive. In addition, written information about medieval field-patterns can be found in field-books, which variously date from the medieval or later centuries and record the holders of strips in each furlong. Examples from the seventeenth and eighteenth centuries should not pose great difficulties, but some skill is needed to interpret the older ones.

Where open-field farming did not surrender to Parliamentary Enclosure one may expect to find fields produced by early enclosure – which could have occurred at any time from perhaps the thirteenth or fourteenth century to the nineteenth century. As we said, early enclosure fields combine fragments removed from open-field strip cultivation, and so such fields will have sides which correspond to former open-field furrows. Their hedges or walls will normally echo the gently sweeping curves of the former strips and will often perfectly preserve the characteristic reversed-S outline.

Old enclosures in and around a village are likely to correspond to medieval closes or, if they are long, narrow and run back from the through-road, to medieval tofts. Sometimes the abandonment of roadside house-plots led to the amalgamation of adjacent tofts, while small squarish closes beside a village which contains no traces of ridge and furrow are likely to be medieval and may contain the earthwork traces of old homesteads. Away from the village, old enclosures which do not have the shape associated with the early enclosure of field-strips may prove very hard to date. They are a characteristic feature of ancient countryside, and unless they can be related to datable features, like Roman roads or medieval moats, their antiquity may be unfathomable. When puzzled by such fields one should resort to old field-maps giving field-names. Amongst a network of medieval assarts there are likely to be at least one or two with characteristic 'ridding', 'hag' or 'sart' names. Similarly, if the fields have actually resulted from early enclosure, then some old strip-ploughland names, like 'land', 'head', 'rigg', 'butt', 'gore', 'flat' or 'shott' may have been preserved, while names like 'dole', 'hide', 'pole' and 'rood' were associated with common meadows.

Fields arranged around the margins of an old common are likely to be intakes. Ancient and medieval commons often had their boundaries marked by a prominent man-made divide – a hedgebank and ditch, double hedgerow or hedge-girt holloway. If the boundary between the open common (or common divided by straight Parliamentary Enclosure walls or hedges) has a ragged moth-eaten appearance, then the frontiers of the commons are likely to have been pushed back by piecemeal intaking. Relics of a continuous boundary lower down the hillslope may reveal the original limit of the common.

Parliamentary Enclosure fields should present the least problems. They will almost always have ruler-straight edges, and a morsel of local historical research will produce the date of the enclosure. The archives may preserve both pre- and post-enclosure maps, showing the before-and-after situation. Tithe-award maps mostly dating from the years 1836–44 were produced after the Tithe Commutation Act of 1836 and they often provide a detailed picture of the early- or mid-nineteenth-century fieldscape in parishes which did not experience Parliamentary Enclosure. The only fields which loosely resemble those produced by enclosure are the rare Roman cases seen, for example, on the Dengie peninsula of Essex. These fields also seem to have been surveyed to produce rectangular networks. However, imperfections in the survey technique and the slight misalignments in hedgerows which are to be expected in fields almost two thousand years old provide a constrast to the uncompromising straightness of enclosure hedges.

We can move from theory to practice by describing the field-patterns around Grassington, which should be a Mecca to all students of the fieldscape. From the archaeological viewpoint the locality is most celebrated for the survival of the lynchet banks and overgrown walls of the 'Celtic' field system which extends across the limestone pasture to the north of the village and covers about 300 acres (c.120 hectares). 'Celtic' fields date from various times from the late Neolithic to the Roman period. Amongst these fields there are the traces of contemporary dwellings – small circular houses with low rubble walls; at map reference SE 995662 one can recognise a small cluster of huts set inside a low wall. Excavation of some of the settlement sites suggests occupation in the late Iron Age and Roman periods, though at this time the associated fields could already have been old. In late Bronze and Iron Age times the deterioration of the climate led to the desertion of many upland farming areas, but here the free-draining character of the limestone and the generally south-facing aspect must have allowed mixed farming to continue. It is strange to think that two thousand years ago a substantial community tilled the ground and drove their cattle along narrow field-tracks in a locality where bare limestone pavements sparkle in the sunlight and rabbits, wheatears and lapwings are far more numerous than people.

In medieval times the area of surviving 'Celtic' fields was considered to be beyond the pale of arable farming and lay within the pasture of the commons that covered the slopes between the village of Grassington and the waste of the Out Moor. The lower land with deeper soils than the other three sides of the village was in open-strip fields: West Field, Sedbur Field and East Field. These fields terminated before reaching the banks of the Wharfe, and a narrow ribbon of common meadowland intervened between the ploughlands and the river. Between the Wharfe and the common to the west of the Old West Field stands Grass Wood, today an important nature reserve, but in medieval times an exclusive deer-hunting preserve for the lord.

Much of the history of the Grassington fieldscape can be observed from a single vantage-point, so let us take a position to the north-north-west of the village on the track to Conistone and close to the site of the former hamlet marked 'medieval village site of' on the Ordnance Survey outdoor leisure map at map reference SE 003651. Looking to the east and north-east over the three lines of straight walls, we find a very large enclosure of a rather oval shape which contains traces of 'Celtic' fields. This is High Close, an area enclosed from the

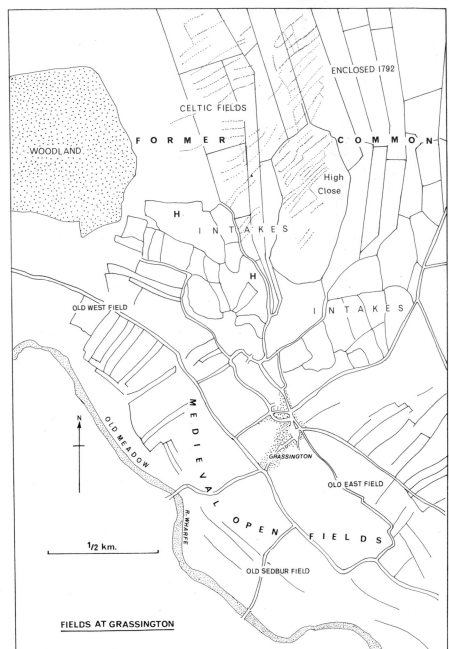

ENCLOSED 1792

CELTIC FIELDS

F O R M E R   C O M M O N

WOODLAND

High
Close

H

I N T A K E S

H

I N T A K E S

OLD WEST FIELD

N

OLD MEADOW

M E D I E V A L

R. WHARFE

GRASSINGTON

OLD EAST FIELD

O P E N   F I E L D S

½ km.

OLD SEDBUR FIELD

FIELDS AT GRASSINGTON

FIELDS AT GRASSINGTON

The map shows the general pattern of 'Celtic' fields, enclosed field-strip, intakes, open field, meadow and Parliamentary Enclosures. The positions of deserted medieval hamlets are marked 'H'. Within the area of the medieval open fields only walls which plainly result from the enclosure of field-strips are marked.

common by the medieval lord for his own use. Smaller walled closes, known as Cove Closes, lie just to the south of our vantage-point, and these were intakes made by medieval peasant families who, deprived of access to Grass Wood, would use some of their intake land to grow hazel, which was coppiced to produce light timber.

Looking southward beyond the Cove Closes one can see elongated fields with curving boundaries which are instantly recognisable as enclosed open-field strips of the Old West Field. The two nearest examples run east to west, and

just beyond them are the members of a larger group running southwards over the brow of a low hill. A written survey of the holdings in Grassington was made for the lord, George, third Earl of Cumberland, in 1603 and revealed a total of 864 strips. The Earl sought to raise his capital by selling short-term leases to his tenants, and around 1605 the strip-holders began a process of swapping and selling which introduced early enclosure into the West Field.

In the seventeenth century enclosure by agreement disposed of the common ploughland, and previous enclosures had produced intakes like High Close, the Cove Closes and some intakes in East Field which were surrounded by plough-land when that field was extended. Apart from the intakes, the common pasture remained open until 1792, when Parliamentary Enclosure divided the grazings. A fine sequence of enclosure walls are seen to the east of our vantage-point, where unusually elongated fields converge on a spring and on the droves which lead to the village.

The view from Cove Closes above Grassington looking across the enclosed medieval field-strips and meadowland towards the River Wharfe, marked by a dark band of riverside trees

129

These walls near Grassington define medieval field-strips which were enclosed in the years after 1603

Looking northwards beyond the Wharfe towards the slopes on the horizon, the step-like pleats in the hillside are the remains of medieval strip lynchets, but to see a more spectacular vista of these features we must walk down through the village and along the road to Hebden for about half a mile and look along the Wharfe at the field-patterns which lie to the east of Linton village. Linton also had its own open fields, and historian Dr A. Raistrick believes that a two-field system existing at the time of Domesday in 1086 was increased with the addition of two new fields, one to the east and one to the west, at some time before 1277, the old open-field land still being surrounded by old walls. Here, as in Grassington just across the river, early enclosure dismantled the open fields, so that when Parliamentary Enclosure came to the parish in 1793 only small patches of open-field land remained to be enclosed.

The Grassington locality is a remarkable open-air chronicle of the history of a fieldscape: I know of none better. Yet every countryside has its field-patterns, and these patterns each tell a story. Hopefully this book will inspire the reader to attempt his or her interpretations. Field-names serve as invaluable sources of information, and interpretation of this evidence is offered in the text accompanying our maps. Some of the names suggest the origin of the field concerned, not only the familiar assart names, but also others drawn from the vernacular of open-field farming, like 'flat', a furlong, or 'hades', a headland, which may reveal that a pasture was formerly under open-field strip cultivation. Field-names tell us about vanished features of the countryside, like the common windmill, dovehouse and warren names, or about the quality of the soil, in names like Stone Ground, Hungry Hill, Starvation or Sweet Leys. Some names describe the shape of fields, like our own Doublet Sleave, Bread Shovel and Boarshead examples. A few recall unusual events; we have recorded Denton's Grave and another oft-described field-name from Northall in Buckinghamshire: Thertheoxlaydede. Names which can seem like gibberish today may have changed out of step with the evolution of our language or may recall forgotten events or jokes. Tar a rat, Hary Man Stones and Tinkletong, all at Burton Leonard, are examples. A few fields can be shown to have kept their names since early medieval times, but one must doubt that the Burton Leonard field named Morcar really commemorates the northern earl who was a contemporary of King Harold and William the Conqueror.

John Field has compiled an excellent dictionary of *English Field Names* which will solve many, though not all, puzzles, and the following table explains many commonly encountered names:

Amad: haymeadow
Applegarth: orchard
Balk: grassy path through open fields
Bang or bong: boundary bank
Barton: demesne land or farmyard
Batch: stream
Bottom: hollow
Brake, breech, breck: waste land brought into cultivation
Byes: inaccessible corner of a field
Cangle: enclosure
Carr: marshy land
Catchland: unclaimed land between two parishes
Catchmeadow: meadow watered by stream from slopes above
Chase: hunting land
Close: enclosure (from open fields)
Clough: a steep valley
Conyger: rabbit warren
Copy, copse: coppice
Crew: a cattle-yard
Denn: a pasture for pigs
Dole, dale, dalt: share in common field or meadow
Dolver: land reclaimed from marsh
Eddish, etch: an enclosure
Ersh: ploughed field

Fall: wood
Farrow: path
Ffridd: enclosed land by Welsh farmstead
Fit: riverside grassland
Flat: furlong
Flockrake: Scottish sheep-pasture
Flonk: pig-sty enclosure
Forschel: land beside a road
Freeth: West Country hedge
Frith: wood
Gall: marshy land
Garston: cattle-yard
Gore: triangle of land between two furlongs
Greeve: grove
Grip: ditch
Ground: land distant from the farmstead or manor house
Hade: headland
Hafod: Welsh summer pasture
Hag: wood, assart
Hale: corner of land
Hamstal: field near the farmhouse
Hatch: fenced land
Haughland, hern: meadow in loop of a river
Hay: hedged enclosure or deer park

Heaf: sheep-pasture
Hendre: winter pasture in Wales
Hollins: holly wood
Holm: water meadow
Hope, hoppet: small enclosure
Ing, eng: meadow
Inham, inning: intake
Jack: small piece of waste land
Lache: pond
Land, loon: strip
Lea, ley, lee: grassland
Lease: meadow (sometimes pasture)
Leasow: enclosed pasture
Low, law: ancient burial-mound
Mains: demesne land in Scotland
Mark, mere, reans: boundary
Moor: marsh or moor
Oldland: former ploughland
Over: slope
Paddle: pasture
Patch, pickle, pightle: small enclosure
Pike, pilch: pointed piece of land

Plachet, plash: wet ground
Pre: meadow
Quillet: narrow strip of land
Rap: narrow strip of land
Reading, ridding, rode, royd, sarch, sart, stubbs, stubbing: assart
Scoot: oddly shaped little piece of land
Severals: land held individually
Sherd, shord: a clearing
Shot: furlong
Sike: a stream or streamside meadow
Slade: valley or damp ground
Slaight: sheep pasture
Slough: marshy ground
Storth: wood
Swale: wet meadow land
Thwaite: meadow or clearing
Tye: small enclosure or large common
Vaccary: cow-farm or -pasture
Wong: enclosure, meadow, garden
Wray, wroe, stitch, plat: a nook of land

FIELD-NAMES, CHIDDINGSTONE, KENT, 1838

This is an area of ancient countryside, with hedged pastures and small woods or 'shaws', which are stippled on the map. Some of the field-names simply express the size of the field. Others are intriguing – was Childrens Field inherited by children? – while the Batfolds group of fields has a name which remains mysterious but may relate to a former owner. Shoulder of Mutton Field takes its name from its shape, and Bean Field from its crop, while Dung Croft was land which required manure. Most interesting are the names which reveal local historical information which might not have survived otherwise: Walk Mead was a meadow by which the medieval fulling of cloth took place (from the Old English *wealcan*). Some of the field-names can help to confirm the discoveries made in rambling across this countryside: Mountfield is close to what appears to be a Norman motte or castle-mound, and near to the motte are the earthworks of

pillow mounds or artificial rabbit-warrens – an identification confirmed by the Warren Field names. This area seems to have experienced a fair amount of medieval woodland clearance, with assarts revealed by the 'Riddens', 'Ridings' and 'Breeches' names. The former existence of medieval strip fields might not be expected in the present landscape of hedged pastures, but the names Calves Flat and Lime Kiln Flat hint at the possible existence of flats or furlongs. Was Denton buried in Denton's Grave Field and, if so, why here and not in the churchyard?

The detail shows the fields around Bore Place as they existed seventy-seven years earlier, showing that field-names can evolve, with Lower Daniel's becoming Upper Donald's Field. Beggars became Young Orchard, and its southern section became Beggar's House Mead.

Overleaf: Just above Grassington,
walls dating from Parliamentary Enclosure of
the common in 1792 converge upon a spring and the
droves leading down to the village farmsteads

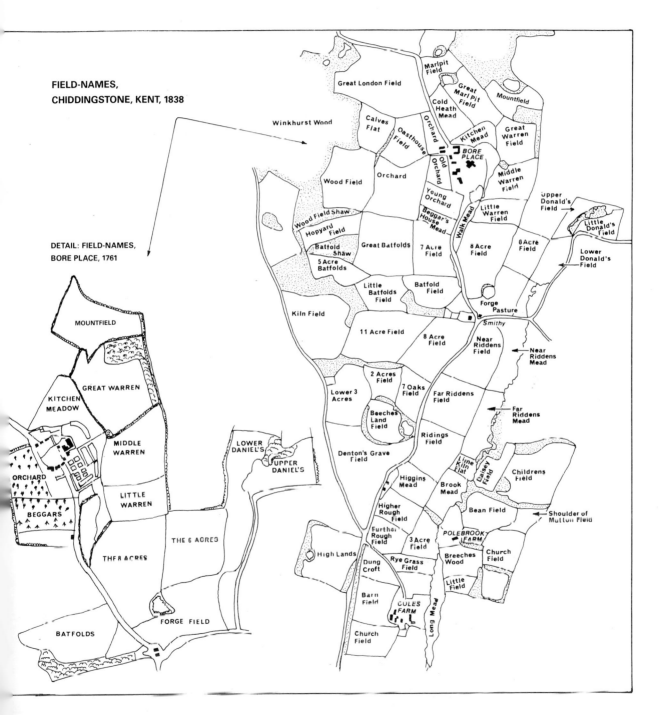

**FIELD-NAMES,
CHIDDINGSTONE, KENT, 1838**

DETAIL: FIELD-NAMES,
BORE PLACE, 1761

CHAPTER 8

HEDGEROWS AND WALLS

Fields must have boundaries to avoid disputes about the ownership of land. These boundaries must be visible on the ground and almost invariably need to be reinforced by barriers; otherwise the horn will devour and trample the corn. In many cases the ditches, which helped to drain wet ground, also marked the actual boundary-line between adjacent properties. Ditches were seldom considered to be adequate barriers, and farmers had a range of different barriers at their disposal: fences or palings; living hedges; dead hedges; hurdles and walls.

Fencing consumes large quantities of perishable sawn posts and rails and, though used in prehistoric, medieval and modern times, does not seem to have enjoyed great popularity. It is not mentioned very frequently in the old records, while the estate maps of the sixteenth, seventeenth and eighteenth centuries show that lowland England was hedgerow country and fencing was unusual. Fencing is indicated on some old maps, like the Moulsham map (p. 48), and it was sometimes employed to fence off new parkland. Hurdles, skilfully made from withies or hazel twigs woven into a frame of hazel or ash poles, were popular as temporary fencing. They could be erected to form livestock-pens or control grazing in a fallowing open field or a meadow. Hurdles and dead hedges were used to close off gaps in living hedges to keep sheep and cattle out of the growing crops. After harvest they could be removed to allow the livestock to graze the stubble. At Minchinhampton in Gloucestershire in 1273, Alan of Forwood was charged with having 'his "hedges" around the field of Westfield carried off before the term'. He replied that 'the reapers and others carried off part of the "hedges" so that in many places there was an entry, so that cattle had a common entry before [he] carried off anything'.

Dead hedges, barriers of posts and brushwood, provided a more permanent and less elaborate screen than a row of hurdles, although dead hedges were probably less common in Saxon and medieval times than is sometimes supposed, for while a dead hedge would consume a large amount of posts, twigs and branches it would soon decay, though a living hedge offered a permanent barrier and would produce valuable crops of fruits, nuts, berries and timber. Sometimes the old records specifically tell us that a hedge was 'quick', or living, but generally the nature of the hedge is not specified, and where the word *sepes* is used the barrier concerned could be a hedge, wall or paling. Old English words like *haeg, hege, gehaeg, raewe* and *hegeraewe* occur frequently in the old charters and documents, and must usually describe living hedges.

It is clear from Saxon records that England was heavily hedged in the centuries before the Norman Conquest, and recent archaeological work is revealing that the prehistoric landscapes were also rich in hedgerows. Julius Caesar provided a detailed description of strong hedges that his armies encountered just across the Channel on the southern borderlands of modern Belgium, and in the 1980s excavation at the Bar Hill Roman fortress on the Antonine Wall in Scotland found that brushwood cut from hawthorn hedges had been used to fill in existing ditches when the fort was built around AD 142. Hedgerow snails have been found in an Iron Age field-ditch excavated at West Heslerton in the Yorkshire Wolds, and the excavation of the ditch of an Iron Age defensive enclosure at Tattershall Thorpe in Lincolnshire in 1986 revealed pollen grains which suggested that a hedge had overhung the ditch. Looking further back in time, it is likely that the Dartmoor reaves originally existed as hedgebanks not unlike those which so greatly enhance the modern Devon countryside. Many of the stone-faced Cornish hedgebanks which still give useful service must have been built in Roman, Iron Age or Bronze Age times – one in the Penwith peninsula was found to contain a hoard of prehistoric bronzework within its fabric.

While most hedges were planted, a minority were 'spontaneous', with shrubs naturally colonising roadsides and boundaries protected from grazing.

Field-patterns of ancient countryside defined by hedgerows below the woods covering the Iron Age Hembury hillfort in Devon

When ditches were dug to mark boundaries it appears that hedges were often planted in the upcast soil beside the ditch. On important old boundaries a double hedgerow could be planted, or a sunken track flanked by hedgerows can also mark an ancient boundary. Current research in Norfolk suggests that the boundaries of vast prehistoric commons were marked in this way.

In the course of time different forms of hedgerow were adopted in different parts of Britain. The best-known form is the Midlands bullock hedge, a stout hedge which is not normally planted upon a hedgebank and which can be found in variations, like the tall Leicester 'bullfinch' or the lower but denser Yorkshire sheep-hedge, throughout most of Midland and northern England. In Devon, the Welsh Marches and most parts of Wales hedges tended to be planted upon banks, with the height of hedge and bank varying from place to place. A Cornish hedge is a thick boulder wall with shrubs sometimes growing in the earth packing between the stones.

Regular maintenance was needed to preserve a strong hedge barrier. In parts of East Anglia hedges were periodically coppiced – cut down close to the ground, a seemingly drastic treatment which actually revitalised the hedgerow and stimulated rapid new growth. In other parts of the country hedges were normally 'laid'. Superfluous twiggy growth was trimmed away from the main stems, and these 'pleachers' were then slashed at their bases leaving just a narrow hinge of living wood between the pleacher and its roots. The pleachers were then laid diagonally downwards along the hedgerow and secured in place by upright posts hammered into the hedgerow at intervals of a few feet. The laying of the hedge was completed by adding a 'heathering' of pliable branches woven between the tops of the posts to stabilise the hedge. New growth would then surge from the base of the hedge, but until the barrier was re-established some protection against browsing was needed. This could be provided by a ditch on one side of the hedge, and sometimes this would be filled with thorny brushwood as added protection. The bushy ends of the pleachers would generally be laid towards the unprotected side of the hedge to keep browsing animals away from new growth. Newly planted hedgerows required special protection, and this could be provided by a thorny dead hedge or by fencing.

Much has been written about 'hedgerow-dating', the notion that the age of a hedge equals the number of species of shrub found in a thirty-yard length of hedgerow multiplied by 100 (so that a count of six different species would reveal a 600-year-old hedge). In a recent book (*Hedgerows: Their History and Wildlife,* Michael Joseph, 1987) we provided a lengthy explanation of why this theory does not work. Perhaps the most telling criticism concerns the fact that, in the days before commercial nurseries selling hawthorn became numerous, peasants and farmers would plant their hedges from saplings and seedlings gathered from woods, roadsides and gardens. So hedges did not begin as single-species hedgerows but as mixed plantings. Mixed hedges were still being planted at the end of the eighteenth century when Nathaniel Kent wrote of Norfolk that: 'Whenever a person can get four or five acres together, he plants a whitethorn hedge around it, and sets an oak at every rod distance [every 5½ yards (5 metres)].' Customs which have gone back to times immemorial were quoted by Fitzherbert in 1534: '. . . gette thy quicksettes [living shrubs] in the woode countreye and let theym be of whyte thorne and crabtree for they be

beste, holye and hasell be good. And if thou dwelle in the playne countrey, then mayste thou gete both ashe, oke and elm, for those wyll encrease moche woode in shorte space.'

A second major criticism of hedgerow-dating concerns the fact that certain invasive shrubs will spread along a hedgerow evicting their neighbours and thus depressing the species-count. Elm and blackthorn are the most frequently seen invaders, but holly and bird cherry will also expand under favourable conditions. It is true that the Parliamentary Enclosure hedges of the eighteenth and nineteenth centuries do tend to be composed of hawthorn with a few pioneering colonists, like elder, wild roses, bramble and sycamore, but their straight forms and well-recorded histories make these hedges easy to identify without any recourse to species-counting.

Field-walls have proved popular wherever quantities of tough rubble are available, and such places are often damp, rocky and not conducive to vigorous hedgerow growth. Walls are more durable than hedgerows, so that traces of field-walls survive at scores of prehistoric sites. However, until recently little was known about the age and evolution of field-walls. In the 1970s Bronze Age reaves on Shaugh Moor and Holne Moor on Dartmoor were excavated, and it was found that the stone banks were preceded by fences of oak staves, which

Laying a hedge: the pleachers have been laid and a 'heathering' of willow is being used as a woven binding between the tops of posts. Such work is done in winter when the hedge is dormant

were ripped out when the reaves were built along the fence-lines. The reaves survive so well because the moor has never since been as effectively colonised as it was in the Bronze Age. In Saxon and medieval times boulders cleared during attempts to resettle the moor were incorporated into clearance-walls, which were elongated piles of boulders. Norman Forest Law forbade the creation of fences or hedges which would restrict the movement of deer, so peasants built 'corn ditches', earthen banks faced in stone and fronted by ditches, to protect their crops against the deer. When Forest Law was lifted from Dartmoor in the mid-thirteenth century wall-banks were built, consisting of a boulder-and-rubble wall with the centre packed with earth allowing a hedge to crown the stonework. The latest stage in the building of enclosure walls on Dartmoor dates from the eighteenth and nineteenth centuries; these walls resemble the Parliamentary Enclosure walls of northern England, though the use of granite rather than limestone or gritstone gives a lumpier, more uneven appearance.

A stone wall in the making, from *Wiltshire Village* by Heather and Robin Tanner, Collins 1939

A remarkable advance in our understanding of field-walls has resulted from very recent research at Roystone Grange near Ballidon in Derbyshire. The earliest walls identified, dating back as far as the New Stone Age, are recognised as foundations consisting of elongated boulders around 2 yards (*c*.2 metres) in length which were simply placed end to end. During the Roman occupation a very different type of wall was built, consisting of double rows of boulders placed up to 2 yards (2 metres) apart in a shallow trench and with the core of the wall packed with rubble and with low facing stones between the boulders and the edge of the foundation ditch. At this time lead-miners and sheep-farmers were apparently being encouraged to exploit the Peak District. The third wall-type recognised dates from the twelfth and thirteenth centuries, when Cistercian abbeys were developing sheep-ranches in the region. These walls consist of a single row of massive boulders upon which smaller stones are balanced to produce a rather untidy-looking wall. Walls built at Roystone Grange in the sixteenth century, when the holdings of the dissolved abbeys were being subdivided by private owners, consist of double faces of stones chosen and placed in such a way that the wall tapers upwards the single row of topstones. The walls that were built during the Parliamentary Enclosure movement – by Napoleonic prisoners of war in the case of Roystone – resemble those of the sixteenth century except that a filling of pebbles and stone chips was packed

Patches of lichen gradually colonise the stones of field-walls. The ring-like markings slowly expand as the colonies grow, enabling lichen to be used as a rough-and-ready guide to the age of walling

between the rows of facing stones while the white limestone used was quarried and contrasts with the brown limestone employed in earlier walls.

In the Lake District, where walls, defining fields, funnelling sheep driven down from the fells towards pens or guarding the edges of precipices, are a key component of the scenery, most result from the Parliamentary Enclosure of fell pasture and common. A few date back to the monastic era and were built to

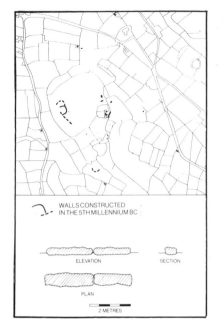

WALLS CONSTRUCTED
IN THE 5TH MILLENNIUM BC

ELEVATION

SECTION

PLAN

2 METRES

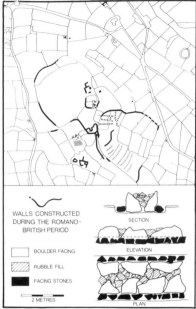

WALLS CONSTRUCTED
DURING THE ROMANO-
BRITISH PERIOD

☐ BOULDER FACING

▨ RUBBLE FILL

■ FACING STONES

SECTION

ELEVATION

PLAN

2 METRES

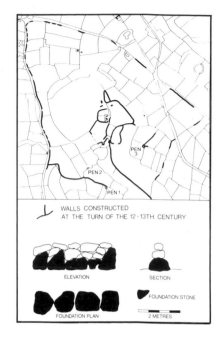

WALLS CONSTRUCTED
AT THE TURN OF THE 12-13TH. CENTURY

ELEVATION

SECTION

FOUNDATION PLAN

■ FOUNDATION STONE

2 METRES

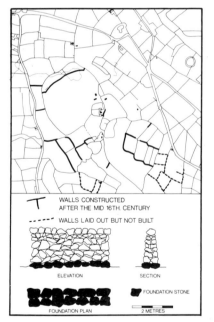

WALLS CONSTRUCTED
AFTER THE MID 16TH. CENTURY

- - - WALLS LAID OUT BUT NOT BUILT

ELEVATION

SECTION

FOUNDATION PLAN

■ FOUNDATION STONE

2 METRES

WALLS FIRST CONSTRUCTED
IN THE EARLY 19TH. CENTURY

-MANY OF THE EARLIER WALLS WERE REBUILT AT THIS TIME

ELEVATION

SECTION

FOUNDATION PLAN

■ FOUNDATION STONE

2 METRES

Field walls of different ages surviving at
Roystone Grange in Derbyshire, as
recognised by M. Wildgoose on his
Roystone Grange Wall Project

heights which would contain sheep but not impede deer, while some others are the product of enclosure in the sixteenth and seventeenth centuries. In Troutbeck township each man was responsible for maintaining a portion of the wall built in 1551 between Troutbeck and Ambleside. In 1680 a hefty fine of 6s 8d (34 pence) was imposed on all those who shirked their duty.

Drystone walls vary according to their age and the nature of the local materials, with walls of slate in herringbone courses being seen in part of north Wales and upright sheets of flagstone being used on Orkney. By the enclosure era, however, the craft of walling had been somewhat standardised, and most walls were built as double rows of stones set in a shallow trench. The footing stones were largest, and the stones become smaller as the wall tapers upwards, with a filling or 'hearting' of small stones packing the space between the two faces. At the top the tapering wall is narrow enough to be spanned by a single row of topstones, known as 'cam stones' in the Lake District and 'combers' further south. Through-stones, which run from one side of the wall to the other, are incorporated to strengthen the structure. In the base of some northern walls gaps known as 'hogg-holes' allow hoggs (yearling sheep) to move from one enclosure or common to the next, while pits at the wall base covered by trapdoors are 'smoots' for trapping rabbits. The stones used for walling were gathered or quarried locally and taken to the site in tumbrils if the gradients were gentle, while sleds were employed on steep ground.

Much walling was done by farmers and their labourers, but during the Parliamentary Enclosure era the demand for walling was enormous, providing work for many professional wallers. Usually the award specified the dimensions of the walls required and the dates for their completion. The award concerning Kirkby Moor near Kirkby Lonsdale, quoted by Dr William Rollinson, specified a foundation trench 6 inches (15 centimetres) deep:

The foundation to be three feet six inches [about 1 metre] wide at the bottom. To be set on three Inches [8 centimetres] on each side upon the foundation stones and to be carried up gradually to sixteen Inches [40 centimetres] at the Top. The Height of the Wall to be six feet [1.8 metres] from the higher side of the foundation including the top stones to be set edgewise and not more than six or seven Inches [15 or 17 centimetres] deep. The Wall to contain three rows of Throughs in height the first row of which to be laid on the first course of stones above the setting on and the other two rows of Throughs to be at equal distance and not laid nearer the top stones than one foot [30 centimetres] and the wall to contain nine Throughs in each row in every rood. . . .

SOME PLACES OF INTEREST

Devon contains many of the finest expanses of hedgerow country, with the old hedges usually growing in earthen hedgebanks. Some of the best views of rolling hedged countryside can be enjoyed by travelling along country roads and lanes from Honiton (ST 1600) to Cullompton (ST 0207) via Luppitt and Ashill or from Newton Abbot (SX 8671) to Moretonhampstead (SX 7586) via Doddiscombsleigh.

Roystone Grange (SK 2057). The valley lies 6 miles (10 kilometres) to the north of Ashbourne in Derbyshire near the hamlet of Ballidon. Here the Peak Park authority and Sheffield University have laid out an archaeological trail with display-boards which identify agricultural patterns of different ages. A guidebook is available at the park information centre.

Potash Lane Hedge (TL 9940). This ancient hedge, protected in a Suffolk nature reserve, is said (improbably) to have standards dating back to around the time of the Norman Conquest. The hedge also supports some shrub species which are good indicators of age, such as Midland hawthorn, wild cherry, dogwood and crab apple. Between Hadleigh and Boxford, off the A1071.

See also *Cheadle Hulme Trail* (p. 185), *Eakring Meadow* (p. 186) and *Stocking Pelham* (p. 276). A particularly fine expanse of enclosure field-walls can be seen in *Dacre Pasture* (see p. 121); older stone clearance field-walls are best displayed at *Wasdale Head* (see p. 81); and relics of prehistoric walls are clearly seen at *Rough Tor* (see p. 37).

CHAPTER 9

CHALK AND LIMESTONE PASTURES

The environmentalist Marion Shoard reminds us that:

Thirty years ago large tracts of chalk downland turf in Sussex, Hampshire, Berkshire, Dorset, Wiltshire and East Yorkshire provided freely accessible land over which the walker could roam at will alongside the sheep, the butterflies and the kestrels on a carpet of orchid, cowslip and harebell-studded turf. . . . Now the experience of walking over a great wilderness of springy downland turf amid thyme-scented air survives mainly in the writings of Kipling, Belloc, Hardy and W. H. Hudson.

Since 1947 we have lost about 80 per cent of our traditional chalk grassland, mainly to arable cultivation and the 'improvement' of pasture. On the limestone fell grazings of the north the changes have been less devastating, yet still considerable.

Much as we may admire the old scenes and mourn the passing of closely cropped chalk pasture with its spangling galaxies of wild flowers, or limestone upland grazings with nodding pansies and bird's eye primrose, we should not imagine that these grasslands are natural. The pastures resulted from the ancient woodland clearances of the Neolithic and Bronze Age periods, while the frequent traces of 'Celtic' fields in the southern downlands or northern fells tell of prehistoric phases of mixed or arable cultivation. The traditional plant-rich pastures were the result of the establishment of a stable régime of close grazing. In medieval times many chalk and limestone downlands or uplands existed as vast open sheep-ranges. Some areas survive as commons, but over the centuries the extent of unenclosed pastures diminished. After the Dissolution of the Monasteries many vast monastic sheep-walks were partitioned, while increases in rural prosperity in the sixteenth century encouraged many yeomen to expand their holdings. Enclosures by agreement, by the grabbing of intakes and, in due course, by Parliamentary Enclosure all reduced the extent of open chalk and limestone country. According to the Wessex antiquary John Aubrey a Captain Jones enclosed downland near Salisbury by ploughing a furrow and sowing it with crab-apple pulp obtained from a local crushing mill. The apple seeds germinated to produce hedges 'so thick that no boare can gett through them'.

Most enclosures were associated with the keeping of sheep. Cattle, too, have grazed the downlands, and grazing by rabbits has also had an important effect. Following its introduction by the Normans, the rabbit was at first a delicate and valuable animal, but gradually a robust strain developed. Some wild rabbits gravitated naturally to the downs and limestone uplands in the post-medieval period, while other rabbit communities were deliberately introduced, with low banks or 'pillow mounds' being provided for them, some mounds even being furnished with artificial burrows. Close regular grazing helped to maintain the pasture, with a reduction of grazing leading rapidly to the establishment of scrub vegetation as nature sought to re-establish the woodland cover. Both chalk and limestone are composed of calcium carbonate derived from the shells and skeletons of the sea-creatures. The soils which form on these calcareous rocks are rich in lime, and consequently alkaline, but generally poor in nutrients like phosphates and nitrates, both of which are needed for vigorous plant-growth. Also, both rocks are associated with very dry soils, the chalk being

highly porous and the limestone absorbing water through labyrinths of cracks and fissures.

Consequently it may seem surprising that traditional chalk pastures are exceptionally rich in plant species, with 1 square yard (0.84 square metre) of ground often supporting between twenty-five and thirty-five different types of plant. This diversity of species does not reflect the richness of the environment; instead it probably testifies to the precarious nature of existence, which prevents any single species from gaining ascendancy over the plant community. This community remains stable only so long as the harmonious relationship with the grazers is maintained, for the sheep which crop the turf provide essential fertilisers and prevent colonisation by woody plants by nipping off the tips of their seedlings. Once the grazing régime is reduced and scrub colonises the

A chalk escarpment at Westbury in Wiltshire. While chalk soils that were easy to cultivate were one of the first to be tilled by Neolithic man, slopes too steep to plough may still hold the riches of chalk grassland. Once the grazing régime is reduced, scrub colonies and pasture changes are not easily reversed

pasture the changes are not easily reversed. Recent attempts to restore the low-land chalk grassland on the great Dark Age frontierwork in Cambridgeshire known as Devil's Dyke met with difficulty. It appears that hawthorn scrub which had colonised the Dyke had in some way enriched the soils with nitrates and phosphates, so that when the thorns were cleared thistles and goosegrass flourished rather than the traditional species. (Elsewhere on an open section of the ancient chalk embankment is one of the last strongholds of the spectacular lizard orchid, with pyramidical orchids growing in profusion nearby.)

The majority of downland wild flowers are perennial plants. They are all adapted to survive and compete in the thin, alkaline and impoverished soils where conditions are never so favourable as to allow one plant to expand and shade out its neighbours. Each plant struggles to maintain its own little grow-ing-space or to advance into any adjacent territory which becomes vacant. Annuals and biennials die after flowering, surrendering their niches in the turf, while their seeds are deprived of bare ground in which they could germinate and grow. Amongst the grasses, the fescues are characteristic of the traditional downland grazings. Sheep's fescue occurs in different forms on both acid and chalky pastures, but its down-curving thread-like leaves which keep the stomata hidden from the effect of the wind help to reduce water-loss on dry chalky soils. On the less impoverished downland grazings the taller red or creeping fescue becomes more common, its creeping runners assisting its spread. Other grasses of the old pastures include the crested hair, fine bent, creeping bent and the rarer downy and meadow oat grasses, while the lovely common quaking grass with its flowering head of heart-shaped nodding spikelets is an indicator of undisturbed grassland.

Changes in the régime of grazing and cultivation produce rapid changes in the grass community. At its most drastic the change may involve the ploughing-up of the ancient sward and resowing with rye grass, which creates plenty of interest for the livestock but leaves little or nothing for the naturalist. Some of the traditional downland grasses, like fescue and yellow oat grass, are also palatable to livestock, though tor grass, which can be invasive, is avoided by them. Less drastic changes to the pasture result if sheep are replaced by cattle. Thereafter the pasture will tend to be colonised by coarser grasses, like crested dog's tail, upright brome and tor grass, which the cattle tend to avoid. In winter the presence of tough unpalatable grasses is marked by hummocky clumps of the invaders standing like islands amongst the closely grazed sward, and as these clumps expand, so they provide refuges within which scrub can become established to mark a new stage in the disappearance of the old pasture. The ecology of the traditional downland pasture is so finely balanced that even the light trampling and enrichment of the soil by discarded food and dog drop-pings at picnic sites can encourage cocksfoot and perennial rye grass to expand at the expense of the established plants.

Downland pastures are noted for the beauty and diversity of their flora. The various wild orchids are the most celebrated of these eye-catchers, but perhaps the most spectacular plant is the rare pasque flower of the downs of Hertford-shire and Bedfordshire and a few lowland chalk sites in Cambridgeshire. The violet or mauve flowers and the finely divided leaves are clad in silky hairs which help to reduce water-loss by slowing down the drying air-stream. The

Opposite above: Sheep crop the turf of calcareous pastures, provide essential fertilisers and prevent colonisation by woody plants by nipping the tips of their seedlings

Opposite below: When sheep-flocks dwindled on downland their rôle as grazers of the sward was maintained by rabbits. Since myxomatosis great tracts of downland are being invaded by scrub

149

The silky hairs of the pasque flower help reduce its water-loss in the drying downland airstream

flowers are produced in late spring before the leaves are fully unfolded, and some of the stamens develop into nectaries to attract pollinating insects. The seeds of the pasque flower are equipped with feathery 'awns' which aid dispersal by the wind, and the seed head with its plume of grey awns is as attractive as the flower.

Around one-third of all chalk-sward plants conform to the low rosette form. In this adaptation leaves grow in rosettes flattened against the ground, keeping the stomata safe from the wind; other plants are prevented from growing too close; and lying low these plants are better able to avoid munching teeth. The plantains are of this type, the distinctive hoary plantain being distinguished from the ribwort plantain by its broad downy leaves and its plume-like flower spike which attracts insect pollinators. Perhaps the most obvious resistance to grazing is shown by the stemless thistle, which has its leaves not only spread across the ground, but also armed with spines. Other plants do not have leaf rosettes but form a low mat-like growth which carries some of the same advantages, the bird's-foot trefoil and horseshoe vetch being examples. Others have fleshy water-storing leaves, like biting stonecrop. Some plants respond to drought by developing root systems which can penetrate into the subsoil and

bedrock for a yard or more, the salad burnet and rock rose both enjoying this advantage. The downland pastures contain a number of semi-parasitic plants which, though they contain their own green chlorophyll and can therefore manufacture their own foods, are parasitic on the roots of various host plants. Most common are the dainty eyebrights and the hayrattle. A few downland plants are wholly parasitic, like the tall broomrape, which parasitises the greater knapweed.

Amongst the most intriguing but vulnerable of the downland plants are the chalk orchids, short-lived perennials which may flower only once before dying. The orchids flower in late spring and early summer, avoiding the heat and drought of high summer, although some orchids which are rare in Britain are not uncommon in warmer parts of the Continent. Rarities include the musk, man, frog, lizard and lady's tresses orchids. The monkey and miliary orchids are restricted to a small number of protected sites, but pyramidical and fragrant orchids can still be found in sizeable colonies, and the lovely bee orchid is locally numerous, while two reasonably common orchids, the twayblade and common spotted, are often seen in chalky settings. Orchids produce great quantities of minute seeds which supply the young plant with very little nourishment.

Salad burnet, here iced with frost, is adapted for living in downland: a low-lying rosette form with leaves close to the ground to reduce evaporation and an extensive root system to reach the water lying deep below the surface

151

Opposite above: The bizarre lizard orchid is rare and localised in its appearance in rough calcareous grassland

Opposite below: Woolly thistle has a distinctive distribution in rough grassland of the limestone outcrops extending from Dorset and Somerset to north-east Yorkshire, but also occurs in scattered localities on chalk. As grazing animals avoid it, the plant can grow up to 6 feet (*c.*1.5 metres) tall, but it is the woolly flowering heads that are the most characteristic feature of this plant

Above left: The summer-flowering bee orchid is usually found in the short turf of unimproved calcareous grassland. Despite its mimicry of the bee, insect pollination is rare in Britain, the plant being almost always self-pollinated

Above right: The rare and localised early spider orchid is confined to a total of about thirty locations in the short turf of old chalk grassland in Dorset, Sussex and Kent. Although the flower resembles a bee rather than a spider, there is uncertainty as to which insect actually pollinates it. Here an ant is seen visiting a flower, but it is unlikely that these insects play an important rôle

The tiny orchid can only develop in an association with a fungus, which invades its roots and supplies the plant with nutrients derived from dead plant material from the surrounding soil. Meanwhile the developing orchid is itself at risk from the fungus, whose thread-like hyphae have invaded its roots. The orchid gains its independence when it succeeds in producing leafy shoots, but years will pass before the first flowers are produced. Consequently the picking of wild orchids is a particularly serious offence against the countryside.

In most downland pastures one will expect to find some plants, like harebell, knapweeds, yellow bedstraw and restharrow which are not confined to these specialised habitats. There will be others which will only flourish in a chalky soil, like the musk orchid, the pasque flower or the small scabious.

The most northerly exposure of chalk in England is eastern Yorkshire, beginning just north of the Humber and stretching to the Vale of Pickering; much of this land is under cultivation. However, the late J. E. Lousley, who is widely considered to have been an authority on calcareous flora, wrote that 'in general, Yorkshire chalk lacks many of the attractive southern plants and has very few additional northerners by way of compensation'. West and further north are the green pastures and wooded dales of Carboniferous and magnesian limestone. Many of the plants which thrive in the chalk soil of the southern downlands can also be found in the lowland limestone pastures – wild thyme, marjoram, rock rose, salad burnet, bird's-foot trefoil and lady's bedstraw being a few examples. The more severe climate of the northern limestone uplands is associated with a rather different range of plants. Perhaps the most characteristic plant is the mountain pansy, which is usually common in rough limestone pastures. Although it is associated with limestone country, it is only able to flourish where free calcium carbonate, which inhibits its ability to take in potash and phosphate, has been leached from the soil. Typically the mountain pansy is a butter-yellow colour, but in Teesdale there is a violet form.

Much more localised is the beautiful globeflower, cultivars of which are often grown in moist gardens. The wild form is confined to damp upland pastures and woods on the northern limestone, where it provides a most striking addition to the May flora. The bloody cranesbill, whose crimson flowers can be seen in high summer, is another beautiful plant of limestone country where it grows in pastures, scree and light woodland at heights up to about 1,200 feet (c.370 metres). Other gems of the limestone fieldscape which can grow in profusion include common lady's mantle, giant bell flower, melancholy thistle and drop wort. The characteristic wild rose of limestone country is the burnet rose, distinguished by its creamy-white blossom and dense thicket of thorns. It may be found growing in thin limestone soils or bare rock exposures in the north of England and also in the downland grazings of the south.

Naked exposures of bedrock are uncommon in chalk country but can frequently be found in the high limestone pastures of the northern uplands. The Carboniferous limestone is riddled with a multitude of cracks and crevices which are gradually enlarged by trickling rainwater. As the trickles dissolve paths through these crevices the surface water soon finds its way to subterranean streams and rivers, carrying away the thin soil with it. This soil is usually a form of glacial drift eroded from the tops of the blocks, or is peat. Some of it settles in the shallow clefts or 'grikes' to provide special niches for plants, giving shelter from grazing and a more shady and humid microclimate. Mosses and liverworts thrive in these niches, as do a few hardy plants like thyme, yellow and rue-leaved saxifrages, herb robert, sanicle, bloody cranesbill, wild strawberry and several ferns. Robert Gibbons explains that the wild flowers of limestone pavements are 'something of a mixture, with woodland flowers, cliff-dwellers, plants of chalk grassland and others. There are no species that are totally confined to this habitat, but several specialise in these areas, and are more likely to be found here than anywhere else.' Rigid buckler-fern is a national rarity but quite common on pavements east of Morecambe Bay. Solomon's seal, baneberry and lily of the valley, flora of limestone ashwoods, are often also a feature of limestone pavements, the former two being quite local.

Many of the high limestone pastures are too thinly soiled and windswept to have experienced great damage, although the removal of limestone pavement for sale as rockery stone has had an adverse effect in many places. Originally excavation of limestone with crowbars was a laborious task, but subsequently tractors with winches and other such machinery led to rapid efficient extraction. When the Wildlife and Countryside Act was being considered in 1981 the concern for the dwindling limestone pavements resulted in specific clauses in the Act to prevent further destruction. The total area of genuine limestone pavement in the United Kingdom is estimated at a little under 5,000 acres (c.2,000 hectares). While designated areas are protected under Sites of Special Scientific Interest (SSSI) legislation, other areas can be protected under the 'limestone pavement order' granted by the Secretary of State if the Nature Conservancy Council or the Countryside Commission perceive a threat of destruction. But, as Robert Gibbons points out, 'the loophole in all this legislation is that destruction can go ahead where planning permission has been granted'.

Many lower enclosed limestone pastures have been 'improved' (see Chapter 11) by the application of fertilisers and by reseeding, so that old herb-rich meadows and pastures are becoming rarities in the more accessible areas. However, the brunt of the destruction has been borne by the chalk downlands. Here the damage has not only been inflicted upon the wildlife and plant life, but often upon the soil itself. Over the millennia farmers accepted that the downlands existed as grazing country. During the two world wars, when U-boat operations threatened to sever our lifelines with the food-exporting countries, quite extensive areas of virgin downland pasture were brought under the plough. More recently and more seriously, the Common Agricultural Policy has encouraged the ploughing of vast tracts of traditional downland for cultivation of high-yielding autumn-planted 'winter' cereals.

As a result the bare soils of new ploughlands are exposed to the erosive effects of winter rainstorms. Dr John Boardman of the Countryside Research Unit at Brighton Polytechnic points out (and we use his metric calculations) that, while soil is only renewed at the very slow rate of 0.5 tonne per hectare per year, the soil losses on the Downs in the autumn of 1987 frequently exceeded 30 tonnes per hectare, sometimes exceeded 100 tonnes per hectare, while one 9-hectare field studied shed its soil at the staggering rate of 270 tonnes per hectare. So it seems that in the long term we may be witnessing a switch not from flower-rich pastures to arable fields, but from stable productive grassland to arid chalk deserts.

Overleaf: Malham in the Yorkshire Dales. Many of the high limestone pastures are too thinly soiled and windswept to have experienced cultivation. Naked exposures of bedrock can frequently be seen in pastures. The soil that settles in the cracks provides special niches for plants sheltered from grazing animals and the elements. In the middle ground, shrubs have established in such niches and beside the stream issuing from the foot of Malham Cove

SOME PLACES OF INTEREST

Box Hill Country Park (TQ 1751). A large National Trust property of downland and woodland and part of the North Downs Way in Surrey. There are several woodland types, but the most notable is full of yew and box, which gives this great shoulder of chalk its name. Centuries of grazing have created the open downland where nearly 400 species of plant have been recorded including lime-loving flowers such as milkwort, salad burnet, horseshoe vetch, kidney vetch and sainfoin. Look out for fragrant, spotted, pyramidical and bee orchids, and in September the lady's tresses orchid. The areas of scrub shelter the small man orchid, and the shrubs here are wild cherry, with its early blossom heralding spring, and with dogwood, wayfaring tree, white beam and traveller's joy all contributing their splendid colours at other times of the year. A dozen species of grasshopper and bush cricket have been recorded here as well as chalkhill blue, skipper, ringlet, green hairstreak and dark green fritillary among the butterflies, while of more interest to gourmet readers is the edible snail – a creature limited to chalk and limestone areas by its calcium requirements for its shell. Scrub and woodland shelter attracts plenty of bird life. One mile (1.6 kilometres) north-east of Dorking off the A.24. Close to Ranmore Common (TQ 1450) and Norbury Park (TQ 1653).

Devil's Dyke (TL 5766–6558). This linear chalk earthwork (about 8 miles/13 kilometres long) is a reserve managed by Cambient and Cambridgeshire County Council. The flora is varied, ranging from scrub to chalk grassland including survivors from the lost Cambridgeshire downs. It has many plants characteristic of southern lime-rich soils such as purple milk vetch, bloody cranesbill, squinancywort, horseshoe vetch and dropwort, but it is famous for its spring-flowering pasque flower, rare spring-sedge and even rarer lizard orchid. The development of open blackthorn and hawthorn scrub has changed the nature of the flora in some patches, but the scrub is maintained and continues to provide a suitable habitat for birds. This linear wildlife-haven, now surrounded by arable land, reminds us of the riches that have been lost to the plough. A public footpath runs along the crest of the Dyke: access is from the B1102, the B1061 and the A11.

Gait Burrows (SD 4877). This Nature Conservancy Council reserve in Lancashire is generally reckoned to be the best example of a lowland Carboniferous limestone pavement in Britain. But the area of about 175 acres (70 hectares) includes a range of limestone habitats including deciduous scrub and woodland on the edge of the pavement, wet and dry grazed meadowland and a small tarn, Little Hawes Water. The pavement resembles a natural rock-garden with bright green ferns (including the rare rigid buckler fern) and colourful flowers, and from the larger crevices rise small shrubs of yew, holly, spindle and dogwood among others. This area is also important for its scrub community of spindle, wild privet, buckthorn, dogwood and small-leaved lime, all of which are near their northern limit. A permit is required from the NCC away from the footpaths. The reserve is best approached via the A6, turning off at Beetham on to the unclassified road to Silverdale.

Graig Fawr (SJ 0680). This is a National Trust property near Offa's Dyke in Clwyd. The site is a limestone hill looking over the Vale of Clwyd. The western and northern slopes are craggy, sometimes spectacularly so, while scrub and large grassy fields clad the gentler eastern and southern slopes. The shallow turf is rich with small herbs and lime-loving plants, but of particular interest is hoary rock-rose, limited to only a few Carboniferous limestone sites in Wales and northern England. The colourful limestone plants attract common blue, meadow brown and small tortoiseshell butterflies, while where gorse and small trees have become established birds of scrub such as stonechat, linnet and whitethroat, among others, have been recorded. South-east of Prestatyn, take minor roads off the A547 and the A5151.

Great Ormes Head (SH 7883). On this spectacular peninsula of Carboniferous limestone in Gwynedd, trails lead through limestone grassland above the coastal cliffs and areas of pavement. The grassland has typical limestone flowers such as rock-rose, salad burnet and wild thyme, while in the crevices of the pavement are a variety of ferns. Butterflies include grayling and silver studded blue. The breeding colonies of birds are a delightful feature of this site; some eighty-five species may commonly be seen around here mainly nesting in the cliffs. These include the sea-birds such as kittiwake, guillemot and cormorant but also jackdaws and ravens. Coast-road A546 from Llandudno.

Ivinghoe Beacon (SP 9616). A National Trust property on Chiltern downland in Buckinghamshire. Here the gentle slopes of chalk grassland and scrub show the curving beauty of the chalklands. The spectacular views of the beacon attract many pairs of feet, and so the slopes are well trodden. Here model aircraft compete with hovering kestrels. The flora is richest on the thinner soils of the steeper slopes that face north and on the banks of old cart-tracks, and here, too, are a range of chalkland butterflies. It is not unusual to find the common-spotted and fragrant orchids on the steeper slopes, but more widespread are salad burnet, common rock-rose, the vetches and even cowslips. Grazing keeps some check on the ever-invading scrub, gorse and coarser grasses. But competition from these is greater where the soil is locally deeper and the chalk is topped by clay with flints. Five miles (8 kilometres) north of Leighton Buzzard, off the B489.

Malham (SD 9068). This well-known Yorkshire site is a wonderful mixture of upland and lowland habitats including limestone grassland and pavement which carry a wide range of lime-loving plants, trees and shrubs, particularly on the ungrazed pavement. The uplands tend to be overgrazed, but stone walls and bird life offer a good deal of interest. Much information about the area is readily available from the Yorkshire National Parks Committee or from the information centre at Malham. Off the A65 from Skipton.

Pewsey Down (SU 1163). This site in Wiltshire is one of the few remaining splendid examples of herb-rich turf and is known to be one of the longest-grazed downland sites now left. From the sheltered arable fields below rise expanses of open grassland on steeper slopes. Plants indicating ancient turf include bastard toadflax, field fleawort, chalk milkwort among others which are common on chalk, such as cowslip, hoary plantain, quaking grass, yellow rattle, restharrow, small scabious, kidney vetch and sainfoin. The reserve protects a wealth of orchid species including burned, common-spotted, bee, frog, frag-rant, green-winged and pyramidical orchids as well as other rare species such as tuberous thistle and early gentian. The wealth of plants are enlivened with col-ourful butterflies such as brown Argus, chalkhill and little blues and marsh fri-tillary, the last occurring here because of its food-plant, the devil's bit scabious. (This plant species, together with betony and saw-wort are apparently rare on chalk outside Wiltshire and Dorset.) There are plenty of other insects, and ant-hills are a familiar feature covered by their own little gardens of tiny flowering plants such as eyebrights, mouse-eared hawkweed, rock-rose and wild thyme. Scrub is confined to a few areas of deeper soils lower down on the slopes, and it is particularly noticeable for its absence higher up. Hence the wide fields inter-rupted only by fencing give a stunning impression of old grassland. Approached from minor roads between Malborough and Devizes.

Queen Elizabeth Country Park (SU 7118). At this park in Hampshire a good variety of habitats may be observed from the trails which lead through beech and coniferous woodland and 540 acres (218 hectares) of open downland on Butser Hill (see also p. 34) with typical chalkland flowers and butterflies. Ex-cellent information leaflets are available from Hampshire County Council. Four miles (6 kilometres) south of Petersfield, signposted off the A3.

Totternhoe Knolls (SP 9821). The history of the knolls (in Bedfordshire/ Huntingdonshire) reflects an area much changed by the hand of man since a Norman castle was built to crown the site. These gentle chalk hills were cleared of their woodland and grazed by sheep for several centuries. Subsequently the hard Totternhoe 'clunch' stone was quarried for building and the softer chalk for cement, creating a topography of hills and holes. The abandoned quarries became covered with a thin turf to form a refuge for chalkland flora, and below the old castle site the grassland is maintained by grazing. While lady's bed-straw, eyebright, basil, thyme, yellow wort and quaking grass are very evident, less common plants and several orchids also occur. Typical chalkland moths found here include small purple-barred and dark pyrausta, and the little and chalkhill blue butterflies have also been recorded. Some forty species of bee and wasp, including species from a family of shell-nesting mason bees, may also be found. Two miles west of Dunstable via the B1354.

Cuckmere Valley (TV 5199). One of the finest views of this valley of rolling open grassy fields and smooth curves is from Firle Beacon in Sussex. Chalk grassland rises from the valley floor, a pattern of short and tall species-rich swards varied by scrub and hay-cropped fields. Early purple, pyramidical and common-spotted orchids occur among gentian, salad burnet, common centuary, squinancywort, thyme and carline and dwarf thistle, while in the deeper swards on the valley floor are viper's bugloss, weld and yellow rattle. The 970 acres (390 hectares) of the Haven include a chalkland estuary and cliffs. Nature trails through the various habitats of the Haven lead from the Seven Sisters Country Park Centre where leaflets and displays of the natural history and development of the area are available. The Country Park is east of Seaford on the A259 by Exceat Bridge.

CHAPTER 10

SHADES OF GREEN

In contrast to the lime-rich pastures described in Chapter 9, neutral grass-lands are much more widespread and varied, occurring on soils formed of clays, loams, alluvium and marls that are neither particularly base-rich nor acid. As these are the grasslands of much of Britain's agricultural regions, they owe their character not only to their soils and other local environmental factors, but also to the way in which they have been managed. Management, past and present, has modified the intensity and type of grazing régimes, whether the grassland is mown and during what season, or 'improved' by influencing the nutrient status of the soil or by deliberately changing the composition of the sward. These grasslands form a wide spectrum of fieldscapes, from traditional-ly managed hay meadows enclosed by hedges or stone walls and characterised by a wide variety of grasses and colourful herbs to wet meadows on flood plains, and from old multi-species pastures and ditch-dissected grazing marshes to those that are heavily 'improved' or to artificially created grass crops, consisting of a few dominant or specifically chosen species. The difference between meadow and pasture concerns the form of management to which they are sub-jected: the former is regularly mown for hay or silage (with mixed régimes of cutting and grazing) and the latter is mainly grazed by farm animals.

In the Yorkshire Dales the proportion of grassland within enclosed farmland far outweighs arable land. A survey of the Yorkshire Dales National Park by R. G. H. Bunce and colleagues in 1985 showed that of the 12,661 enclosed fields 29 per cent were hay meadows, most of the remainder being permanent pasture, with very little arable. The 3,746 hay fields ranged from intensively managed lowland hay meadows, often reseeded and subject to chemical control, to small herb-rich hillside meadows on limey soils which are relatively undisturbed by management apart from cutting. Some 129 different plant species were found in the latter type in contrast to only sixty-nine in the former. Only 185 of the 3,746 fields could be regarded as herb-rich, and even of these 125 failed to qualify for SSSI status, their score of 'indicator plant species' being below the level qualifying for protected-area status.

A survey of northern upland meadows by R. S. Smith revealed sites in Wharfedale and Cumbria which had been maintained in the same way for so long now, their vegetation being composed almost entirely of native species, that they may be regarded as semi-natural. Hardly any fertiliser, save for infrequent manuring, is applied to the swards on thin limestone soils, and the

Tor grass, cocksfoot and brown knapweed capture the drowsy warmth of a summer meadow on chalky soil

frequent summer droughts experienced allow only occasional cutting when particularly wet weather has produced a reasonable yield. Those on wet sites on boulder clay and peaty soils suffer from waterlogging. Though the botanical composition of each type of sward reflects its environmental conditions, both are species-rich. This is because the nutrient supply in both areas is low, allowing large numbers of species to coexist without any achieving particular dominance: each meadow-type has an average of just under thirty species per square yard.

While the existence of hay meadows depends upon continued agricultural use, the most highly valued meadows, as far as naturalists are concerned, are those that have been maintained traditionally, that is, where fertility is low and where disturbance, or management, serves to maintain species diversity. But as farmers have sought to increase the productivity of their hay fields the great majority have been improved to some extent. Little more than the application of drainage and additional nutrients from farmyard manure has converted semi-natural wet meadows to the now more common buttercup meadows of the Dales, averaging about twenty-six species per square yard. However, buttercup meadows that are only occasionally cut for hay and are, for most of the time, cut for silage or used as pasture inevitably see a further reduction in the average number of species (to about twenty-three per square yard). They also see a change in the main species present. As the march of agriculture has progressed, the practices of using mineral and artificial fertilisers, of spraying with herbicides and of reseeding have become so widespread that the traditional herb-rich meadow is arguably considered to be the most threatened British ecosystem.

Where hay meadows have been part of farming practice the detail of management régimes has varied according to the constraints imposed by the farm in which the meadowland is situated. Here we examine how management of a traditional Dales meadow from which a moderately productive yield of hay could be obtained can have affected the nature of the sward. The manure collected from livestock overwintering in barns was spread on the meadow early in spring. This together with the dung dropped by the grazing animals during the autumn and winter months replaced nutrients leached from the soil by rainfall and removed in the hay crop. The additional manure encouraged an 'early bite' for farm animals and will have been particularly beneficial for ewes prior to and during lambing. At this time of year it is the grasses that suffer the brunt of defoliation, reducing their competitive ability so they do not dominate the herbs which begin to grow later. The differences in the grazing methods of livestock, their trampling and the effects of their dung and urine patches all add to creating species diversity. Cattle roll their tongues around the grass and so may uproot it in the process. Their large patches of dung may first smother the vegetation under the pat and then create a niche for species characteristic of fertile conditions. Sheep move across the sward eating the uppermost parts of plants first and in this way gradually reduce its height. Sheep are not particularly selective, though they prefer the young green leafy material to the drier old stem material. Hence there will be some selectivity depending on the changing palatability of the sward. Trampling opens up germination sites, but around more heavily trodden areas, such as water- and food-troughs, only those species tolerant of disturbance may find a niche: here annuals such as knot grass and rayless camomile may establish.

Some time early in May grazing ceased and the meadow was shut for the hay crop to develop. (Spring grazing is not suitable for early-flowering species such as fritillaries because the flowers are removed before there is time to set seed. Where fritillary meadows have developed in the south, spring grazing will not have been part of the management pattern and the meadow will have been shut to livestock by February.) The rise in temperature and the nutrients from the manure encouraged the now undisturbed flora to grow in rapid sequence, beginning with the early-flowering species such as daisy, wood anemone and lesser celandine which would be shaded out by the later-maturing species by the time the hay crop was taken. The diversity of the developing mosaic would therefore, to some extent, have been affected by the previously grazing livestock and also by the partitioning in the growth period between the different species.

The hay crop was taken some time between July and early August, depending on the weather and altitude. Meadows higher up at the heads of the Dales were often cut later than those lower down. The time at which cutting occurred could also influence the components of the sward, for in years of early cutting late-flowering species such as cocksfoot could not set seed: a succession of early cuts in this competitive habitat could result in less vigorous later-flowering species becoming eliminated. While mowing and removing the hay crop is a considerable disturbance to the vegetation, it stops any course of dominance that taller vigorous species may exert over others by mid-summer by removing most of the above-ground parts of all but the ground-hugging plants. As there

Overleaf: Hay harvest in Nidderdale, Yorkshire. While haystacks have long disappeared with the advent of modern machinery, even hay-making scenes such as these are becoming rare where silage-cropping is preferred

163

The hay crop has just been removed from this meadow, but uncut field-edge and hedgerow offer shelter and add diversity to the wildlife of the fieldscape

is no build-up of litter over the years the low-growing plants can establish as components of the sward and, as the examples above show, these are the first to flower. So in order to maintain diversity, allowing a full sequence of flowering to be followed, the annual cut is a significant factor. R. S. Smith has shown that, other factors being similar, the vegetation of the uncut meadow has, on average, only two-thirds the number of species that one might expect to find in a meadow cut for hay.

After the hay was removed livestock were returned to graze the meadow. The regrowth of the vegetation, known as 'aftermath' or 'foggage', ensured more palatable leafy growth for sheep, which was said to increase their rate of conception. During the autumn and winter months the animals were moved around pasture and meadow according to the weather and availability of grass, the stored hay supplementing their feed when the grass stopped growing. Cattle, oxen and horses usually overwintered in barns. On farms with ploughland, in the days before the tractor, oxen and horses would be drawing the plough in early spring and had to be properly fed during this period of hard work. Hay meadows were thus important features of farms, for while staple crops were grown on arable land they could not be produced without animals to pull the plough. An average eight-ox team which could plough about 60 acres (24 hectares) per year would need some 8 tons of hay to maintain them during the winter months.

While traditional management contributes significantly to maintaining species diversity, a meadow's environmental site conditions provide the framework. A large meadow with a range of site conditions can accommodate not only a diversity of species but also different plant communities. Such variation can be demonstrated at Yellands Meadow nature reserve in Swaledale. A study by E. J. Cross revealed not only two habitats within the meadow itself – the hay crop and the uncut edges – but also four additional habitats which contributed to the overall diversity: hedgerow, stone wall, riverbank, and a small stream running across the meadow. The total number of species in the locality added up to more than 120. Of these fifty-three were found in the main crop area and seventeen in the uncut edges. However, a detailed analysis of the hay crop revealed that it subdivided further into groups of flora owing to localised variations in wet, damp and dry areas of different degrees of neutrality.

Records of meadows began appearing during Anglo-Saxon times in many charters. There is no doubt that grasslands were put to use as meadows and pasture long before then, and field- and place-names (see Chapter 7) and Old English terms for grassland (*mæd, teah*) may give clues of this. Though scythes have existed since at least Roman times and may well have been used on meadow, *storing* hay for winter food became a more common practice in medieval times. Among the few old northern meadows which are almost semi-natural in character there may still be fragments which link back through time to early medieval meadows, and the areas involved will have been grassland for much longer. Floral components of swards may be woodland species, possibly remnants of the original woodland which once stood where grassland eventually developed. Bunce and colleagues explain that the transformation of woodland to grassland during the successive periods of settlement in the north was so very gradual that there was sufficient time and opportunity for some of the wild flowers associated with woodland to adapt to the developing open fieldscape. Wood cranesbill, wood sorrel, wood angelica, greater butterfly orchid and bluebell are a few examples of an old Dales meadow sward, and there are also components of woodland-edge flora, such as cow parsley and hogweed. Some species-rich old meadows and pastures have unequivocal records showing their previous use as ploughland, such as those that lie on ridge and furrow (see Chapter 3). Within the same square yard the flora of the ridge can vary from that in the damper furrow where water may lie. For example, at Thorpe Marsh reserve in Yorkshire, where ancient ridge and furrow is still visible, the frequent species on the ridge are pepper saxifrage, sneezewort, great burnet and occasionally cowslip – herbs of damp-to-dry habitats; while in the furrows grow cuckoo flower, meadow buttercup and tubular water dropwort, indicating damp-to-wet niches.

Grassland is relatively easy to produce from arable land, for even a stubble field, if grazed and then left unploughed, will revert to some sort of pasture, poor though it may be, within a few years. Good pasture will have taken many more years to produce, although the deliberate sowing of pasture was known to take place by the seventeenth century with suitable seed developing by then. However, it will have taken several generations for grassland to have gained many of the characteristic meadow plants. Once the rich variety of meadow flowers was welcomed by farmers for the sweetness and nourishment they

Wild primroses have become established in this old Cornish pasture which is closed to grazing animals in spring

added to the hay. Hence meadow was an essential feature of traditional mixed farming and was considered to be a permanent precious fixture. Muddy damaged areas would be carefully patched up by scattering the sweepings from the stored hay, reintroducing the seed into the sward.

Most hay-meadow plants are perennials making growth in rapid succession through spring and early summer, their fruits ripening in sequence until around haytime. As we have already stated, precise plant associations for any single hay meadow will depend on its environmental factors and management history, so an account such as this can only give a general impression of some of the characteristic species. The small semi-natural upland meadows, on light calcareous soils, have many species that are more typical of low calcicolous grasslands. Though the grasses that grow here are individually of low nutritional status, the diversity of the sward may produce a decent hay crop. Quaking grass, purple moor grass and sheep's fescue will add delightful tinges to the colour of the sward; but while the last, a variable species, is nourishing enough in pasture, its lack of foliage does not allow a good hay crop. Brown bent grass, Yorkshire fog and sweet vernal grass are also characteristic species of old meadows, though in productive improved pastures they may be considered weeds. The two former are tuft-forming and play a better rôle as fodder grass. Sweet vernal grass, which contains courmarin, imparts a characteristic spicy scent, but bitter taste, to new-mown hay, but in pasture sheep will readily eat it. About 150 years ago it was erroneously recommended in seed mixtures and has

Left: A traditional buttercup meadow beside the author's home. Manuring encourages the growth of the buttercups
Above: Poppies growing among the grain give this Kentish arable field a traditional appearance

The meadow grasshopper is common on all types of chemical-free grassland

A pearl-bordered fritillary on old herb-rich grassland in the Mendips

The common blue can be seen in most old grassland as it has a variety of food-plants of the pea family

The small skipper favours long grass with numerous wild flowers

Cowslips (*left*) and green-winged orchid (*right*) are good indicators of old meadow or pasture and are among the first flowers to appear in spring

been flourishing ever since. Cocksfoot may also be found here. Although a coarse grass, if unmanaged, it is a very useful species for regularly cut hay because it grows tall and has a high yield. It is also excellent for pasture because the young shoots remain green throughout the winter, when their growth is briefly arrested, but resume growth at a rapid pace in spring. While herbs of semi-natural and traditionally managed meadow are numerous, few achieve dominance. A species-count by R. S. Smith in semi-natural upland hay meadows in Wharfedale and Wales revealed that 70 per cent occurred with a frequency of less than 5 per cent. On the well-drained soils swards contained species such as rough hawkbit, mouse-ear hawkweed, cat's ear, sealheal, burnet saxifrage, bird's-foot trefoil, heath bedstraw; while fragrant orchid, betony, cowslip and common milkwort were reasonable indicators of old meadow. Damper meadow, as a result of imperfect drainage on boulder clay, was differentiated by sedges, including carnation, glaucous, common, flea, bladder and brown. The herbs included woodland species such as bluebell, bugle, wood anemone, wild angelica, violet and others, like tormentil, marsh thistle, harebell and bitter vetch. Gems such as devil's bit scabious, yellow pimpernel, common spotted and twayblade orchids indicated old grassland, and the presence of globeflower was interesting because it is mainly a northern species.

Moving towards nutrient-rich meadow, there are those that are heavily manured but not treated with herbicides, such as the traditional buttercup meadows. Here grass species, such as crested dog's tail and red or creeping

Opposite above: A colourful garland of weeds of cultivation with the blue cornflower and yellow corn marigold, both now threatened, and with red poppies and ox-eye daisy, the last-named sometimes spreading from hedgebanks

Opposite below: Mayweed, a frequent weed of arable crops on light soils

169

fescue, may become obvious. The last can often be the dominant species of this type of meadow; but, while it produces good grazing, it is not an important component in the hay crop as it lacks bulk. The presence of rough meadow grass and perennial rye grass in the sward will reflect richer soils which hold moisture. Perennial rye grass is particularly important, for it is a highly nutritious food for cattle. Although it has naturalised widely in Britain, perennial rye grass is not indigenous but it has been cultivated here for at least the last 300

An old buttercup pasture forms the foreground with traditional Dales hay meadows in the background of this panorama near Summerbridge in North Yorkshire

years, probably originating in Europe and western Asia. Also not native, yellow or golden oat may sometimes be an important component of the sward. It was formerly used in seed mixtures for pasture and hay, being well liked by cattle and sheep, and therefore it may be indicative of old grassland.

The predominant yellow colour of buttercup meadows is maintained by the flowering of a number of species in sequence: bulbous buttercup, meadow buttercup, yellow rattle and rough hawkbit, while the variable dandelion

flowers continuously from March to October. The last is well suited to colonising almost any open habitat. It is able to succed without pollination; like all *Compositae* it produces numerous plummed seeds and it is able to regenerate vegetatively from fragments. Autumn hawkbit is also late-flowering, and if undisturbed it will continue blooming with dandelion well into October. The presence of several other species, such as meadow cranesbill, bistort, lesser knapweed, ox-eye daisy, yellow and blue forget-me-nots, germander speedwell, tufted and bush vetch, and meadow vetching will colour the sward and reflect the lack of chemical control. The latter leguminous species are capable of growing tall amid supporting vegetation and are valuable for the nitrogen they accumulate in their root nodules. Red clover is a much more prized pea species. It is a very variable species; several varieties are commonly cultivated as forage crops and have become widely naturalised. Red clover grows tall and adds significantly to the fodder value of the hay crop. White clover is also grown as a fodder plant, but its persistent root stock may enable it to spread at the expense of other meadow plants. The leaves of some previously cultivated strains have been found to contain glycoside, which produces prussic acid when eaten by animals, and in large quantities this can cause poisoning. Other toxic or

Dandelion is well suited to colonising almost any open habitat: it is able to set seed without pollination; it produces numerous plumed seeds that are dispersed widely by the wind; and it is able to regenerate vegetatively from small fragments

troublesome species may also be present in untreated swards, such as ragwort, containing an alkaloid which acts as a cumulative poison in cattle and horses. Meadow saffron is poisonous in parts, though regrettably the pink crocus-like flower of this species, which rose from the autumn aftermath, has now all but disappeared from many grasslands owing to improvement and changes in the cutting régimes. Its foliage develops in spring to build the corm throughout the summer, and by the time the flower appears the plant is leafless. Though the fresh leaves are toxic, with colchicine, when cut and dried in hay they are supposedly safe for consumption. Buttercups, though bitter when eaten fresh, are no longer so when dried in hay. Crow garlic and yarrow are quite safe for consumption by livestock but are nevertheless unpopular with dairy farmers because they are said to taint the flavour of milk.

The floral components in chemical-free meadows and pastures on fertile alluvial soils on flood plains will vary according to the duration of flooding and the amount of waterlogging of the soil. Damp meadows prone to short periods of flooding in wet winters and managed along traditional lines can accommodate a range of species which enjoy the natural fertility of alluvial soils and reflect varying degrees of tolerance to damp and wet conditions. Dominant

Fritillary thrives exclusively in our ancient flood meadows

grasses will include those that do well on fertile soils, such as meadow fescue, meadow foxtail, rough meadow grass, tufted hair grass and perennial rye grass among others. The fritillary thrives exclusively in our ancient flood meadows. The inverted tulip-like flower of the fritillary seems almost exotic and has no doubt always fascinated gardeners. The name is from the Latin *fritillus*, a dice-box, the bloom's allusion being that of a chequered board upon which the dice may have been thrown. In common with many bulbous species it flowers comparatively early and so is able to seed by July before hay-making. Though the species had been recorded in twenty-seven counties before 1930, today few fritillary meadows remain, the best lying along the upper Thames valley and in East Anglia.

The most famous site for fritillaries is, of course, North Meadow in Wiltshire, with perhaps 80 per cent of the total British population. North Meadow is 'lammas land' (see Chapter 3) where management has remained more or less unchanged for the last 800 years. The existence of common rights, granted in perpetuity to the people of Cricklade, has served as an effective stabliser for the habitat, as no individual has been able to obstruct the rights of others by changing the land-use of his allotted area – by arable cultivation, for example. The fritillary is no doubt the most striking and abundant species of the meadow when it flowers during April and May, but up to a hundred other plant species have also been recorded in this stable habitat. Also in Wiltshire, the Upper Waterhay reserve, on private land, was established especially to protect its display of fritillaries: the flowers here are unusual because many of them are white. The Suffolk Trust for Nature Conservation has taken responsibility for the conservation of several small hay meadows which have enjoyed traditional management for a few hundred years, as reflected in their colonies of fritillary, meadow saffron and green-winged orchid; and the presence of lady's mantle at one of these sites is significant, for it is very rare in East Anglia. Fox Fritillary Meadow is the best-known of the Suffolk meadows, said to be the second-best fritillary meadow in the country with a density in excess of 100,000 plants per acre. Another private five-acre hay meadow in Bedfordshire, also maintained as a county nature reserve, is an unusual fritillary meadow because the plant has been deliberately introduced here. It has become well established because of sympathetic management, as reflected by the other species present, which include cowslip, pignut, wild angelica and meadow cranesbill.

There are many herbs that are more commonly characteristic of damp meadows. In spring the bright yellow marsh marigold will be one of the first to catch the eye, while if the creeping plant butterbur has established it is unmistakable, its peculiar flowering head emerging straight from the ground, well before the large rhubarb-like leaves are fully developed. It is said that butterbur leaves were used for wrapping butter, making it useful on dairy farms, and this is presumably how the common name came about. Towards summer the diversity of a meadow can become apparent. Cuckoo-flower, ragged robin and meadow saxifrage flower late in spring, and then species such as marsh cinquefoil, water avens, bugle and comfrey will bloom by May. By June marsh speedwell, devil's bit scabious, bistort, meadow cranesbill, skullcap and great burnet may be components of the sward, the last being more widespread in damp meadows in the north. The later-flowering corn mint, wild angelica,

A variable species, early marsh orchid occurs throughout Britain in wet meadows, marshes and other damp habitats It flowers during May and June and is probably pollinated by bees

meadow rue and common fleabane will only succeed in propagating their species if their seeds are allowed to set before the hay crop is taken. Old meadow is indicated by the frequent presence of certain species such as those encountered in the above-mentioned fritillary meadows and others like pepper saxifrage, adder's tongue, a dwarf shrub, dyer's green weed, and orchids. While the green-winged orchid is very localised, other orchids are quite common in damp grassland: early marsh appears in late spring, followed by common twayblade, common spotted and the northern and southern marsh orchids, the last two each being more widespread in their respective halves of Britain. Annuals may find a niche in this competitive habitat, and particularly those with special adaptations. Red rattle and the related lousewort are partially parasitic, battening on to the roots of grasses from which is extracted their requirements of water and mineral salts, enabling them to exist without large root systems of their own. Nodding bur-marigold is an annual which succeeds very well where the ground is under water during winter and dry in summer, because water aids the dispersal of its seeds. Marsh beds, ditches, and streams will add further diversity of meadow flora, with sedges and rushes as well as taller herbs such as

meadowsweet, common valerian, purple loosestrife and hemp agrimony growing here.

More specialised flood meadows may be seen in the fenlands where 'wash-lands' have been deliberately created to accept river overflow. The Ouse Washes are the largest and most important of these. The 'meadows', which lie between the two parallel channels of the River Ouse, the Old and New Bedford rivers, receive and store the surplus flow of winter floodwater, and gradually re-lease and channel it towards the sea, thus preventing serious flooding on the adjacent productive arable land. Though widely referred to as wet or flood meadow in our definition, the wash fields are, strictly speaking, pasture or, more correctly termed, grazing marsh. Other types of grazing marsh are formed by the reclamation of fen and estuarine saltings. The fields of these grazings are divided by drainage ditches. The botanical interest of such pas-tures is very varied (many being better-known for their bird life), grasses, sedges and rushes being predominant, and most colour and herbs are associ-ated with their drainage ditch systems. The Ouse Washes consist of about 4,700 acres (1,902 hectares) of small fields divided by nearly 90 miles (145 kilometres) of operational dikes. As the terrain of the washfields slopes margi-nally upwards between the two rivers there is some transition from wet pasture to marshland to water flora. Although grazing takes place during the brief drier summer spell, there is some respite for the plants, because it is deliberately con-trolled to maintain the various vegetation types for the washland bird life (see Chapter 14). Moving towards dry land, the principal grass species include reed sweet grass in the wettest ungrazed spots, while marsh foxtail and floating seed grass can tolerate the grazed waterlogged fields. As the pasture dries out, creep-ing bent, meadow grass, rough meadow grass, red fescue and tufted hair grass become more frequent. Rush and sedge species are obviously plentiful, particu-larly in the marshy transition zone between water and moist mud. The timing of grazing can be critical for these species as spring grazing will destroy reed shoots whereas winter grazing does not affect the overwintering buds. How-ever, where grazing creates openings in rush and sedge beds, niches are cleared for herbaceous species like yellow flag and marsh marigold, while ditches and river banks which enclose the fields are coloured with ragged robin, hemp agrimony, common valerian, water mint, comfrey, nodding bur-marigold, meadowsweet and purple loosestrife.

More widespread were water meadows which were designed to increase the productivity of the river-valley grasslands by various systems of deliberate flooding (see Chapter 5). Those in the valleys of chalk streams benefited parti-cularly from the warm alkaline water, leaving warmth and nutrients in its wake. The intensive régime of grazing, mowing, drowning, and the practice of weed-ing out those species that made poor grazing, will have taken a botanical toll on these habitats during their early working history. In the Wessex chalklands the maintenance of water meadow was an intricate part of the 'sheep-and-corn' sys-tem of land management. Each depended on the other in the following way: the sheep were folded on fallow ploughland during the night, revitalising it with their manure and transferring nutrients from the water meadow to the arable land before the spring sowing; while in the water meadows drowning periodi-cally throughout the winter ensured an early flush of grass, enabling more

Opposite: Grazing at Wicken Fen in Cambridgeshire. Riverbank, pasture and hedgerow offer a range of opportunities for wildlife in a small area

177

sheep to be kept. During the early spring grazing, 1 acre (0.4 hectare) was said to support 400 ewes and their lambs for one day. When the meadow was shut in April the irrigation began again for the hay harvest. The warm temperatures of the chalk stream encouraged rapid growth for a first harvest by June and sometimes a further second and even third harvest if the meadow was not to be used by cattle for summer grazing. With decreasing British grain prices owing to cheaper imports and the introduction of chemical fertilisers, few sheep were needed and early grazing became less important. Thus the system became progressively less intensive until many water meadows gradually reverted to their former state as flood meadows used for non-intensive grazing. With this declining intensity the number of plant species increased.

At Lower Woodford and Britford in the Avon valley there are working examples of the water-meadow system, and the flora here is dominated by grasses with relatively few herbs. In contrast, those that have long since been abandoned and have survived agricultural improvement are floristically much richer. This is less so where the meadows are completely unmanaged and have reverted to botanically poor marshy habitats, though nevertheless rich in animal life. But where they are managed for hay or non-intensive grazing they can be botanically rich. In the Winnal Moors Nature Reserve, the water-meadow system was abandoned about a hundred years ago, during which time the meadows have been mainly grazed and occasionally cut for hay. Now the Hampshire and Isle of Wight Trust maintains it for hay and aftermath grazing. Over a hundred species are regularly recorded here, including many declining fen-meadow species. Most water meadows have been drained but are still recognised by their water-carrying earthworks where they have been converted to permanent pasture. Under arable crops or put to other land-use, such as housing development, all traces are usually lost.

As the increased use of imported food for stock lessened the need for hay production the balance of agricultural grassland has changed to permanent pasture. On farmland, fields under pasture are usually significantly larger than hay meadows. While old permanent pasture – land that has never been ploughed and reseeded or treated with artificial fertiliser and herbicides – is floristically more impoverished than hay meadow, many indigenous herb species, particularly those that are tolerant of grazing, may also be present, but with far less frequency, the grasses being predominant. On uneven ground, variability will increase with a depression here, a damp patch or hillock there, but decrease with grazing pressure. Grazing slowly eliminates those species that cannot withstand it, and R. S. Smith describes how a shift from meadow to permanent pasture has seen the traditional autumn hawkbit/sweet vernal grass/buttercup meadow convert to common tormentil/brown bent top buttercup pasture.

The remaining vestiges of unimproved meadow or pasture enjoy relative security if protected by SSSI or nature reserve status, but grassland poses particular conservation problems, for it is expensive both to acquire and to manage: the very nature of these ecosystems relies on man's routine management of the land. It is therefore far better if landowners can be persuaded to maintain their land without change or improvement. Grasslands can be particularly vulnerable to changes in land-tenure. Unimproved grassland can persist where farmers belong to an older generation and are not under economic pressure and continue using the traditional methods of management out of habit. Younger farmers tend not to be able to ignore economic realities as easily. The Berkshire, Buckinghamshire and Oxfordshire Trust (BBONT) recently reported that they had failed to purchase an important old meadow through lack of funds, but 'luckily the new owner is sympathetic to conservation, and the Trust is hoping to be able to advise on management'. In an appeal on behalf of BBONT for substantial funds (£1 million) for reserve purchase, the Trust's executive chairman, Richard Fitter, wrote that old grassland had been

... under serious and sustained threat from agricultural policies that until extremely recently have almost deliberately set out to destroy them. They are 'uneconomic' in today's Alice in Wonderland agricultural economics which depends on state subsidies. for 'uneconomic' read 'not earning a state subsidy' ... the only way to be sure of any piece of land not being developed is to own it. Even then you can still lose your land to a bypass or a motorway, as happened when much of Osney Mead was lost to the Oxford Western Bypass, and may yet happen to valuable old grassland on Otmoor with the M40. Though BBONT leases a grassland reserve on Otmoor, our position would be much stronger if we owned it.

(Subsequently the inspector reporting for the Secretary of State recommended that the route should avoid the threatened environmentally sensitive areas, but at the time of writing the decision remains to be settled at a future public inquiry. However, a representative of the Nature Conservancy Council has stated that Otmoor is in fact over three-quarters of a mile away from the original proposed route.)

Elsewhere sites are being lost to other forms of development. In 1984, Gloucestershire lost one of its finest hay meadows when a development company destroyed Hucclecote Meadow. Although the Nature Conservancy Council emphasised the importance of the site to the development company, informing them it was of SSSI quality, the Wildlife and Countryside Act did not protect sites 'awaiting designation', and so before the status could be officially granted the site had been sprayed with fast-acting herbicide and ploughed up. The 11-acre (4.5-hectare) site contained no less than sixty different wild flowers, including uncommon species such as green-winged orchid, dyer's greenweed and corky-fruited waterdropwort. In the last few years this is only one of the increasing number of cases in which valuable old grassland sites have been damaged by activities other than agriculture.

Not many results of detailed surveys are readily available to interpret the scale of change, though work is being carried out in earnest by the National Parks Authorities, the Nature Conservancy Council, nature trusts and others. From the few results available, there is little doubt that the percentage of remaining unimproved agricultural grassland is now often in single figures. In 1971 a survey in Cambridgeshire showed that only 3–4 per cent of the 33,467 acres (13,544 hectares) of permanent grassland was found to be botanically rich. (This figure is no doubt now much outdated and probably even lower.) Surveys in 1982 by the nature trusts of the counties of Worcestershire and Herefordshire revealed that 5.7 per cent of the total of 435,368 acres (176,191 hectares) of permanent enclosed grassland was unimproved. In Cumbria, 82 per cent of farmland is enclosed grassland, but only 3 per cent of this remained

179

unimproved, while in Yorkshire this figure is around 5 per cent. In some counties the changes have been most significant within the last decade. Surrey Nature Trust's recent survey has shown that 9,884 acres (4,000 hectares) of 'high value wildlife habitat' have been lost in the last ten years: this includes 25 per cent of unimproved grassland. The pastures of grazing marshes have taken less of a toll, but nevertheless even the seemingly awesome task of conversion of such difficult land has been encouraged by grants from successive British governments and the Common Market. Timothy O'Riordan explains:

During the late 1970s and early 80s these policies worked in such a way as to penalise livestock, especially beef cattle, and to favour cereal production. Net annual profits for Broadland graziers rarely exceeded £100 per acre from beef, but could easily top £300 per acre for winter wheat. In addition the MAFF [Ministry of Agriculture, Fisheries and Food] was willing to pay grants to Internal Drainage Boards and individual farmers to assist in the expensive costs of improving drainage.

By the early 1980s the following losses had been recorded: the north Kent marshes 48 per cent to urban development, mineral workings and arable land; in the fenland basin marshes 49 per cent to arable land; in the Yare Basin (including the recently controversial Halvergate Marshes) 35 per cent to arable land.

The 'improvement' of grassland has entailed the heavy use of artificial fertilisers on existing grassland, or ploughing and reseeding with grasses of high nutrient value. Varieties of the following cultivars (wild grasses adapted for cultivation) have been particularly popular: cocksfoot, perennial and Italian rye grasses, timothy, meadow and tall fescues. Fields may be sown with a monoculture or mixture, the variety and mixture chosen according to their particular purpose. As we have seen, cocksfoot grows on light well-drained soils and is drought-resistant. A course species, it was widely used for hay. The rye grasses falter under dry conditions, so are never mixed with cocksfoot. Short-term 'leys' (see below) were often seeded with monocultures of a rye grass. Perennial rye grass, being leafy, produces good grazing, while Italian rye grass grows taller and is therefore more suited to silage. Timothy and the fescues provide better grazing than cutting varieties, though all have been common in seed mixtures for hay. A good pasture mix to fatten sheep is rye grass with timothy and white or Dutch clover. Cultivars respond better to nitrogen fertilisers than do wild grasses. However, sheep cannot tolerate a high nitrogen content, for it gives them diarrhoea, so the application of nitrogen fertiliser is much less intensive where sheep are grazed. The clover serves the purpose of fixing nitrogen from the air to fertilise the soil. On the other hand, the milk yields of dairy cattle benefit from the intensive use of nitrogen, and therefore the animals may be grazed on pasture which may have experienced several applications of the fertiliser and be fed on silage which has also been treated in this way.

Monocultures and other forms of reseeded pasture are generally very dull for the naturalist, and the herbs that usually exist are the uninteresting weedy species that livestock ignore, such as nettles, thistle and dock species. The first two are avoided for obvious reasons and the last apparently because of their acid taste. The odd bare patch exposed by trampling may create a niche for annuals which are more common on arable land, such as chickweed or the annual speedwells, and the occasional perennial may also establish briefly, particularly if there is an adjacent seed-source from the plants of adjacent ditches, walls or hedgerow verges. In the Yorkshire Dales (and elsewhere on estates and parkland: see Chapter 5), although many pastures have been reseeded, they are still punctuated by old oaks which are originally likely to have been planted for sheltering livestock and providing timber. Wild grasses and herb species have often established in small clumps around the trees in the areas that are inaccessible to mowing machinery. While these oaks remain to shelter the livestock, they also offer a valuable microhabitat and, together with hedgerows which may still enclose the pastures, can add woodland wildlife to the field ecosystem.

The sowing of fallowland with grass seed had been common practice to serve as a short-term 'break crop' or 'ley' to replenish the richness of arable land after it has been exhausted by cereals or other arable crops. Leys may stand for between one and six years. Short-term leys are normally monocultures, and those that are long-term are a mixture of grasses and clovers. They may be grazed and/or cut for silage during the course of their duration, though during the final year it is usual to graze the pasture intensively so that a large quantity of manure may build up to be ploughed back into the soil. Since the war years, and particularly during the last couple of decades, the trend encouraged by the Ministry of Agriculture has been to 'take the plough round the farm' (which we understand

While pastures are floristically more impoverished than hay meadows, on this dairy farm livestock-density, early cropping for silage (background), and short, mechanically trimmed hedgerows all reduce opportunities for wildlife

Above: Although some of these pastures have been reseeded, the hedgerows and oaks remain to confine and shelter livestock, offering niches for woodland wildlife in the field ecosystem

Right: Leys are usually monocultures devoid of botanical interest but, where manure has been spread or farm animals grazed, toadstools growing on old dung may provide interest

182

is a slogan actually coined by them!). The well-intentioned advice of agricultural experts, research workers and farming journals resulted in the widespread
ploughing-up of permanent grassland, to replace it with high-yielding pastures
sown with a few vigorous species or grass monocultures. However, the advantages to be gained from such conversions were often quite different in reality as
compared to experimental test-plots. An initial outlay of capital was required
for grass seed, fertiliser, tractor fuel, labour wages and the inconvenience of
having the land out of use for several months before any returns were seen. In
some areas cultivars were found to be less resistant to the effects of weather
than the original wild grasses. Cultivated varieties of rye grass, for example,
were often found to crop poorly in the first season and, having shallow roots, in
a dry season they became parched and bud-bound when grazed. If such a reseeded field was not intensively maintained, it would revert to wild grasses
within five years.

By the 1980s it became clear that the consensus 'replanting was better than
renovating' did not always apply, and it really was not worth all the extra effort
unless there was a specific purpose, such as for ley or silage. Silage is generally
cut in May, so an early, high-yielding, predictable crop is desirable. The recession in livestock farming and milk quotas by then also made it become more
economical to maintain original pasture than to replace it. Experimental research about this time also began to show that old pasture could compete with
new for productivity when treated correctly.

A trial in Shropshire compared a permanent pasture of perennial rye grass,
fescues and bents to a newly sown area of rye grass, timothy and white clover.
Both fields were fertilised in the same way. While the new grassland produced
extra dry matter per acre, this was considered to be too small a difference to
cover the inconvenience and cost of converting; and, besides, the protein crop
from the permanent pasture was significantly higher.

The intensive use of fertiliser was also found to be questionable in another
trial organised by the Weed Research Organisation at Taunton. Instead of
ploughing up a meadow, or applying fertilisers, furrows were made at intervals
through the existing turf and sown with the seeds of red clover. The rest of the
sward remained undisturbed. The control field was not sown in this way but
instead heavily fertilised. Over a period of two years the yield from the
clover-sown field equalled that of the fertilised control meadow, indicating a
more benign and less costly alternative to the application of nearly 440 lb (200
kilograms) of fertiliser per 2.4 acres (1 hectare) which was required to equal the
yield. New grass seed can be introduced in the same way to revitalise old pasture
or meadow that will otherwise already contain (by natural selection) those species
best adapted to its environmental conditions. While naturalists may be concerned
about the increasing use of nitrogen fertiliser on wildlife, the rising nitrate levels
from farm drainage and seepage into our water courses, which then affect our
drinking water, is perhaps a cause for wider concern. The use of nitrogen
fertilisers in the United Kingdom has increased eightfold from the annual average
of about 200,000 tons in the mid-1940s.

The trend in wild-flower gardening is increasing rapidly, and the demand for
wild-flower seeds for parks and gardens in both rural and urban areas is said, at
the moment, to outstrip supply. Meadow mixtures are selling at anything up to

£25 per pound, while rarer species such as cowslip can earn a supplier a few hundred pounds per pound weight. Although suppliers are attempting to meet the need in earnest, and the market is becoming progressively more competitive, species-rich meadows could be a source of income from the production of wild-flower seeds, at least perhaps while the present recession in livestock farming continues.

The Government's recent renewed agricultural policies (discussed in more detail in Chapter 11) are intended to encourage farmers to look in new directions and to try to integrate farming with nature conservation. In his quarterly 'comment' in 1985, Dr Ian Presst, the director of the Royal Society for the Protection of Birds, wrote:

At last there are signs that official attitudes to land drainage are changing for the better . . . when [government] decisions about drainage are made, greater weight will be given to nature conservation. . . . For five years we have criticised the system of cost benefit to appraisal for land drainage, because we believe it to be biased in favour of drainage. . . . MAFF has now reformed the system. For the first time, guidance is given on the appraisal of costs and benefits that cannot be measured financially. . . . In a key test case in Yorkshire, a pump-drainage scheme at Duffield Carrs was refused grant aid because of the predictable impact on wintering wildfowl and breeding waders. Without ministry backing the internal drainage board decided not to proceed with the scheme. . . .

The RSPB and other conservational bodies are also lobbying the MAFF to introduce a three-tier system of payments in ESAs (see Chapter 11). The scheme would work as follows: in the first tier a flat-rate payment in return for 'acceptable limited constraints', such as reducing stock densities; second-tier payments would encourage the sympathetic management of threatened habitats, such as hedgerows and hay meadows; with third-tier payments for 'creative conservation'—for example, replacing arable land with flower-rich grassland or flooding pasture to create water-bodies and flood meadows.

Such changes are seemingly already taking place here and there, but have yet to catch on more widely. Mary Marston, the farming adviser in the RSPB Conservation Advisory Unit, recently took a look at seven farms which have introduced wildlife conservation projects as part of their policy. A farm in Lincolnshire had created two new wild-flower meadows. While one was composed of the usual flora of hay meadow, such as ox-eye daisy, yarrow and autumn hawkbit, the other was a mixture of arable annuals akin to fallow land, featuring cornflowers, corncockles, corn marigolds and poppies. The preparation involved in the creation of these 'meadows' is as intensive as that for reseeded pasture, but for wildlife and visual appeal far more worthwhile. Herbicides were used to clear the existing arable weeds, while ploughing turned the topsoil under to *lower* fertility and discourage vigorous plants such as docks and nettles. The 'meadows' will be maintained specifically for their wild flowers, and while the one sown with grassland seed will be treated as a hay field, but mown late to give the late-flowering species a good chance to set seed, the 'meadow' sown with annual species will be cultivated each spring to provide the bare ground necessary for germination.

SOME PLACES OF INTEREST

Although grasslands are generally more accessible to the rambler than arable land, particular care must be taken in hay fields while the crop is growing. Some of the best remaining hay fields are now nature reserves, and permission to visit must be sought from the appropriate trust or relevant managing body. Addresses have been supplied for those mentioned here (and details of others can be obtained from the Royal Society for Nature Conservation (RSNC), The Green, Nettleham, Lincoln LN2 2NR. Tel. Lincoln (0522) 752326). Many trusts hold open days when the flora and fauna are at their most interesting, but one must keep strictly to the marked trails.

Allimore Green Common (SJ 8519). Small hedged fields of unimproved damp and wet pasture. A sequence of herbs with marsh marigold in spring followed by ragged robin; greater bird's-foot trefoil, marsh bedstraw, devil's bit scabious speckle the meadow grasses, which include quaking grass. Summer-flowering orchids include marsh and common spotted. Watermint, marsh pennywort and grass of Parnassus grow in the wet areas. The shrubs in the scrub and hedgerow resound with birdsong, and insects abound: alder buckthorn ensures the presence of the brimstone butterfly. Permission is required to visit this reserve near Stafford, from the Staffordshire Trust (3A Newport Road, Stafford).

Boynes Meadow near Great Malvern in Worcestershire is a delightful ancient meadow on ridge and furrow. In early summer species such as dyer's greenweed, pepper saxifrage, adder's tongue and green-winged orchid may be found. Few open days usually restricted to trust (and RSNC) members. Otherwise permission to visit this site must be obtained from the Worcestershire Trust (The Lodge, Beacon Lane, Rednal, Birmingham B45 9XN).

Cheadle Hulme Trail (SJ 8785). A leaflet for this delightful pasture and hedgerow trail beginning south of Cheadle can be obtained from the Stockport Metropolitan Borough Council (Town Hall, Stockport SK1 3XE). While the ecology of grassland is enjoyably discovered, the old hedgerows are more accessible, consisting of several species of shrub and climber. The hedgerows provide ideal nesting-sites for the farmland birds, and chiffchaff, willow warbler, blackbird, wren and robin are recorded in large numbers.

Coe Fen (TL 4457). A nature trail runs beside the River Granta through pasture which has been used for grazing for centuries. A good variety of pasture and riverside flora attracts a range of insects and birds. Some public access all year. Leaflets available from Cambient (1 Brookside, Cambridge CB2 1JF). Off Fen Causeway, south of Cambridge city centre.

Ireland: Clonmacnoise Callows (NO 131). In the flood meadows of the Shannon valley north of the old abbey at Clonmacnoise, traditional farming practices are still carried out. The meadows are enriched almost entirely by the river, and hay is cut comparatively late in the year; 120 plant species have been recorded here, and all sorts of flying invertebrates abound before the hay is taken. Many bird species have also been recorded, including the corncrake, and local birds are supplemented by those species which use the Shannon valley as a migration route.

Cribb's Meadow near Wymondham in Leicestershire has an open day in May for trust (and RSNC) members. Two fields of unimproved meadowland lie either side of a disused railway line. Cowslips and green-winged orchids are the first to appear in spring, and later in the year the yellow hue is lent by bird's-foot trefoil, yellow rattle and lady's bedstraw. The presence of green-winged orchid followed later by adder's tongue, pepper saxifrage and common spotted orchid confirms this to be an old meadow site. Hedgerows and scrub on the railway embankment include ash, blackthorn, crab apple, dogwood, hawthorn, oak, willow, bramble and wild rose. Through the ballast emerge herb-robert, ox-eye daisy, perforate St John's wort and rosebay willowherb. The variety of habitat attracts many invertebrates and birds. The butterflies easily seen are common blue, and small copper and warblers and yellowhammer sing from the hedgerows. Details about open days from Leicester and Rutland Trust (1 West Street, Leicester LE1 6UU).

Eades Meadow. This meadow in Worcestershire lies between Droitwich and Bromsgrove. Access on open days only for trust (and RSNC) members. Permission from Worcestershire Trust (see Boynes for address). Meadow with damp and dry areas and old hedgerows. Old oak trees mark a line of the hedge that has disappeared. Floral gems include green-winged orchid, adder's tongue and cowslip. Although there is evidence of ridge-and-furrow ploughing, the grassland has been uncultivated for several centuries. In July the meadow is cut for hay, and by September the reserve's speciality, meadow saffron, colours the aftermath.

Eakring Meadow. This damp meadow near Kersall in Nottinghamshire is open one day in May. While the meadow has a good variety of plants, including pepper saxifrage, the best feature of this reserve is the old hedge containing over forty plant species, including guelder rose. Details from Notts Trust (The Whimbrels, Goverton, Bleasby, Nottingham NG14 7FN).

Epsom Common Nature Trail (TQ 1960). A circular 2-mile (3.5-kilometre) walk in ancient commonland in Surrey passes through meadow grassland and damp pasture as well as woodland and scrub. Details of trail and wildlife can be obtained from Epsom and Ewell Borough Council (Parks Department, Ewell Court House, Ewell, Surrey). Trail begins north of Epsom. Minor roads off the A24.

Fox Fritillary Meadow. This fine fritillary meadow in Suffolk is open one day a year (in April/May) as advertised in the local press and national botanical journals. Further details from Suffolk Trust (St Edmund House, Ropewalk, Ipswich IP4 1LZ).

Langdon Hills Country Park (TQ 6886). Old pastures occupy a small section of this park in Essex which is essentially farmland and woodland. South-west of Basildon off the B1007.

Leyburn Old Glebe Field (SE 1089). Bound by stone walls, this small pasture is a fragment of Ellershaw, a district known to naturalists since the early nineteenth century. The flora reflects the calcareous nature of the soil, and species recorded include quaking grass, primrose, agrimony, salad burnet, milkwort as well as notable ones such as the green-winged and burned-tip orchids. Ten species of butterfly are known here. Lapwing and curlew can be heard nearby. Off the A684, minor road east through Wensley.

North Meadow (SU 0994). Although there is no public access off rights of way, the wonderful mosaic of meadow plants can nevertheless be fully appreciated. It is best visited in April–May for its fritillaries, but until the end of June a rich mix of meadow plants, including adder's tongue, great burnet, cowslip, ox-eye daisy, southern marsh orchid and many damp-loving species. Near Cricklade in Wiltshire. Off the A419.

Pool Hay Meadow (SO 8230). This recent acquisition by the Worcestershire Trust is managed traditionally for hay. Public footpaths cross the meadow. Minor roads to Coarselawn off the B4211.

Thorpe Marsh (SE 5909). Ancient wet pasture along the River Don in north Yorkshire (see text). North of Doncaster. Off the A19, minor road to Barnby Dun.

Wheldrake Ings (SE 7043). The meadows and pastures of this reserve are managed traditionally, without agricultural chemicals, by the system of hay-cropping and grazing. The land is enriched with the river silt in the winter floods. Flora varies from species such as reed sweet grass in the wetter parts to indicators of old meadow: sneezewort, pepper saxifrage and an uncommon dropwort (*Oenanthe silaifolia*). Butterflies are numerous and include small copper. The autumn and winter flooding provides a refuge for wildfowl which come to the Derwent valley in huge numbers. Barn owls and short-eared owls recorded in the reserve. South-east of York. Can be approached from Wheldrake or Thorganby villages. During bird breeding season, April–June, access confined to RNSC members.

White Moss Common Nature Walk (NY 3406). This short trail on National Trust land leads through pasture land, open fell, woodland and by lake and stream, providing a cameo of Cumbrian lakeland. A leaflet is available from the National Trust. North-west of Ambleside off the A591.

Willsbridge Mill (ST 6670). A wildlife and countryside centre in the steep-sided valley of the River Avon including meadowland, scrub and woodland supporting a range of wildlife. A leaflet prepared by the Avon Wildlife Trust (209 Redland Road, Bristol BS6 6YU) available on site. East of Bristol off the A431.

Yellands Meadow (SD 9197). This meadow (see text) by the River Swale is a fine example of a typical Dales meadow, and the Yorkshire Wildlife Trust ensures it will continue to be worked in the traditional manner. Permission must be sought from the Yorkshire Trust to visit the reserve between March and July. Near Muker off the B6270.

CHAPTER 11

THE ARABLE SCENE

By clearing the vegetation and exposing the soil by ploughing, farmers introduce new opportunities for wildlife. In the process of natural succession open ground will, over time, be recolonised by vegetation. On land under the plough this process is continuously being interrupted, and the wild plants that are best able to establish in this artificial habitat of frequent disturbance are the rapidly growing, pioneering colonisers of the early stages of the plant succession. On arable land these wild flowers compete for soil nutrients with the crop monocultures which man has planted and are therefore branded 'the weeds of cultivation'.

Many weed species are now so totally dependent on the arable-land habitat that their natural origins are unknown. Some are almost certainly native. It is known that dock and ribwort plantain flourished in the barren glacial soils at the end of the Ice Age until being gradually replaced by the more permanent vegetation. By the time man first broke the surface of the ground, the British vegetation had recovered from the devastations of the Ice Age, and the greater part of the land-surface below 1,300 feet (400 metres), save the extreme north, was clothed in forest. But the opportunist plants were surviving in odd corners of the landscape, ready to make a comeback when tillage gave them the openings. However, as the Ice Age exterminated a very high proportion of plant species, it is very probable that the majority of our common weeds of arable land are not indigenous but of southern European origin introduced, some very early on, as impurities in imported seed. Their association with this man-made habitat can sometimes be traced back to antiquity. For example, plant remains from cultivated ground at a late Bronze Age house site at Minnis Bay in Kent have thrown some light on the early presence of weeds and other plants in southern England. The following species were found to preponderate and are thought to represent the residue from threshing: poppy, pennycress, thyme-covered sandwort, corn spurrey, purging flax, silverweed, bur chervil, coriander, ox-tongue, smooth hawk's beard and stinging nettle.

Some wild plants turn up with such increasing regularity and in such large quantities in excavations that it is possible that they were collected as food-plants, if not actually grown as crops. Collections of carbonised seeds of fat hen and black bindweed, for example, have turned up regularly. The former may have served as a nutritious green vegetable before the introduction of cabbage and spinach, and in fact is said to have a higher food value than the latter vegetables. It may also have been used as fodder for cattle, sheep and, particularly, pigs, who find the leaves quite palatable. The North American Indians are known to have collected fat hen seeds for flour-making, and the same may have been done here. The triangular seeds of black bindweed, resembling those of buckwheat, are also thought to have been ground up for flour. However, the archaeologist Peter Reynolds puts things into perspective by suggesting that carbonised seeds cannot necessarily indicate their function or purpose, or indeed if they were deliberately collected; for, 'apart from the cereals for which there is a clear case in support of cultivation, the vast majority of other carbonised seeds could well be the result of bonfires built to burn the weeds gathered from the fields at the end of the harvest' (see below).

Today there is no doubt that many of these plants are loathed weeds, and few arable fields have escaped the herbicide treatment to eliminate them. In England and Wales about 15,000 tonnes of herbicide are now used on the 10–12 million acres (4–5 million hectares) of agricultural crops. Although hedgebanks, field-edges and other such niches may now offer the only available refuges for wildlife in the arable landscape, a survey at the Royal Show in 1985 revealed that 60 per cent of the farmers questioned used herbicides in the hedge bottom because they feared that arable weeds established here, and 75 per cent cultivated their land right to the field-boundary. However, no arable weed has yet become completely extinct through the use of herbicides, although some plants have been made much rarer. Moreover, work being carried out at

Hedges and field-edges may offer the only available refuges for wildlife in the arable landscape. However, they may also accommodate arable 'pests' – the bare patch in the cereal field has been created by rabbits which have their burrows in the protected Dark Age frontierwork of Fleam Dyke. This bank forms a ribbon of interest in a monotonous landscape of prairie fields

Only about a quarter of the plant species found in the hedgebank are arable weeds. Lady's mantle, a variable species, has found a niche in this field-edge bank where, if the plant-density is maintained, there will be few openings for arable weeds to establish

experimental stations in Boxworth (Cambridgeshire), Manydown Estate (Hampshire) and Bovingdon Hall (Essex) indicate that only a quarter of the plant species found in the hedge bottom were in fact arable weeds. This seems to suggest that if these edge habitats were maintained as part of the field management policy, encouraging their plant density and diversity, there could be fewer arable weeds. Being mainly annuals needing bare surface on which to grow, they cannot become as easily established in densely covered ground where there are very few open spaces to be occupied. So it appears that by cultivating land right up to the edge farmers are not only reducing the prospect for wildlife, but also possibly creating opportunities for the colonising annuals.

Many weeds are very suitably adapted for persistence. Ephemeral annual species complete their life-cycles in a few weeks and produce large numbers of lightweight seeds which in turn germinate very quickly under suitable conditions. The following examples will indicate the seed-production capacity of single plants: dock, up to 25,000 seeds; corn poppy, 20,000; yellow-horned poppy, 24,000; toadflax, 29,000; scarlet pimpernel, 12,000; mullein up to 700,000. Large numbers of seeds are an insurance against heavy or total loss, and their lightness and in some cases special adaptations, such as the plummed fruit of the *Compositae*, like the dandelion, ensure their widespread dispersal. Quick-maturing plants have the potential to produce several generations a year: for instance, the *Cruciferae* family have such a short period between germination and the production of seed that they can perpetuate their species between one weeding and the next. Shepherd's purse is a self-pollinating member of this family, enabling it to reproduce throughout the year. In some species germination of the new seeds can occur almost immediately they are shed by the parent plant. Seedlings of dandelion have been raised just eight days after their removal from the parent plant, though seeds of some plants were found to retain their vitality for up to three years when kept dry. Fat hen and corn poppy are also examples of species with seeds of varying dormant periods. Staggered germination ensures the species' survival, for at least some seeds are likely to germinate under favourable conditions. The buried seeds of some plants can remain viable for very long periods: kidney vetch for more than ninety years and corn poppy for more than a hundred years. Dormant seeds contain much less water than most other parts of the plant, and because of this relatively dry condition they can withstand great extremes of heat, cold and lack of moisture. Germination may be induced by light as the plough turns the seeds up to the soil-surface, provided, as every gardener knows, sufficient moisture is available and the temperature is adequate to provide the necessary warmth.

Given such pertinacity it is not surprising that the farmer has always had such a battle with weeds of cultivation. The changing trends of modern farming to mechanisation, chemicals and specialisation have, all too often, been too rapid for the animal life to keep pace or even adjust, but the wild flowers seem never to have been completely subdued as there are always some colourful clumps breaking the monotony of the monoculture. At present about 200 plant species can be found growing on arable land, of which about ninety are virtually unknown in other habitats. Traditional farming techniques of hand-weeding,

Large areas of the fieldscape are now golden prairies of barley and wheat monoculture, which offer little to our native wildlife

Poppies are persistent cornfield weeds, producing large numbers of seeds ensuring a few survivors annually where weedkillers fail to reach

unintensive recropping, rotation and low input of fertilisers inadvertently encouraged wild flowers and resulted in botanically rich arable habitats which were also of great value to wildlife. Before the days of herbicides cheap labour – such as children – was employed to 'walk the wheat' and pull out the weeds. Geoffrey Young describes how in Gwent it was customary for the children to do this on Easter Day: 'Cider and cakes were handed out at the end of the day, with double rations for those who found any corncockle. The plants were then ceremoniously burnt.' In this way, more often than not, it will have been the spent parent plant that was removed. Crop rotation required ground to be left fallow, and this, too, will have encouraged weeds. When the ground was subsequently ploughed in, this green manure will have enhanced the fertility of the soil. However, the offspring of the weeds will have grown with doubled vigour on the enriched ground. Many organic farmers and gardeners today prefer that weeds should be hoed out and left to die rather than destroying them by burning or weedkiller. This has the advantage of adding to the soil humus, but hoeing is only effective if the weeds are tackled when young and when the weather is dry enough to shrivel the young plants. In wet weather they merely lie on the surface and send down new root shoots. John Clare's celebrated poem 'May' makes this point:

> Each morning, now, the weeders meet
> To cut the thistle from the wheat,
> And ruin, in the sunny hours,
> Full many a wild weed with its flowers. . . .

Once weeds have got to the flowering stage their seeds may have already dispersed to perpetuate the species even after the parent plant is destroyed.

Weeds of arable land include some of the most showy of our wild flowers, and when growing *en masse* in the cornfields are a proliferation of colour. Those with conspicuous flowers include the poppy varieties, mayweeds and the now rarer corncockle, cornflower and field cowwheat. The golden glow of species such as charlock, corn marigold, field pennycress and the rarer woad, while 'troubling the corn fields with destroying beauty' (John Clare), are surely more uplifting in their variety than the yellow monocultures of black mustard and rape. Of the many more diminutive flowering species, those such as common fumitory, common field speedwell, field pansy, scarlet pimpernel and the now rare pheasant's eye are more colourful than others and therefore likely to be noticed. Arable fields on calcareous soils have characteristic species such as pale poppy, viper's bugloss, red hemp-nettle, wild candytuft, basil thyme and red bartsia. Weed flora capable of tolerating dry, well-aerated, sandy soils often deficient in calcium and acidic in nature include storksbill, sand spurrey, shepherd's cress, treacle mustard and sheep's sorrel.

The vigorous adaptations of some weeds have enabled them to remain common and troublesome in spite of cleaner seed, selective herbicides and post-harvest stubble-burning, but these practices have resulted in many of the more beautiful arable wild flowers becoming scarce. As the majority of our endangered wild flowers may be found elsewhere in the world, and usually no further than Continental Europe, at the purely scientific level the concern at their loss may not be very significant. But as Dr Max Walters, previously of the Cambridge Botanic Gardens, points out: '. . . the cold calculations of science do not provide the motivation for the widespread concern to "preserve our flora", and it is right that aesthetic and emotional factors play their part.' However, the truth of the matter is that, although we as visitors to the countryside may regret the disappearance of fields full of hues of reds, yellows and blues, we can hardly expect farmers to share our enthusiasm for 'weeds'. Some may also question the significance of these losses, as nearly all of them are aliens introduced by agriculture in the first place, but the alternative of the developing bleakness of our countryside and a sterile environment for wildlife is decried by many like ourselves. Besides, as it is British taxpayers who are presently heavily subsidising the farmers to enable surpluses and savings in the costs of using chemical sprays, we might question the changing nature of the arable habitats of our countryside on both financial and health grounds. More than nine-tenths of all grain and vegetables are sprayed with chemicals, often many times over. In 1984, Geoffrey Lean and Arthur Osman of the *Observer* reported that 600,000 acres (242,816 hectares) of Britain are sprayed with *toxic* chemicals each year and in the same article revealed several incidents of resultant serious health problems.

Twenty years ago a farm may have used only half a dozen chemicals at the most, today the number is around thirty, each more specific. Pesticides have been particularly effective in increasing yields. A Nature Conservancy Council report has calculated that if their use ceased in the United Kingdom (not considering the alternatives practised in organic farming) the yield of cereals would fall by 24 per cent in the first year and 45 per cent by the third. Before the use of insecticides it was often necessary to sow a crop more than once because of the damage done by insects. Depending on the technique of application to the crop, a large proportion of the pesticide can be wasted, leading inadvertently to the contamination of the environment. For example, it has been calculated that only 0.03 per cent of the regular dose of the foliar chemical dimethoate, used to prevent aphids on beans, would be necessary to kill the infestation if it could be applied directly to the pests instead of being sprayed on to the beans.

When in the years of postwar reconstruction farmers were asked to grow more food, the change and conflict that were to result in the countryside could not have been properly envisaged. This was hardly surprising as then organic farming with high levels of employment, crop rotation, natural fertilisers and only small quantities of chemicals and pesticides was more the norm. But to meet the challenge, and armed with subsidies and grants, a most dramatic swing took place, most notably in East Anglia, to growing expanses of monocultures, particularly wheat and barley, where previously there had often been a mixed patchwork of several fields under cultivation and pasture. According to the Countryside Commission's survey, *Monitoring the Landscape*, in 1980 half the total farmland in England and Wales comprised arable land, compared to just over a third in 1947. Presently in Britain barley occupies nearly 5.4 million acres (2.2 million hectares) and wheat 4.2 million acres (1.7 million hectares). The results are enormous surpluses stored at public expense. In 1985 it cost the Common Market taxpayers £700 million to buy British surplus grain, while storage charges in 1986 were calculated at £150 million a year. As a result of technological advances it is said that the same area of land under cultivation in Britain now could produce 50 per cent more grain by the year 2000.

With the need to eliminate surplus production there are changes in store for our countryside. While there are not yet the signs of the expansionist mania of the Common Agricultural Policy being strenuously reversed, the Ministry of Agriculture seems to have taken a new rôle towards encouraging the repair of at least some of the damage it has sponsored in the past. New schemes and proposals for making agricultural policy and practice more environmentally benign are being introduced as part of the Farmland and Rural Development Bill and 'Environmentally Sensitive Areas' (ESAs) have been designated on grounds of landscape, historic importance and the value of wildlife habitat. Announcing the scheme in 1986, Mr Michael Jopling, the Minister for Agriculture, said: 'In the selected areas we shall be offering farms incentive payments to continue the more traditional methods and maintain the beauty and wildlife value of their farms.' This may serve to halt further intensification and conversion to arable land in those areas which have been under threat and environmentally controversial in the last decade, but as Mr Andrew Lees of the Friends of the Earth remarked: 'The whole countryside is environmentally sensitive. Until farmers everywhere become eligible for special payments to maintain practices which benefit conservation, most of the countryside remains exposed to environmentally damaging agricultural development.' Six million pounds have been earmarked for the present ESAs scheme where traditional methods already largely exist and essentially need only to be maintained. A Nature Conservancy Council report in 1986 predicted that on the best land, such as that in East Anglia, there will be further amalgamation of farms. The cost of taking land out of production or converting to low-intensity 'landscape farming' may be far more costly, and there may simply not be the money to 'bribe' landowners into reshaping the land in an environmentally acceptable way. Marion Shoard comments: 'In any case, why should the taxpayer continue to underwrite the scandal of the agricultural subsidy in another guise? The mistaken approach of subsidies-for-conservation is one of the main failings of the Wildlife and Countryside Act.' No doubt the debate will continue over the preference of subsidies for the changing agricultural practices that are compatible with conservation to special payments for increased production and maintenance of farm incomes (seemingly at all costs).

While token gestures towards conservation encouraged by the available grants (such as replacing grubbed-up hedges, maintaining ponds, planting trees in corners of fields) are all to the good – for at least they offer islands and corridors for some less fussy wildlife – a real difference is made when replacing involves the landscape of the *whole* farm. And it is truly heartening when one reads in a report from Christopher Probert that a group of East Anglian grain producers, the United Framlingham Farmers (UFF), have recently collected two major conservation awards. With the intention of doing more to sustain the environmental value of their land, the group have appointed their own conservation adviser to devise appropriate management plans for each farm. The loss of income from the reduction of cereal production is to be offset by fully using the farms' resources of land, woodland, water and access, by business diversification directly related to conservation – such as the maintenance of existing woodland by restoring traditional practices – and by developing farm-based tourism. The management plans have incorporated the identification of existing wildlife habitats to ensure that these are safeguarded and maintained, and to indicate the potential for creating new features. This aspect of the plans includes planting areas of broad-leaved woodland, the better management of marginal areas of uncropped land, banksides and verges, and the restoration of ponds. The co-operative has set up its own employee-training operation to provide general conservation awareness and retraining in traditional techniques, such as the craft of coppicing and charcoal manufacture. Farm employees carry out the non-food-production activities during the winter months when few jobs would otherwise exist on these predominantly cereal farms. While the UFF group do not have plans for going organic, a more enlightened use of pesticides has shown results. Edges of fields and uncropped land have seen an increase in wild flowers. This has also been the result of field-margins being considerably widened for public access, and sometimes wild-flower seeds are deliberately sown. As business diversification develops some members will open up their

Overleaf: Parts of Britain are so intensively used for arable farming that hardly any space remains for wildlife. Winter is a harsh time for fauna anyway, and such an environment may offer few chances for survival

195

The Yorkshire Wolds. Although Yorkshire chalk lacks many of the attractive southern plants, there are few areas where these can be discovered for oneself as much of this land is now under cereal cultivation in thinly soiled and eroding prairie fields

farms so that visitors can see the practical benefits of the measures being carried out. Christopher Probert writes:

In the longer term one of UFF's objectives is to promote a series of countryside trails with visitor facilities . . . the public will be able to come out into the countryside, enjoy themselves and maybe take home wildflower seeds or plants, aquatic plants, wood crafts and farm foods – all produced . . . using new skills developed as a result of the need to diversify into line with the growing commitment by group members towards countryside conservation and associated rural prosperity.

(The Countryside Commission has formed a partnership with a range of working farms, from a Northumbrian hill farm to an arable one in Essex, to create the Demonstration Farms Project. The aim is to encourage and involve farmers, landowners, land managers and conservationists to integrate farming and conservation through demonstration: see below, 'Some Places of Interest'.)

Organic farming has been practised for quite some time now. Organic farmers aspire to a largely chemical-free environment, often employing nature to fight nature, but fewer crops may be produced by these methods and therefore higher prices are generally charged for their products. On the largest organic farm in the country, at Rushall near Salisbury, expanses of wheat resemble those in the chemically laden East Anglian prairies. However, the crop is grown on an eight-year rotation with animal fertiliser. So although, large-scale organic operations are feasible, the owner of this farm claims the yield is only half what it could be if chemicals were used (though this is offset by the higher price he can charge for his organic wheat). Organic farming is otherwise generally small-scale and capital-intensive before returns are visible. One criterion for organic crops is that where land has previously been treated with organic agrochemicals it should be left fallow for three years.

While a strategy for taking land out of production on a large scale is now feasible with our surpluses, the question remains as to whether Britain – and, for that matter, her European counterparts – could take such a radically different path from worldwide competitors. However, although organic farming may still be considered eccentric by some, the UFF scheme does appear to offer a better prospect to serve as a model to show that conservation can be a part of good farming practice. Franklyn Perring, general secretary of the Royal Society for Nature Conservation, writes:

Recent figures on farm income have shown that in terms of profitability, it is the mixed farms which have outstripped all others – pigs, milk or grain ... even greater diversification may be the only protection against the swings and roundabouts of the ECC ... the need to look in new directions means that many farmers will be redrawing their farm plans. This will be the moment to try and integrate nature conservation. ... Those that do not may be missing the chance of a generation to bring back flowers to many an agricultural desert.

We began this chapter examining the nature of the wild flowers in the arable habitat. While for centuries their tenacity has been such that man has been little more than a step ahead in his battle with them, their very existence has depended on his maintaining the arable habitat. In the last few decades we have seen the odds mount up against the wild flowers – and, ironically, while we are losing the more delightful species, the less pleasing ones remain persistent! We cannot expect farmers to sacrifice their livelihood to preserve our visions of the countryside, especially when complicated economic incentives have encouraged them to do otherwise, but things may change with our revamped agricultural policies. Meanwhile, only a short shift in farming management, such as the careful use of chemicals and leaving uncropped land unsprayed, can offer a breathing-space for wild flowers which will in turn benefit other wildlife.

Opium poppy occurs throughout the British Isles, either as a garden escape or as a relic of cultivation. It was introduced centuries ago for medicinal purposes

199

SOME PLACES OF INTEREST

Nearly everywhere in lowland Britain there are examples of arable fields. In some counties such as Devon and Shropshire, and parts of Essex and Norfolk, a pattern of small fields and woods enmeshed in a network of hedgebound lanes is still the attractive physical expression of the countryside (see Chapter 2). By contrast the flat prairie lands of Cambridge and Lincolnshire are almost treeless with monocultures cultivated to the edge of hedgeless fields and stubble-burning a regular practice. As farmers do not always welcome people trampling on arable land, it is organised trails or nature reserves adjacent to farmland that offer the best opportunities to study the ecology of the arable scene. Most county councils and nature trusts have details of these. The following are examples.

Brook Nature Trail (SZ 3983). A countryside trail on the Isle of Wight, organised by the Natural History and Archaeological Society, taking one through downland and farmland showing the contrast of flora. A leaflet can be obtained from the tourist office in Ryde. Brook lies off the A3055.

Broomfield. This reserve managed by the Derbyshire College of Agriculture supports a range of habitats including grassland, marsh, scrub, woodland and disturbed ground on a variety of soils from acid to lime-rich. Permission to visit the reserve must be sought from the principal at the College in Morley (SK 3941) off the A608, north from Derby.

Broomfield Walk (ST 2232). A 5-mile (8-kilometre) walk organised by the Somerset Nature Conservation Trust passing through a range of agricultural land. The walk includes some gentle climbing with rewarding views. Details from the Trust (Fyne Court, Broomfield, Bridgwater TA5 2EQ). Broomfield approached off the A361 south of Bridgwater.

Cambridge University Botanic Gardens. An opportunity to examine British arable weeds and grassland flora that are no longer widespread (among plants from all over the world). Open all year Monday to Saturday and Sunday afternoons in summer. Guided tours available. 1 Brookside, Cambridge.

Grafham Water (TL 1467). This County nature reserve is noted mainly for its waterfowl, for it was designed to provide a refuge from disturbance by sailing boats and fishermen on the rivers. Intensively managed farmland surrounds the reservoir on the reserve giving an opportunity to study how wildlife has adapted to the arable. A few interesting plant species have been recorded at the edge of fields, such as cowslip, great burnet, woolly thistle and sulphur clover. Lapwing, skylark, yellow wagtail, lesser whitethroat and grasshopper and willow warblers are among the bird species nesting in the farmland. The twenty butterfly species recorded here include common blue and small copper. Leaflets and booklets, particularly about the waterfowl, available from Beds and Hunts Nature Trust (38 Mill Street, Bedford MK40 3HD). Approach from the B661 near Perry.

Horton Country Park (TQ 1962). Nature trails offer the opportunity to study the arable, grassland and pond habitat. North-west of Epsom, Surrey, off the B280. Follow signpost to West Park Farm.

Ireland: Johnstown Castle (TO 217). A nature trail on this experimental farm leads through a combination of agricultural land, woodland and garden. An agricultural museum helps explain the practices that have shaped the landscape and nature. South of Wexford. Northward on the road to Castlebridge are the *Wexford Slobs* where reclaimed polders were transformed into arable fields in 1850. The present large fields of arable land and pasture are dissected by drainage channels. The area has become well known for birdwatching.

Little Burstead (TQ 6793). A 3.5-mile (5.5-kilometre) trail organised by the Basildon District Council, Essex, in spring and early summer along old hedgerows with pollarded oaks and past farmland where lapwings dive. Water habitat is also included in the trail. Leaflet available from Basildon District Council (Fodderwick, Basildon, Essex SS13 2EX). East of Brentwood off the A129.

Loughrigg Fell Nature Walk (NY 3704). A 2.5-mile (4-kilometre) fell and farmland trail from Ambleside to view the patchwork of grassland and arable fields in the Cumbrian lakeland. Woodland and riverside wildlife may also be seen. Leaflet from National Trust information centre at Ambleside.

Market Drayton Nature Trail (SJ 6834). A 4-mile (6.4-kilometre) habitat trail organised by the Shropshire Trust for Nature Conservation in spring and midsummer to study hedge-ridges and farmland. River and woodland offer further interest. A booklet is available from the trust (Agriculture House, Barker Street, Shrewsbury SY1 1QP).

Norton's Farm Museum (TQ 7815). A fruit and arable farm in East Sussex which is said to be 'typical of the south-east'. A farm trail offers the opportunity to study flora and fauna. There is also an interesting collection of old farm implements. Open mid-June to September. Kent Street, Sedlescombe.

Skelmersdale and Tawd Valley Nature Trail (SD 4806). A leaflet from the Lancashire Trust for Nature Conservation (Dale House, Dale Head, Slaidburn, Clitheroe, Lancashire BB7 4TS) guides and informs about the wildlife interest of the valley, exploring a corridor through farmland to urban Skelmersdale.

Bird Farm (TL 4256). A small working farm which has opened its gates and invited the public in. Mixed farming has been maintained here whereas elsewhere in the area the landscape has changed to that of prairie farming. The farm has fine old hedges with spindle and buckthorn, old pasture, arable land, water meadow and a stream. Walking around the farm is encouraged, but the public are requested to keep to marked trails so that wild flowers can develop without being trampled and birds can nest undisturbed. Twenty-two species of butterfly have been recorded on the farm, foxes breed in the hedgerow, and a pair of hobbies have successfully reared their young in the area. Open from late spring to early autumn, Tuesday to Sunday. South-west of Cambridge off the A603 at Barton. Junction 12 exit from the M11.

Demonstration Farms. Working farms co-operate with the Countryside Commission. Groups sharing an interest in land-use, management and conservation from an agricultural perspective may be able to visit certain demonstration farms. Contact the Commission's Conservation Branch, John Dower House, Crescent Place, Cheltenham, Gloucestershire GL50 3RA.

CHAPTER 12

INVERTEBRATES, AMPHIBIANS, REPTILES

INSECTS AND INVERTEBRATES

The great majority of the invertebrate life of the fieldscape is small, even minute, easily passing unnoticed unless deliberately sought for. But nevertheless little creatures are there in their hordes: on average 5 acres (2 hectares) of grassland are said to contain about a ton of invertebrates, the same weight being accommodated in about 20 acres (8 hectares) of arable land. Invertebrate life is so successful because, taken together, the range of their specialised feeding habitats allows them to consume almost anything organic. There are some that chew solids, others that suck liquids. Some eat plants, some eat other animals. Others eat both, and others still are parasitic. Then there are the scavengers which consume dead and waste matter. Therefore, a habitat in the fieldscape might have a considerable number of different invertebrate animals living in it, each species depending on others to some extent. Together they form numerous taxonomical groups, many of which still remain to be studied thoroughly. As it is, the conspicuous species or those that draw attention to themselves by the evidence of their destruction that are best known we have chosen to concentrate on a few of these within the space available.

In Chapter 10 we have shown how environmental conditions and grazing-management régimes impose certain structural patterns on the grasslands, and this in turn will affect the invertebrates present. Climate, topography, aspect and vegetation all create restrictions for some fauna and offer special niches for others. Many insects benefit from the effects of grazing, but timing is important. Plants benefit from the absence of summer grazing, and therefore so will the insects they host. A tall diverse flowering sward will provide a better food-supply, dense cover (offering protection from predators and a humid micro-climate) and an accumulation of litter. The presence of grazing animals ensures a supply of dung (and carrion) and adds to the invertebrate diversity. In such a habitat, affording several zones of niches, a range of species from plant-eaters to parasites can be accommodated in both the vertical and horizontal dimensions. In their largely hidden world we will discover that the invertebrates of the fieldscape play a much greater part than many people may appreciate.

Above ground it is the herbivorous invertebrates that form the bulk of the fieldscape fauna. Together they will eat all parts of the majority of plants, but in individual species a good deal of specialisation takes place. Many plant-eaters

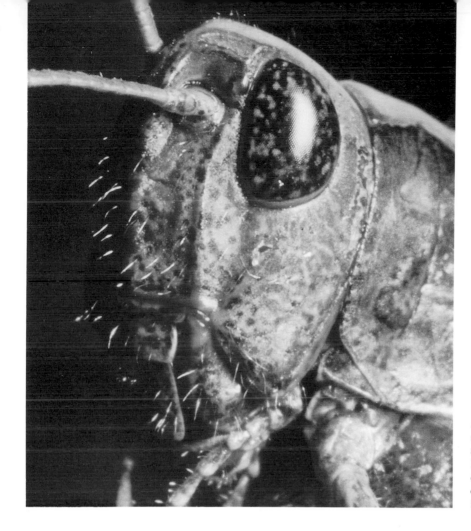

A prey's eye view? Although short-horned grasshoppers are almost entirely vegetarian, long-horned species will seek out other invertebrates and are even known to devour weak individuals of their own kind

restrict themselves not only to certain plants but also to particular parts of those plants. In some, such as moths and butterflies, diet changes with the development of the insect: the leaf-eating caterpillar turns to a nectar-sucking adult, but the latter may seek the flowers of different food-plants to avoid competing with their young. When several species share a single host plant they will tend to specialise on various parts of the plant. The caterpillars of orange tip and green-veined white butterflies share many wild members of the cabbage family and avoid a measure of competition on the same plant because the former eat the flowering parts and the latter feed on the leaves. Ecologist B. N. K. Davis found that as many as forty-four invertebrate species exploit the stinging nettle: twenty-seven species were almost entirely dependent on this plant, and a further seventeen used it as a food-source. Both larvae and adult forms exploit the plant but are separated by subtle variations in feeding habits and lifestyles. For instance, the larvae of weevils feed and hibernate in the rhizomes and stems; adult weevils and larvae of butterflies and moths use the leaves; pollen-chewing beetles roam the male flowers; and the piercing and sucking abilities of bugs enable them to suck juices from fruit, stem and leaf.

If readers were asked to pick one insect to represent grassland, we suspect most would choose the grasshopper. Indeed, the short-horned grasshoppers, which are exclusively vegetarian, having a wide variety of grass and herb foods, live mainly in grassland, and the two most widespread species are the common field and common green. The former is the larger of the two. Both have a number of colour variations; and this adaptation, together with their long thin bodies, enables them successfully to blend against the landscape of grass stems and varied herbs. The meadow grasshopper prefers most lush vegetation. It can easily be identified by its short wings, which are insufficiently developed for the creature to be able to fly; but it can, nevertheless, effectively escape danger, for grasshoppers can jump twenty times their own body length. Although young grasshoppers (nymphs) resemble adults, they have no functional wings, and during the three months of immaturity after hatching they remain concealed low in the vegetation. During this time their bodies are soft and vulnerable, becoming more scaly with each of the four skin-changes after they have reached adulthood. From mid-summer onwards the adults can be spotted easily, for they will readily jump or fly away if disturbed, but as the creatures do not become active until they have warmed up by basking in the sunshine chirping is more common on sunny days. It is generally the male that 'sings' the song, a vibration produced by the rapid to-and-fro movement of the hind leg. The nature and frequency of the song vary. A group singing together are males rivalling each other to attract females. When successful, a quieter wooing song is performed. On chalk downland grasshoppers tend to favour south-facing slopes; and two rare species, the rufous and stripe-winged grasshoppers, found mainly on chalk and limestone grassland in southern England only, are restricted to this aspect. Bush crickets, the long-antennaed relatives of grasshoppers, prefer to remain concealed in rank vegetation and favour hedgerows and scrub. They are also less visible because they tend to show a leaning towards the nocturnal way of life and their songs are usually too high-pitched for the human ear to pick up. The females are instantly recognisable by their awesome-looking ovipositors. Bush crickets serve a useful rôle as predators of soft-bodied pests but they will also eat plant material.

Small snails and slugs may well be preyed on by bush crickets but they also constitute tasty morsels for larger animals from carnivorous beetles to the song thrush – which has become adept at dealing with snail shells, having adopted the habit of deliberately smashing them to remove the flesh. In contrast to grasshoppers the gastropods prefer a moist north-facing aspect (*gastropod* literally means 'stomach foot', referring to the way in which these creatures creep along by wave-like rhythmic contractions on the belly surface). As slugs lose moisture easily they usually feed in the cool of the night and during wet days. Their file-like rasping tongues enable them to cope with both flesh and rotting plant materials. While three species of slug – black, garden and field – are ubiquitous, snails are more numerous in calcareous areas. As their shells are made from lime-rich substances it follows that alkaline soils will accommodate the largest colonies. A good time to study these creatures is on an early summer's day after a shower has raised the humidity, for they are particularly active then, but the most widespread Helicidae are even conspicuous during dry weather and drought. In dry sunny conditions they will attach themselves to plant stems to escape the heat of the ground and remain inert for long periods. All snails are able to retire into their shells and seal the entrance with several layers of mucus, which sets hard and waterproof. A location with a wide variety of habitats with-

in a small area, including niches offered by stone walls and pavement crevices, can often accommodate a rich variety of species. But as many snails are tiny and there is much shell-colour diversity within a single species identification can be quite challenging. One of the most distinctive species is, of course, the large Roman snail. It is thought originally to have been introduced by the Romans, but present populations in a few places in southern England, mainly on the North Downs, in Herefordshire and on limestone in Gloucestershire, are probably the result of more recent introductions to the wildlife of large estates for their curiosity value. The main populations are restricted to southern calcareous soils because they spend several years – they may enjoy a lifespan of up to nine years – increasing their size and calcium is said to be more easily absorbed at high temperatures. In some European countries they are readily collected for consumption by man, but in Britain their numbers are kept in check by other animal predators ranging from foxes, field mice and shrews to predatory beetles which seem to cope quite well with smaller, immature specimens. Roman snails are very much vegetarian, and unlike many other snail species show a preference for flowering plants, particularly hardhead and greater knapweed – hence a flowering sward offers a better habitat.

Though too tiny to be as easily visible, some invertebrate herbivores will draw attention to themselves by the evidence of their destruction. The tiny larvae of some moth, fly and beetle species may be hidden between the epidermal layers of leaves but, while tunnelling through the soft tissue within, their mining activities are visible in the form of curious blotches and squiggles. For example, dock leaves are commonly disfigured by the leaf-mining larvae of a fly

The Roman snail is a large distinctive mollusc. The largest populations are on calcareous soils in southern England because they spend several years increasing their size and calcium is said to be more easily absorbed at high temperatures

205

species (*Pegomya*), and bramble leaves are attacked by a species of moth (*Nep-ticular aurella*). Galls are a form of plant deformity caused when plant tissue reacts chemically to the activities of the parasitic insects within, usually by swelling up around the creature and providing it with accessible nutritious food. Species of mites, worms, beetles, aphids, midges, moths and wasps are all responsible. Familiar examples include the stem galls on ground ivy and hawk-weed caused by a reaction to gall wasps (*Liposthenus latreilles* and *Anlacidea hieracci* respectively). The downy 'beads' on common speedwell are in fact de-formed leaf buds protecting the larvae of a gall midge (*Jaapiella veronicae*). Some of the most interesting galls are those that can be seen on hedgerow shrubs and trees, such as the 'robin's pincushion' on the wild roses – deformed leaves resembling a bunch of red moss – a reaction to a gall wasp (*Rhodites rosae*).

It is the caterpillars of butterflies and moths that are best known for their spe-cific relationship with their food-plants. But the immature stages of nearly all species of the butterfly are usually difficult to spot because they are so well camouflaged. The spiny caterpillars of the 'aristocrats' and fritillaries may be easier to find, and also perhaps the gregarious hairy ones of the small tor-toiseshell, which live under the protection of home-spun 'tents' on stinging net-tle. The butterfly's scientific name, *Aglais urticae*, reminds us of its association with the nettle, *Urtica dioica*. Anyway, most people are more familiar with the butterfly adults on the wing. With many moths it is often the other way round. As most are nocturnally active and many adult specimens have a nondescript dark coloration, their identification is usually a job for an expert or someone with a great deal of patience and a good identification guide (Bernard Skinner's *Colour Identification Guide to the Moths of the British Isles* comes to mind). However, the caterpillars of some of these species may be found quite easily, for they can be quite bizarre in their woolly forms or sport bold colours in their attempts to deter predators. Examples of widespread woolly caterpillars in the

Although the tiny adult vapourer moth is nondescript enough to be overlooked, the caterpillar is bizarre, covered in bunches of fine hair and four tufts along the back

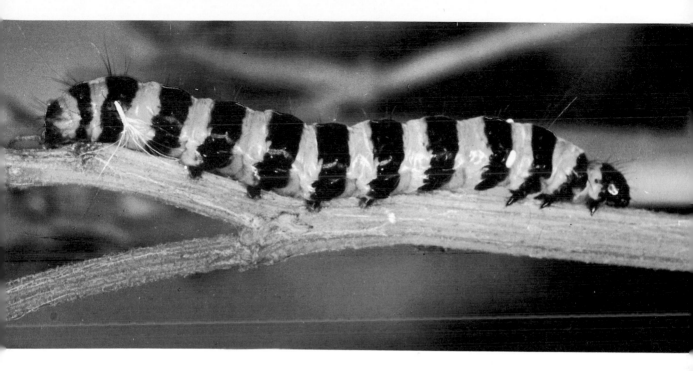

herb layers include those of the fox moth on grasses, the ruby tiger and buff ermine on docks and dandelion, and those of the tiger moths. Of all the tiger moths, it is the caterpillar of the garden tiger, often described as 'woolly bears' by children, that are most familiar, for they are commonly found on garden plants in parks and gardens. In the field they feed on dead-nettle and plantain. The gregarious hairy caterpillars of the brown-tail tussock are a common feature on hawthorn in hedgerows, for they spin large silk tents around several leaves and twigs. Black and yellow is a standard combination of warning coloration, mimicking wasps and bees, and the moth caterpillars of the buff-tip on deciduous shrubs, the scarlet tiger on various meadow plants, the six-spot burnet on bird's-foot trefoil, and cinnabar on ragwort and groundsel are banded in these hues. Ragwort and groundsel are rich in alkaloid poisons which are stored in the caterpillar's body without harming the creature itself. While the yellow bands and black spots on the caterpillars of mullein moths may serve to deter predators, these larvae are heavily parasitised by the ichneumons (see below). And there are always some predators that can assimilate the poisons of insects. The cuckoo, for example, is able to eat caterpillars other birds leave alone, but as this bird has a relatively small population the survival of the invertebrates is not severely threatened.

A walk through a field or along verge and hedgerow will invariably flush out odd adult moths resting in the vegetation during the day. If luck has it, these may well be one of the colourful day-flying species (and there are also many interesting nocturnals which may be disturbed in this way), but more often than not it will be one of the 'micro-moths'. The crambids or grass moths haunt grassy places in large numbers, perched with wings folded and often head downwards. Their tiny caterpillars are rarely seen, for they live in the litter layer from where they make a vertical silk lined gallery down into the soil to feed on grass roots and the base of stems. These moths can breed to pest proportions

Caterpillars of the cinnabar moth feed on ragwort. Their black and yellow warning coloration serves to deter predators. As ragwort is a damaging weed, experiments in its biological control have been attempted with the caterpillar

to threaten both pastures and cereal crops. Another small moth, the common footman, is also easily flushed from vegetation near a hedgerow and may be mistaken for a crambid, but when resting it can be distinguished by the way it folds its forewings, one held lop-sided over the other so that only one wing is visible. The disappearance of a species of footman from an area is said to indicate rising pollution, for their caterpillars feed on lichens which require a high degree of clean air. The tiny white-black-and-yellow hairy caterpillars of the muslin footman may just be visible on lichens and algae on stone field-walls in south-west and central England, southern Scotland and north-west Ireland.

Among the beetles and bugs are numerous species of herbivore. Many bugs (mainly the division *Heteroptera*) resemble beetles, but if one can get close enough to examine the wings they can be distinguished. When folded against the body the bug's outer pair of wings (the front pair) known as the 'elytra' are tough and leathery at the root but membranous at the tip – so the insect appears to have only half a wing. Also bugs' wings visibly overlap each other, while the elytra of most types of beetle meet in a straight line along the middle of the back, the hind wings usually well hidden under the tough leathery armour of the forewings.

The chafers and chrysomelids are examples of leaf-eating beetles, and each group has rather spectacular species that cannot fail to be noticed. The best-known of the former is the rust-coloured cockchafer, which, because it is active during May and June, is often confusingly known as the 'May bug' or 'June bug' (confusing because it is a beetle). A swarm of these large buzzing creatures can appear quite alarming, but the danger may only be to the plants they damage. The adults eat the foliage of shrubs and trees, but do not do as much damage as their larvae, which feed on grass roots. Many of the chrysomelids are bright green, blue or golden in colour, and the reed, dock-leaf and tortoise beetles are among those that may be found in grasslands. A mainly southern species, the bloody-nosed beetle has the startling habit of ejecting a drop of fluid when irritated, probably a deterrent to small predators, such as lizards, mice and birds. The adult is usually seen on bird's-foot trefoil and broomrape to avoid competing with its larvae on bedstraw food-plants, particularly goosegrass. Not all ladybirds are carnivorous. The 24-spot is vegetarian, feeding on campion, clover and vetches. In fact various parts of the protein-rich leguminous plants are popular food items for many invertebrate species. Those beetles characterised by a long beak or 'rostrum' which extends forward from the head and carries the jaws at the tip are the weevils. With this adaptation they are able to drill through plant tissue. Bugs, too, have beak-like mouth-parts, but theirs are adapted to suck on plant sap. The most notorious are the *Aphidae*, so warred against by farmers because they infect cultivated crops (see below). Arable land represents in effect a drastic change in the balance of nature, for by overproducing one type of vegetation an extensive food-source is created for certain invertebrates that are able to flourish better than they would in their natural setting because predators and other natural checks may not have been able to develop as well in the artificial setting. While they serve as prey for a range of insectivorous fauna, ranging from ladybirds, bush crickets, hoverflies, lacewings, wasps to shrews and titmice, the relationship of root aphids with the meadow ant is symbiotic.

Adult root aphids tap the sap of plants, and when stroked by ant antennae they are persuaded to exude a sugary waste product known as 'honeydew'. Meadow ants actually 'farm' several types of root aphid for this substance. Aphid eggs are collected and carried to their food-source close to the ants' nest and are tended until they hatch. The adult aphids graze on the plant roots protected from their enemies by the ants. The aphids have become so dependent on the ants that they are unable to excrete without the ants' assistance. (The larvae of the *Lycaenidae* family of butterflies, to which the hairstreaks and blues belong, have a similar association with ants of the *Myrmica* genus, of which the most highly developed is the relationship between the brown ant and the large blue: see page 000.) Although the meadow ant is rarely seen because of its predominantly subterranean habit, its mounds or hills are prominent and will invariably characterise old pasture. As mounds make mowing difficult they are usually cleared from hay meadows and improved pastures. There are several places on the Wiltshire Downs where huge thyme-covered mounds are evident. It will have taken several generations for them to have reached their present size, and it is thought that they may be 150 or more years old. The domes conceal a network of passages and chambers, each mound accommodating a colony of up to 25,000 ants. Calcareous grasslands are inhabited by a number of ant species, the red ant being particularly common. A large ant-hill may be shared by both red and meadow ants, coexisting because of their different foraging habits. The former largely hunts and scavenges above ground, seeking decomposing matter, oil-bearing seeds, nectar and tiny invertebrates, while the latter feeds on soil fauna, making up for the protein lacking in honeydew.

The presence of ground-dwelling beetles is encouraged by a litter layer and dung. Most of these creatures are scavengers feeding on plant debris, seeking out soft-bodied invertebrates, and some species depend largely on dung. Many of this group, though large and conspicuous, are nocturnal, hidden in the debris or under stones during the day. If disturbed, they will rapidly scurry away on their long legs, for several species lack hind wings and are completely flightless. Being creatures of the night, they tend to be predominantly black, though some have interesting metallic sheens, such as the violet ground beetle and its relatives. Features suited to their ground-living lifestyles include large jaws, powerful and spiny limbs adapted for digging and numerous fine bristles on the front part of their bodies which detect prey by sensing vibrations.

Ground beetles are only one group of an enormous army of decomposers, serving the useful purpose of turning litter, carrion and dung back to pasture – and without their help it would take a long time for this waste matter to be converted to accessible plant nutrients in the soil. In fact they bridge the gap between the decomposing material and the true nutrient-converters: the microscopic bacteria and fungi which feed on the by-products of the larger creatures. The dung beetles of the genus *Aphodius* specialise in mammal waste matter. Those with a catholic dung diet such as *Aphodius fimitarius* and *Aphodius rufipens* are widespread, but others with more conservative tastes may be localised. *Aphodius obliteratus* prefers horse droppings, and *Aphodius lapponum* enjoys sheep waste. Some dung beetles actually suck the dung, while others graze on the fungi which develop on it. For others still it is the food for their larvae, eggs being laid into this food-source. The dor and minotaur beetles lay their eggs hidden underground so they will collect balls of dung, roll these into burrows which are often as much as a couple of feet deep and lay their eggs in the balls. The larvae of dung beetles have to compete with the grubs of other dung-feeding species such as those of the dung fly. Adult male dung flies are a common sight on cowpats in summer, where they congregate to await the arrival of females for mating. Like all flies they feed on fluids by pouring digestive juices on to the food-source and then drinking the partially digested slime that results. They are also carnivorous, and grubs on cowpats, including their own, are therefore vulnerable, for the flies will plunge their 'beaks' into the prey to suck their juices. Male butterflies have also been seen lapping up juices oozing from mammal dung, Adonis blue and purple emperor being examples. As this is apparently a male indulgence it seems something is sought that is required by this sex alone. Sodium and nitrogenous compounds are possibilities.

Although they are rarely seen, the creatures of the litter layer play a remarkable rôle, for they serve to convert to pasture the pats of 13 million cows and droppings of 35 million sheep on our grasslands. Any threats to their existence may lead to severely fouled pastures – as recently revealed by research at Bristol University's Zoology Department. An antiparasitic drug used to control the pests in livestock is found to act as an insecticide in the dung after egestion. In an experiment on calves 16 pats from non-treated animals were found to accommodate a population of 1,229 beetles (in immature and adult stages), 286 flies, 36 earthworms and 7 other invertebrates after 100 days. By this time these pats had virtually degraded away. By comparison, 17 pats from the treated calves had only 29 beetles, 40 flies, 44 earthworms and 8 other invertebrates after the same time, and these pats were largely intact.

While mammal dung may serve to add to the diversity of the litter and soil fauna, trampling by farm animals creates its own effects. It reduces the numbers of some species, but others may actually increase. The creatures of the litter zone will take a toll, for they are vulnerable to being crushed underfoot and exposed to predators. In pastures, birds, such as wagtails, starlings, crows and blackbirds, can often be seen following in the wake of grazing livestock, snatching up the insects disturbed by their trampling. Soil fauna may actually benefit. Trampling has the effect of shredding and crushing the litter, thus helping to break it into smaller pieces for the decomposers. Also, species that lay their eggs directly into the soil may find it easier to have gaps opened up in the herbage where they may deposit their eggs. The ovipositors of bush crickets are easily recognisable, but in fact all female grasshoppers possess such a structure, which serves like a drill to make holes in the soil. Female craneflies actually hack out their holes using the ovipositor like a pickaxe. The female arches her abdomen high in the air, then strikes the ground with it forcefully. The task is exacting, for a deep hole may take up to half an hour to dig, so moist ground is usually desirable. Grasshopper and cranefly larvae live on roots, and large populations may seriously impair the productivity of grassland.

The scorpion fly is another insect that lays its eggs in soil; but in this species it is the male that is more noticeable, for his abdomen is shaped like a scorpion's tail. It functions not to sting but as a genital claw to hold the female while mating. The females of some parasitic invertebrates have jagged needle-like ovipositors. Eggs are injected into the live bodies of invertebrates and on hatching the

Adult craneflies which fly amongst the grasses and flowers in summer are harmless, though their larvae, familiarly known as 'leatherjackets', are soil fauna feeding on the roots of grasses and arable crops to which they can cause extensive damage

grubs rather gruesomely consume their host leaving a hollow husk. Species of the braconid wasps and the ichneumon and chalcid flies are important in regulating the populations of many pests in this way. The larvae of the large white butterfly are a favourite host for several species of parasitic wasp and fly, and in some years they may be responsible for 80 per cent of caterpillar deaths.

A good many spider species are able to exploit a diverse habitat. Spider expert Dr Eric Duffey reveals that of the 140 grassland species most will be found in the litter zone. Many are minute – possibly revealed, if the litter layer is carefully explored, by their tiny webs spun in crevices between fragments of plant debris. In the litter layer on well-drained light soils one may discover the visible portion of the unusual cocoon-like web of the purse web spider, which extends at a right angle into a vertical burrow below the ground where the spider waits for a meal to walk over the sticky silk. When the spider detects such movement it rushes up, seizes its prey by making a slit in the web and drags it down through the tube. However, it is spiders above ground that offer more interest, because many are conspicuous without one having to get too close, for there seems to be a very widespread aversion to the creatures. A tall herbaceous layer is required from which to suspend the sheet or hammock webs of the 'money spiders' of the family Linyphiidae. These webs may shroud large areas of a field. The spider usually hangs underneath the hammock waiting for insects, such as craneflies, moths and grasshoppers, whose low blundering flights render them prone to crash into the strands and become ensnared in the tangle of threads. Adorning hedgerows and bushes, or in their vicinity, vertical orb webs are more familiar. The garden spider is the commonest orb-web architect, but the webs are also constructed by about ten other related species. These webs are usually very visible and numerous on autumn mornings when laden with jewels of dew highlighted by frost, making one appreciate just how many spiders there are in a habitat. Not all spiders construct webs. Some have actively to hunt their prey, while others are able to rely on their camouflage to the extent that unsuspecting victims come so close that they are able to be seized easily. Those species of wolf spider that are mainly ground-crawling prefer open short turf, but *Pardosa nigriceps* has the agility and is suitably disguised in dark and pale striped markings to hunt high in a tall sward. Wolf spiders run after prey and jump on them, and the female is instantly recognisable when carrying her silk-ball egg-sac around with her under her body. These spiders do not catch their prey in webs but will weave a kind of nursery web where eggs are placed before hatching. Nursery webs of the very common species *Pisaura mirabilis* are a common sight amongst the herbs in July and August; and the female may also be visible, for she guards the nursery when the young have hatched.

The flowering heads of plants attract their own group of fauna. There are numerous minute herbivorous bugs, beetles and grubs which exploit the food-sources of this zone, but most are well camouflaged or hidden from view. The familiar serrations around the leaf margins of plants belonging to the clover family are the responsibility of the adult clover weevil, but it is the larvae that are far more destructive, for they will bore into the growing seed-pods of the clover flower and feed, well hidden, on the small succulent seeds inside. Oil beetle larvae may hide in flower-heads in order to attach themselves to visiting wild bees. They are carried to the bee's nest where they enter the brood cells, devour the egg or young grub in the cell and then use the honey and pollen food for their own development. Only those larvae which introduce themselves into a bee's nest in this way will survive, and to ensure proliferation the wingless female lays several thousand eggs close to low-growing and creeping plants with flowers near the ground so that the hatchlings can work their way into the flowers to await bees.

The most conspicuous invertebrates on flowering heads are the large nectar- and pollen-seekers or those that display warning colours. The bright and boldly contrasting colours of many beetles warn predators that they are distasteful. Ladybirds, for example, have poisonous blood which oozes out from the knee joints when attacked. While one ladybird may not harm a predator, several can cause the poison to build. Other black and red beetles on flowers include soldier and sailor, variable long horn and cardinal. The cinnabar and burnet moths are examples of those that fly during the day, and as they flutter they are easy to spot and catch. However, predators learn to leave them alone, warned by their

The soldier beetle is found all over the country in early summer on nettles, umbellifers and grass, in fields and hedges. The brown or black wing-cases and red or black thoraxes are said to resemble nineteenth-century military uniforms, hence the name. While they are mainly carnivorous, feeding and scavenging on other invertebrates, birds avoid them because of their warning colours

red-spotted black wings, for they secrete an armoury of poisons including alkaloids and prussic acid. Bee and wasp species abound, as do their mimics such as the broad-bordered bee hawkmoth, another diurnal species, hoverflies and the wasp beetle. Crab spiders await their prey on flowers but are masters of camouflage. The species *Misumena vatia* is able to change its colour to blend with the flower where it chooses to wait in ambush with legs splayed at the ready to spring on unsuspecting prey. On grass stems this stance enables them to hold their legs parallel to the stem thus concealing them in profile.

The most visually pleasing nectar-seekers are inevitably the butterflies. Although their specific food requirements will have a direct effect on their distribution, many species are also sensitive to the way their habitats are managed (see p. 223). About five years ago a national survey carried out by members of the Royal Society for Nature Conservation (RSNC) and WATCH revealed, as expected, that the highest counts and variety came from old, unimproved southern grasslands. Not only are most adults warmth-loving, but so, too, are some larvae, and many of the food-plants are better-established in the southern semi-natural grasslands. The south-west had the highest total number of butterflies and most browns, while the blues were commonest in the south-east. The whites, mainly cabbage, were common everywhere and particularly in the Midlands. In the north there tended to be fewer butterflies over all, though the rare Scotch argus, a northern species, was found to exist in locally dense populations. The larvae favour purple moor grass. Improved pastures were usually species-poor, and those that were recorded there were the most mobile species such as the white, brimstone, red admiral, small tortoiseshell and peacock, which may not necessarily have bred there. Brimstone, red admiral and small tortoiseshell are open-scrub species, and the peacock favours woodland-edge settings. Red admiral is also a migrant. The more sedentary species, such as the browns, blues, skippers and small copper, that rarely fly far from their breeding-grounds were tellingly absent from improved pastures, indicating the unsuitable breeding conditions of this sort of habitat.

The larvae of the browns and skippers feed mainly on grass and, in stable habitats where wild grasses are abundant, species from these families may be among the most common butterflies. In improved grassland their grass food-plants may be reduced or eliminated; for, as we have seen, certain grasses respond better to nutrients. Also, the grasses favoured in improved pastures are mainly those that are palatable and therefore readily nibbled down to the ground. In lightly managed grassland coarser grasses, such as cocksfoot, are ignored by sheep when they become unpalatable and form grass tussocks. The caterpillars of browns usually overwinter as larvae, and grass tussocks form an important place of refuge for them. Obviously, heavily grazed pastures and temporary grass leys are too disturbed for any grass-eating fauna to develop a stabilised population. Also, the leys consists of no more a handful of grass species. However, although a hay meadow rich in flowering plants may appear to have a rich invertebrate fauna because of the winged nectar- and pollen-seekers it will attract, the practice of hay-cropping in mid-summer followed by aftermath grazing is probably sufficient to keep the population of herb-zone invertebrates quite low.

The common browns, abounding in suitable grassland, are meadow brown, small heath and wall. The last two produce two generations. Their first adults may be seen by May and those of the second generation around August. The meadow brown has a single generation, the adults appearing on the wing in mid-season, between June and August. The marble white also has a single generation and flies in July and August in a few locations in southern Wales but mainly on the warm slopes of the Downs, where it tends to be localised. The adult butterfly looks very different from the rest of the browns family, for it has black-blotched white wings. All other browns are decorated with various forms of eye-spots. These markings near the wing-margins are thought to divert the predator's attention away from the vulnerable soft body-parts. Large eye-spots, such as those carried by the female meadow brown and gatekeeper, may work as deterrents because attackers believe that the insect is part of a large animal. The largest brown butterfly, the grayling, appears to have a canny knack of camouflage: it is a localised species and prefers well-drained locations where the vegetation is sparse, such as heathland, coastal clifftop grasslands and those on chalk and limestone, for it conceals itself on the ground. When chased it will suddenly alight on bare ground, flashing for an instant the bright eye-spots on

the forewings. While this distracts the pursuer, it swiftly slides the conspicuous forewings behind the hind wings which resemble the stony surroundings and thus it immediately blends into the background, becoming difficult to see. It then leans over at an angle to reduce the length of its shadow. While some have argued that this last movement completes the effective defensive action, others have suggested that it is no more than an attempt to regulate the insect's body temperature on the warm ground.

In the lively little skippers the tawny colouring predominates, and they may be mistaken for moths. The dingy skipper even rests like a moth with the wings folded on the abdomen, but others such as the small, large and Essex skippers rest in a fashion peculiar to butterflies, holding their forewings partially raised and hind wings horizontal. The large and small skippers may be seen on the wing between June and August in the central and southern grasslands of Britain. The occurrence of the dingy skipper extends to Scotland, but its distribution is patchy all over Britain. The caterpillars of this skipper are not grassfeeders, but have only one food-plant, bird's-foot trefoil, which, though widespread, grows best on calcareous soils.

The meadow brown is one of the commonest butterflies of grassland, the adults appearing on the wing between June and August

215

The larvae of the common blue also feed on this trefoil but are not confined to this plant and may also be found on other wild members of the pea family, such as the clovers and vetches, possibly explaining why this blue is widespread. Other blues are relatively restricted in range, not only because of their less adaptable food requirements and the fact that blues are not particularly mobile, but also because their lifestyles are so intricately linked to the special character of their local environment. Hence, while blues are able to form dense local colonies in a suitable environment, they are a good example of insects that have been very vulnerable to change in the structure of the grassland in their habitat. In some areas their leguminous food-plants have been swamped by more vigorous species where grassland has been improved for grazing. Elsewhere it is the *lack* of grazing pressure that has changed their environment. The elimination of rabbits by myxomatosis and reductions in the numbers of sheep have resulted in the disappearance of the brown ant and therefore of the large blue, too. The Adonis blue has been affected in another way. Adonis blue and chalkhill blue caterpillars feed solely on horseshoe vetch; and, although this plant is a strict calcicole and therefore restricted to calcareous grasslands, it is widespread locally. However, while the chalkhill blue may be found in most

The Adonis blue butterfly has a restricted range because of its food requirements and a lifestyle that is intricately linked to the special character of its local environment

places where the vetch grows, the Adonis blue is much more localised. As the latter originates in central Europe it requires a warm dry microclimate. Its caterpillars and chrysalids need to be close to the warmth of the sun-baked ground, so the female never lays her eggs on a plant that is over a couple of inches tall. Hence in Britain the Adonis blue does best on the south-facing hills of the South Downs on very short-cropped or sparse turf. With its restrictive breeding habit a colony easily disappears if no short horseshoe vetch plants are available.

The whites in contrast are so successful because they are strong long-distance fliers and adaptable to a number of food-plants, and the 'cabbage whites' succeed to the extent that they are considered pests. 'Cabbage white' is the popular name given to the small and large white butterflies. Their caterpillars readily feed on the cultivated brassica crops but have also been recorded on sixty wild members of the cabbage family. Though the larvae of the more colourful orange tip are restricted to only the wild plants, they, too, have been recorded on as many as thirty species. The caterpillars will not succeed equally on all the plant species. Cuckoo flower, creeping yellow cress and garlic mustard seem to be among those most favoured, possibly because the

Though the larvae of the orange tip are restricted to only the wild members of the cabbage family, they have been recorded on as many as thirty species. Here the female is seen depositing her eggs on cuckoo-flower. By the time the caterpillars have hatched the seed-pods will have developed and the larvae, resembling the seed-cases, will be well camouflaged

blue green caterpillars are so effectively camouflaged against the seed pods along which they lie and feed.

The RSNC/WATCH survey found that hedgerows were avoided by butterfly species which prefer more open situations, but where the hedges enclosed old pasture they added to the butterfly variety of the whole habitat. In intensive arable areas fewer species were recorded at hedgerows, although if these were along roadside verges they were richer. According to Dr Moore, only three butterfly species feed on shrubs and two on trees, and so the herbaceous zone of the verges will have contributed to the increase. The brimstone butterfly is an example of a shrub-leaf eater, feeding on buckthorn and alder buckthorn, while the spring generation of the holly blue eat the buds of holly or the flowers of gorse. Members of the browns family, the gatekeeper and ringlet, are more likely to set up territories near hedgerows. Although their larvae feed on grasses, they prefer slightly shaded, damp niches. The adults of both species seem strongly attracted to hedgerow bramble flowers to drink the nectar. The gatekeeper is often mistaken for the meadow brown, but is smaller, more orange and rarely seen far from shrubs. The caterpillars of the green hairstreak have as many as ten food-plants, which include shrub species, such as dogwood, and open grassland plants, such as rock rose. But even if their eggs are laid on the latter the adults are always in the vicinity of shrubs, which are essential perching vantage-points for the strongly territorial males.

Although the Glanville fritillary is now found only on the Isle of Wight, on rough grassy slopes near the sea, large local colonies can develop. The larvae feed gregariously on sea or ribwort plantain and tend to keep together when adult on the wing in May and June. They are said to have once been common on parts of the English mainland, but attempts to reintroduce them have so far failed

While most of the butterflies belonging to the families of the browns, whites, skippers and blues are open-ground species, those more familiar in other habitats may also be seen in the fieldscape, depending on the general setting of the location in relation to the surrounding countryside. The nectar-feeding adult butterflies usually seek different food-plants to avoid competing with their young and may choose to exploit the flowers of adjacent habitats once their breeding responsibilities are over. The same site may also see a range of adults during the course of the season, different species being on the wing at different times between April and September because of their staggered breeding periods. The few that hibernate as adults are earliest to appear, such as small tortoiseshell and peacock, and their new generation of adults will appear again later in the same year. Some, such as small tortoiseshell and small copper, have a short development period, and so there is time for two broods a year – their adults may therefore be seen throughout the season. Strong fliers and migrants may turn up anywhere. Large numbers of painted lady, a migrant, travel northwards from their winter headquarters in North Africa, and a few individuals have even been recorded on the shores of the Arctic Ocean. Hence they may be sighted anywhere in Britain. The migrants usually cross on the southerly winds, so it is in the south and east that these species are most frequently spotted. Kent in particular benefits from its relative proximity to Continental Europe; for, together with regular populations of painted lady, red admiral and clouded yellow, many unusual moths are carried across to the county. The hawkmoths are swift and powerful fliers, and many of them are able to migrate long distances.

However, apparently suitable habitats may not have the butterfly (and indeed other insect) species one might expect, and an investigation into the recent history of the habitat may reveal why. Nevertheless, the creatures sometimes seem to be able to increase as quickly as they decline when suitable conditions return and are maintained, provided that there are some individuals to propagate the population. The eliminated species may have to be reintroduced. Jeremy Thomas found that even the fussy Adonis blue could be returned to an area after it had completely disappeared. When Old Winchester Hill reserve became a tangle of scrub after sheep-grazing was reduced and the rabbit population decimated, the butterfly vanished. In order to restore the herbaceous floral diversity grazing régimes were deliberately reintroduced and maintained. Although the site subsequently became suitable for the butterfly, it was too far away to be reached by existing colonies elsewhere; so, in 1981, Mr Thomas with the Nature Conservancy Council reintroduced sixty-five individuals of this species. The results were spectacular, for eighteen months after the introduction there were 5,000 individuals on the wing (and as far as we know this colony still exists and at the time of writing will have produced fifteen generations – there being two generations a year).

If the reader was not already aware of this, he or she may now realise that grassland is not always as benign a habitat as it may seem to be for invertebrate fauna. However, by comparison arable land can amount to a battle zone, for here the invertebrate casualties are not only those species deliberately warred on by farmers for their destruction of arable crops, but also the harmless and helpful bystanders, so to speak, the predatory invertebrates and decomposers.

In the much disturbed environment of an arable field it is the more permanent features, such as streams, ditches, ponds, unsprayed headlands and hedgerows, that may offer the most interest. Permanent water-bodies accommodate a variety of aquatic invertebrates, but even if they appear to form islands in the fieldscape they are not the closed microhabitats they might seem. Two common water beetles, the diving beetle and water boatman, are strong fliers; and apparently secondary creatures such as water snails can colonise new areas with help from the larger fauna when their slime-covered eggs attach themselves to their transport. However, it is the sight of dragonflies and damselflies which will draw most attention to the water-body, for they are sensitive to pollution and disturbance (see p. 223) and like some butterflies are good indicators of a chemical-free, relatively stable habitat. With their preference for still or slow-flowing water with plentiful marginal vegetation, most dragonflies are heavily dependent on ponds and ditches for their survival (as are many amphibians: see below).

Dr Pollard has shown that, while hedgerows provide food and shelter for some woodland insect species on arable land, they may also play a significant rôle in the life-cycles of pests which exploit the changing availability of food in hedgerow and crops. As we have seen, hedgerows encourage the presence of butterflies, and so they will other nectar- and pollen-seekers, for in arable land hedgebanks and verges may be the only source of a succession of flowering plants. These insects can in turn serve to pollinate arable crops, such as field beans. Several aphid species have complicated life-histories which involve exploiting the hedgerow in winter and spring and dispersing to crop hosts in summer. However, hedgerows also accommodate predatory invertebrates which serve to keep pest populations down, for their life-cycles and lifestyles overlap those of their prey. The common flower bug and species of ladybird and hoverfly which feed on aphids and red-spider mites produce a spring generation on deciduous shrubs and a later one on arable crops.

Pest species are able to reproduce at alarming rates – one hectare of sugar beet may hold over a million aphids – and, as the biological control of a pest by its living enemies is not always predictable and can therefore be considered inefficient, modern agriculture has become highly dependent on the use of chemicals. More than nine-tenths of all arable crops eaten in Britain are sprayed with pesticides. However, vast populations like those of aphids are never completely destroyed, because amongst such large numbers certain individuals which are more capable of assimilating the pesticide are bound to develop and subsequently give rise to future populations of resistant individuals. But pesticides, particularly those that are non-selective, can have a more lasting destructive effect on the useful predatory insects. A few years ago para-oxon was used against the cabbage aphid. It effectively killed off a substantial proportion of these pests, but also the insect predators. Subsequently the small proportion of unaffected aphids soon gave rise to a new population (cabbage aphids can produce a new generation of fifty young every two weeks, and therefore a single female could potentially have a family weighing about 250 million tons in a single year); but the predator populations, their life-cycles being much slower, had not caught up, and this resulted in the largest cabbage aphid outbreak ever recorded in England.

Opposite: On summer evenings the air around damp pastures, ditches and ponds may swarm with mayflies. The adults take no food and live, only to breed, at the most for three or four days. They make easy prey for swallows and martins, for their flight is weak, while when they attempt to lay their eggs in streams and rivers the trout engage in a frenzy of feeding

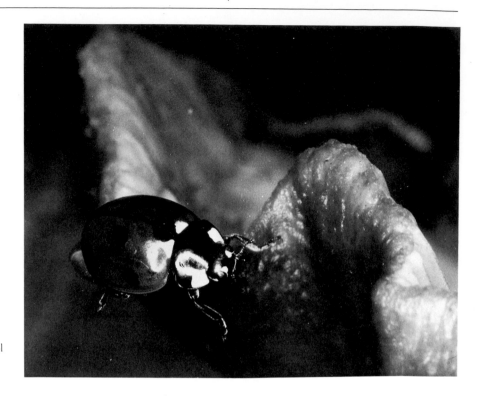

The predatory seven-spot ladybird will aid the arable farmer in the biological control of invertebrate pests such as aphids

Some chemicals can indiscriminately destroy pollinators, such as bees, and earthworm populations, which can result in the texture of the soil becoming adversely affected. The invertebrate fauna of microhabitats, such as hedgerows and water-bodies, can also be affected – and in other chapters we have seen the indirect effects of pesticides on vertebrate field fauna. Some forms of 'cultural control' such as crop rotation, stimulating the growth of crops with fertiliser, and stubble-burning are also practised to destroy pests. However, burning can deplete populations of predatory ground insects and soil fauna (including vertebrates such as amphibians and reptiles) unable to move quickly to unburned areas. The Ministry of Agriculture and the Nature Conservancy Council recommend integrated control programme systems of pest management in which chemical, biological and cultural methods are combined. In such systems the use of pesticides is limited and highly selective, with the effect that little harm is done to the natural enemies of pests. For example, with the sparing and selective use of herbicides the destruction of wild flowers in uncultivated areas, such as hedgebanks and headlands, is avoided, providing food and breeding-grounds for predatory insects. However, under warm conditions, as the reproductive powers of pests such as aphids is such that its enemies cannot prevent serious infestation, a selective insecticide can reduce their population until the numbers of their natural enemies have caught up successfully to combat the reinfestation. Warm humid weather encourages a fungal attack on aphids, and so during such an occurrence chemical treatment may be completely unnecessary.

Decline in Resident Butterfly and Dragonfly Populations in Britain since 1950

Of the various groups of invertebrates monitored, butterflies and dragonflies have shown the biggest losses as a result of agricultural intensification in Britain since 1950. The possibilities that these insects may be indicators for wider problems among the less-studied groups of invertebrates is worrying.

Butterflies		*Comments and reasons for decline*
Adonis blue	*vulnerable*	Loss of chalk grassland to ploughing; lack of grazing on many remaining sites
Brown hairstreak	*declining*	Loss of hedgerows, extensive mechanical cutting, alteration of woodland edge by ploughing meadows, coniferisation, etc.
Chalkhill blue	*declining*	Loss of chalk grassland to ploughing and lack of grazing
Dingy skipper	*declining*	Loss of grasslands, lack of suitable management
Grayling	*declining*	Loss of inland colonies; ploughing or lack of grazing of chalk grasslands; destruction or coniferisation of heath
Grizzled skipper	*declining*	Loss of grasslands and lack of suitable management
Large blue	*extinct*	Ploughing of grasslands, absence of grazing and cessation of gorse-burning
Large tortoiseshell	*endangered*	Reasons for decline not understood; loss of hedgerow trees including elm and change in agricultural landscape
Marbled white	*declining*	Loss of grasslands and scrubbing-over
Marsh fritillary	*vulnerable*	Loss of wet meadows to modern agriculture (woodland sites lost as rides close in)
Silver-spotted skipper	*vulnerable*	Loss of chalk grassland and lack of suitable grazing
Silver-studded blue	*vulnerable*	Lack of suitable grazing on chalk grassland sites (and loss of open heathland)
Small blue	*declining*	Most colonies are very small and lost to ploughing, grazing and development
White-letter hairstreak	*vulnerable*	Loss of elms
Dragonflies and Damselflies		
Brilliant emerald	*declining*	Loss of ponds (improvement of ponds)

Butterflies		Comments and reasons for decline
Hairy dragonfly	declining	Agricultural improvement of grazing levels
Norfolk aeshna	endangered	Pollution of Norfolk Broads; overmanagement of ditches on grazing marsh including drainage schemes for agriculture
Ruddy sympetrum	declining	Removal of emergent vegetation to improve fishing and amenity
Coenagrion armatum	extinct	Deterioration of the Norfolk Broads
Lestes dryas	extinct	Agricultural drainage, intensive ditching, loss of ponds (migrants appeared in 1983 but may not succeed in permanently re-establishing)

Adapted from: *Nature Conservation and Management* (NCC, 1984)

AMPHIBIANS AND REPTILES

Pastures, meadows and commons are the abode of a variety of amphibians and reptiles, although like many invertebrates these creatures are usually invisible amongst the vegetation. Frogs, toads and newts are most commonly seen in farm ponds and field-ditches during the spring breeding season, while snakes and lizards may be glimpsed basking on the hedgebanks and walls which form the field-boundaries. All these creatures, however, spend a considerable part of their lives hidden within the fieldscape and safe from the eyes of man.

Amphibians need both warmth and dampness. Like the reptiles they are cold-blooded and need the warmth of the sun to vitalise their bodies. At the same time their moist skins are prone to desiccation, so much time must be spent in damp habitats. Even so, the palmate newt is common in heathland environments as well as in rugged uplands and wetlands. Slightly smaller than the smooth newt, the male can be recognised by the thread-like tip to its tail and its webbed hind feet. Though quite often found sharing the same ponds, the smooth newt is less tolerant of acid conditions than the palmate. On emerging from hibernation in spring the newts head for their breeding-grounds (like the common frog, the great crested newt may hibernate on the pond floor). During this season the males of all three newt species are spectacular, the palmate sporting a dark blotched coloration and low straight-bordered crest, the smooth with a higher wavy-edged crest, and the great crested looking like a miniature dragon with its serrated black crest and vivid flame-coloured underside. Unlike the great clusters of eggs produced by frogs or long chains of toad spawn, newt eggs are produced singly and attached to the undersurfaces of water-weeds.

With breeding completed, newts spend the remainder of the year on land, often in adjacent pastures and meadows, where they tend to lurk beneath stones or logs during the daytime and emerge at night to prey upon worms and insects. The tadpoles leave the water in late summer and will not return to the water to breed until two or three years old.

The common toad is the most numerous of our amphibians and, although the colour may vary from a pale greenish ochre to a deep brown, its camouflage allows it to escape detection within the fieldscape. With the onset of the autumn frosts toads seek out hibernation holes in the muds of wet meadows or in abandoned animal-burrows in hedgebanks. Around the end of March, particularly after warm rains, they emerge, congregate and follow their traditional migration routes to their breeding-areas. Concealed in burrows or moist sheltered places by day, the toad emerges at dusk to hunt. However, the toad itself is prey to a formidable range of predators, which include hedgehogs, stoats, rats, snakes, crows and several birds of prey. Its defences include stillness and camouflage, and release of a foul-tasting liquid from glands in its skin, and the

Courting palmate newts. The male seen here in its courtship display can be recognised by the thread-like tip to its tail

225

inflation of its body, which may make the creature seem too large a mouthful to be swallowed.

The marsh frog and the edible frog are localised introductions, and the once ubiquitous common frog is now rare or absent in many localities because of the drainage of its breeding-grounds and the effects of farm chemicals. In the damp Romney Marsh sheep-pastures of Kent marsh frogs originally released into a garden pond appear to be displacing the native frog. While resembling the toad in its feeding habits, the frog's long and powerful hind limbs make it much more agile, both in water and on land. It may be found in habitats varying from the lofty acid mountain streams, tarns and marshes to the calcareous lowland wetlands, though it appears to be more sensitive than the toad to the impacts of modern farming practices. Within the fieldscape there are estimated to be about 81,000 miles (c.130,000 kilometres) of artificial ditches and watercourses, excavated to provide land-drainage, field-boundaries and, in the case of some of the wider channels, transport. The use of piped land-drainage, the lowering of the water-table for crop irrigation or domestic water-supplies and the infilling of farm ponds – at least half of which have been lost during the last fifty years – all pose serious threats to amphibian life. Since the 1930s a survey has shown that frog numbers in the Huntingdon area of Cambridgeshire have decreased by more than 99 per cent. Pollution is an additional threat, and the increasing popularity of cutting grass early and green for silage rather than allowing the hay crop to mature has not only damaged the wildlife of traditional

The common toad is the most numerous of our amphibians. While migrating to their traditional breeding-areas, males may sometimes hitch a ride on their chosen mates *en route*

meadows but also led to widespread pollution by silage liquor. The Nature Conservancy Council reports that a 400-tonne clamp of unwilted silage creates as much pollution as a day's untreated sewage from a town of 150,000 people.

Amphibians form the principal prey of the grass snake. Consequently field-ditches and farm ponds are the most favoured abodes of this snake, which may be seen gliding through the moist waterside vegetation or swimming in pursuit of frogs. However, apart from the northern part of Britain, where the summer temperature does not rise to the level of 21°C needed to incubate the eggs, the grass snake may also be found in meadows, pastures, woodland and hedgerow environments. Snakes congregate in places which provide the optimal hatching conditions: either accumulations of decaying vegetation or the haystacks, manure or compost-heaps of farmyard and garden environments. The grass snake is not venomous and seizes its prey in its jaws and swallows it whole. For defence it depends upon a number of ploys, feigning death, mimicking the striking attacks of a poisonous snake and emitting a foul-smelling excrement.

Our only venomous snake is the adder or viper, which also differs from the grass snake in its choice of prey – mainly shrews, voles and mice, though the snake will also seize amphibians and fledglings. These are gradually paralysed by the poison injected through the snake's hollow fangs, stalked until they die and then consumed at leisure. It prefers habitats which are drier than those favoured by the grass snake, such as moors, heaths and woodlands, though it will resort to meadows and pastures during summer. A study of vipers on farmland in the Isle of Purbeck in Dorset revealed that the snakes tended to hibernate amongst the roots of hedgerow trees, emerge and mate and then move

The grass snake is not venomous but for defence depends upon a number of harmless ploys. Here it is seen mimicking the striking attack of a poisonous snake

227

The slow-worm is a lizard which appears snake-like because of the evolutionary reduction of its legs. It frequents drier pastures and hedgebank environments, preferring lank rather than closely grazed grassland

through the network of hedges and ditches to spend the summer in the marshes and damp grassland of the River Frome. The female adders carry eggs in their body until they are close to hatching and return to the hibernation areas to lay them. When the eggs hatch both young and females share the hedgerow environment, where they are joined by the returning males at the onset of the hibernation season in November. The third British snake, the smooth snake, is an endangered species which is confined to sandy heathlands of Dorset, Hampshire and Surrey. This snake preys on other reptiles, notably the sand lizard which has an almost equally restricted range.

The common lizard is found throughout mainland Britain in pastures and meadows, hedgebanks, woodland clearings and gardens. They are most likely to be glimpsed when exposed on a chosen basking-site, which is often a wall, tree-stump or open patch on a hedgebank. Field-walls are favoured because they provide cool shady crannies into which the lizards can retire from the excessive heat of the midday sun. The common lizard preys upon the invertebrates which are associated with the warm dry hedgebank and wall habitats which it frequents, including spiders, harvestmen and insect larvae. It is an 'ovo-viviparous' reptile, which is to say that the eggs mature within the mother and hatch immediately they are laid.

The slow worm, a lizard which appears snake-like because of the evolutionary reduction of its legs, is also ovo-viviparous, producing up to twenty young, about twice as many as the common lizard. It frequents the drier pastures and hedgebank environments, preferring lank rather than closely grazed grassland and basking or burrowing among the tussocks or leaf litter in the daytime and hunting at dusk for slugs, snails, worms and insects. It has a widespread but localised distribution. An isolated colony around our home has made a successful adaptation of man-made change. The original colony favoured the banks and cinder basking-sites of a railway cutting, but when the disused railway was redeveloped the slow worms survived and increased, exploiting the opportunities for hibernation-sites provided by the compost-heaps of new gardens.

CHAPTER 13

MAMMALS OF FIELDS

Fields and hedgerows are man-made environments. They created new niches in which some animals, like the native mole or the introduced rabbit, could flourish. They are also environments in which farming causes disturbances, some of these disruptions declining as agriculture has used much less labour, but other adverse effects increasing with the rise of modern farming methods. The commonest mammals in field habitats are small and inconspicuous or medium-sized and adept at concealing themselves so as to keep out of harm's way. In the daytime their activity requires caution, so many will only become fully active at night. Generally mammals are not restricted to one particular vegetation-type but occur in a variety of different situations. About two dozen of our mammal species are distributed widely throughout the British Isles (though several are absent from Ireland and some small islands off the mainland shores), and it is these which are commonly found within the mosaic of niches offered by the field environments. The natural history of Britain and Ireland is one of change, and this is part of its fascination. The abundance or scarcity of wildlife in a given area will inevitably be governed by the availability and distribution of suitable niches.

Although it leads a subterranean life, few creatures make more mark upon the countryside than the miner in black velvet! 'Untitumps', the west Midlands term for hillocks of soil thrown up during their mining operations, testify to the indefatigable mole's eager pursuit of soil creatures, and particularly earthworms, in a labyrinth of underground tunnels which are forever being renewed and extended. Their habitat is confined almost entirely to the topsoil, and a single creature's territory may occupy an area of up to 1,000 square yards. In winter moles may have to dig deeply in search of worms which have migrated downwards to avoid freezing. This mammal has three periods of activity and three of sleep during the twenty-four-hour day, and it will die of starvation without feeding for even a few hours. However, it is not only hunger which controls the short-term rhythm of activity, but the action of the brain in relation to the physiological states of the various organs of the body.

Although earthworms are their main and preferred diet, when these are scarce, such as in time of drought when the invertebrates are inactive, moles will seek other soil fauna. Otherwise much of their feeding is done when the

A mole emerging from its tunnel. Extremes of drought or wetness may bring the animals above the ground, and the losers in violent territorial battles may escape to the surface

worms burrow through the walls of their tunnels. The mole will accumulate stores of worms which are immobilised by decapitation. Such stores are gathered throughout the year and not just for winter. These rations ensure a regular supply of food, for experiments have shown that moles can consume up to sixty earthworms – about their own weight in food – in twenty-four hours.

Though rarely seen, moles do appear on the surface, particularly during flooding or extreme drought. Being solitary, aggressive, territorial creatures, encounters can lead to fighting, and the loser may have to escape to the surface. It is the youngsters newly dispersed from their nurseries that are most likely to be seen above ground, for until they have become practised builders they are able to construct only very shallow tunnels. At this time the animals are vulnerable to predators, which include owls, foxes, weasels, herons and buzzards. While weasels can pursue the creatures through their tunnels to capture them, herons can extract them from their shallow runs by, it is thought, sensing the vibrations of their underground movement.

During February and March the aggression towards the opposite sex falls temporarily into abeyance when moles will tolerate each other's presence to meet for mating. The breeding-nest may be no more than a large dry chamber at the end of a deep tunnel, suitably lined with leaves, grass and moss. Nesting-

chambers built in a 'fortress', a surface nest below a much larger than normal molehill, are more likely where deep tunnels are liable to flooding.

The hedgehog is also solitary by choice for the greater part of its life, emerging from its den in the shelter of a hedge or an abandoned rabbit-hole in a bank in search of food at dusk and continuing through the night. The creatures do have territories, thought to be marked by their droppings, but these are not as strictly preserved as those of moles (and other insectivores) and vary with their foraging-area. Although solitary and avoiding any social contact – except for a brief period in the breeding season when the pairs stay together for a short time – hedgehogs do not, or cannot, fight each other in an encounter. Both parties will simply avoid each other, or one probably rolls up into an impenetrable ball until the other moves away. Flattened hedgehogs are a common sight on Britain's roads, again because, instead of scuttling away, they approach this danger like any other, by curling up into a ball – an example of a formerly viable defence mechanism which serves the animal very badly in the changing world. There is a theory that those few hedgehogs that run away from vehicles – for these mammals can move at quite a speed if they wish to – will, by natural selection, create a new race of hedgehogs that avoid being slaughtered on the roads. But, we fear, unless this process of natural selection accelerates, the slaughter

The hedgehog emerges at dusk to search for food in fields and hedgerows

231

on the road must continue – for, as Desmond Morris puts it, 'insectivores are incapable of grasping anything awkward, either physically or mentally'.

Although the lesson of the motor-car still eludes them, we are not sure we entirely agree with Dr Morris's statement, with regard to hedgehogs. They certainly have a primitive brain but are nevertheless versatile in their feeding habits. Hedgehogs will search leaf litter and turn over stones and other small obstacles with their snouts in search of earthworms and other soil fauna, while they are able to use their front paws to dig for food. They will also take amphibians, reptiles, young mammals and birds. Seeking carrion on roads is one of the reasons why they lose their own lives. While flesh-eaters by preference, hedgehogs will take other food, including vegetable material and the human gifts of bread dipped in milk. The case widely reported a few years ago of the North Ronaldsay (Orkney) hedgehog population demonstrated that birds' eggs can provide a major source of food. The creatures bite into the egg-shell with their canine teeth and lick out the yolk. We have found records of the creatures being persecuted by gamekeepers in the past for their alleged depredations on the eggs of game birds, while on the other hand naturalists tell us that it is improbable that eggs constitute more than a very tiny fraction of their diet. These days many gardeners encourage these devourers of slugs and other insect pests to live in or visit their gardens – perhaps it is the hedgehog's misplaced confidence in its defence system which makes the animal so easy to tame. Cattle-grids in place of gates on farmland are proving to be another threat if hedgehogs fall through the bars and cannot climb out. Hedgehog-ramps, simple but effective structures, promoted by the Hedgehog Society, ensure that the trapped creatures can escape.

While moles are almost ubiquitous in field habitats except in poor cold soils where soil fauna is scarce (and an experienced mole-catcher tells us that their tunnels are often located under hedgerows), the hedgehog is essentially an inhabitant of scrub or the woodland edge. However, if open grassland includes hedges or scrub the hedgehog will invariably be present using the cover as shelter and foraging in the adjacent open spaces.

The much smaller insectivores, the common and pygmy shrews, are abundant in both types of habitat and, like the other insectivores mentioned, are solitary and aggressive in nature except in the breeding season. Individuals will actually fight on meeting, preceding or accompanying bouts with a screaming match in which much energy is expended. Both species have large territories with extensive runs made in the surface litter zone, but while the common shrew mainly digs its tunnels (though any existing tunnels of other animal species are also utilised) the pygmy shrew only depends on those burrows that are already available. Hence the latter has a much smaller home range: about 100 feet (30 metres) compared to about 475 feet (145 metres) of a male common shrew, though in spring the males of both species may move beyond their home range seeking mates.

The home range of an animal is the familiar area which it regularly uses in carrying out its routine activities. The area must be large enough to cater for the food-energy requirements of an individual, but is determined by the density of the species' population. The requirements of other species sharing the habitat will control its productivity, but this may be offset by different species living on

Above left: The common spotted is the commonest orchid of old pastures in England

Above right: The pyramidical orchid can be numerous on chalky pastures and is pollinated by butterflies and moths

Left: The green-winged orchid is an indicator of old grassland and is rapidly declining with loss of habitat

Corn cockle is a beautiful though now rare weed of arable land.

Field scabious, a plant of hedgebanks, verges and rough pasture, occasionally seen as a weed of cultivation on chalky soils

Betony, a plant of permanent grassland. In medieval times it was regarded as having magical powers against the forces of evil

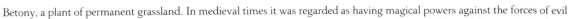

Hawkweed flourishing in an unimproved
limestone pasture in the Mendips

Common ragwort, a poisonous weed in
overgrazed cow-pastures

The common poppy provides a vivid
splash of colour wherever it escapes the
herbicide spray

slightly different diets or occupying slightly varying microhabitats within the main habitat. Home ranges will therefore separate the individuals within species, but do not necessarily separate those of different species. The two species of shrew occupy the same habitat successfully because they are partly separated by their behaviour. The common shrew is more active underground and the pygmy shrew on the surface. Any possible encounter between the two is avoided because of the agility and alertness of the pygmy shrew, which silently escapes before the larger common shrew becomes aware of its presence. Dr L. H. Matthews suggests that, although the pygmy shrew knows about the common shrew, the latter is ignorant of the former's existence. Perhaps this is just as well, because the smaller species would not stand much chance at the mercy of the teeth of the larger shrew. Another marginal difference in their habits is that, although both are active throughout the twenty-four-hour period, alternating periods of activity with periods of relaxation, there is some evidence that the larger species is more active at night and the pygmy shrew relatively more active during the day. Because of their high metabolism, shrews are short-lived and soon drop dead of old age – living not much more than a year – even

The tiny pygmy shrew is fiercely territorial within its home range, where it occupies abandoned burrows

Opposite above: The snake's head fritillary, a now rare plant of damp grasslands

Opposite below: Fallow deer are found in parkland and may escape into the adjacent woods and fields

with plenty of food available. Their food largely consists of invertebrates of the soil and litter zone, and a surplus is stored, like that of the mole, in a maimed form, the shrew having first taken a bite from it.

The larger cousin, the black and white water shrew, despite possessing adaptations for aquatic life, is not confined to water, for it may even be found on dry chalk grassland. Although the common shrew is an agile swimmer if its territory is near water, it is the water shrew that is usually associated with aquatic habitats. However, it only ventures into water on short feeding excursions, otherwise spending a great deal of time grooming on dry land.

The home ranges of our flying mammals may well overlap with those of the aforementioned insectivores, but they extend into another dimension: the air above (and bats do not compete with insect-eating birds, because they fly at dusk and into the night when few birds are active). The commonest species of field and hedgerow are the pipistrelle, the brown long-eared bats and, to a lesser extent, the whiskered bat. As it prefers to hunt for aquatic insects, the Daubenton's bat is an opportunistic hunter in meadows. More locally common, flying high over chalk grassland, is the serotine; while, even rarer, the low-flying greater horseshoe feeds over grassland and hedgerows in south-west England and south Wales. The only large bat in northern England is the noctule and it is quite likely to be spotted not only because of its size, but also because it is usually the first bat emerging in the evening.

Our bats are all entirely insectivorous and, being great opportunists, will exploit any good feeding-site. Flies and gnats that dance in eerie columns in the still air of warm summer evenings afford good hunting over muggy dung-steaming pastures and grasslands. Large concentrations of insects collect in wind eddies created by hedgerows. If species share hunting-grounds, they will seek prey in different places, and the shape and span of their wings will, to some extent, affect their flight and hunting technique. Most prey is taken on the wing, though those species that hunt around shrubs and trees such as the whiskered and brown long-eared bats will pluck their prey from foliage. The greater horseshoe bat has been seen settling in the grass to take beetles on cow dung. If the prey is too large to handle on the wing, bats will carry it to the roost to be dismembered there.

It has long been known that our bat species do not fly all night but emerge at dusk, hunt for a while in the gathering gloom, then return to their roosts to rest. In the middle of summer, when females are suckling young and energy requirements are greater, a second flight is made each night at dawn. The two flight periods correspond with periods when insect prey is most abundant: insect-traps in bat feeding-areas have shown this to be so.

The physiology of these mammals is remarkable in that it is not only during their long winter hibernation that they assume their torpid state; in fact they retreat into this form of 'suspended animation' daily during their periods at rest. Then their temperature falls, the rates of heartbeat and breathing are much reduced and all physiological processes slow down. The warming-up period commences in the roost about half an hour before hunting-time. Enormous amounts of energy are expended when hunting, so the catch must be high – a pipistrelle needs about 3,000 small insects per night. However, as bats spend all winter and nine-tenths of the summer in a torpid state, they are able to live for

twenty years in comparison to an animal of similar weight, the shrew, which is lucky to live for one-fifteenth of that time. Dr Matthews questions 'whether a long life spent mainly in unconscious torpidity is more satisfactory than a short one spent in frequent short bursts of greater activity. Natural selection, or rather natural elimination, has presumably been the cause of the evolution of the different ways of life, both of which, however, "await alike the inevitable hour".'

Because they crowd into their roosts – which may be no more than hollows in hedgerow trees – in large numbers, bats are assumed to be sociable insectivores, but as there is still a lot to be learned about these creatures many of their habits are conjectural. For instance, do bats roost in large numbers for warmth in their frequent state of torpor or because of a comparative scarcity of suitable places? The vocal communication in their roosts is perceptible to the human ear, but when hunting bats emit immensely high-pitched ultrasonic sounds which bounce back in echoes from their prey, and other bats and obstacles, providing a 'sound picture' of their surroundings. Summer roosts are likely to be in different places from winter hibernating-roosts, the former being near their

During the early 1950s myxomatosis reduced the rabbit population by more than 99 per cent. Rabbit numbers are now gradually increasing, although the disease still takes a heavy toll

food-sources. In the summer the sexes separate, the females forming maternity colonies, but they may be accompanied by juveniles of both sexes.

The social behaviour of the rabbit is very familiar, and so widely documented, sometimes delightfully so as in Richard Adams's *Watership Down*, that we need not consider it here. Their prolific breeding habit ensures that they are the most ubiquitous mammal and are widespread in all hedge-rows, grasslands and pastures. In 1936 the naturalist Francis Pitt wrote that the rabbit is 'possibly one of the most dangerous animals on the British list', for at this time their enormous numbers were doing serious damage to crops and competing with sheep and cattle on pasture. Although much of the English landscape has been moulded by sheep, the rabbit has also played a major rôle. While the rabbit has been crucial in preventing the natural generation of wood-lands by eating young saplings and ring-barking older trees, where the crea-tures are extremely abundant their selective grazing turns dense grassland into expansive areas of short turf with vigorous growth of the poisonous or tough plant species such as thistles, nettles and ragwort. On chalk downland, together with the sheep, rabbits have been instrumental in holding the scrub at bay. With the introduction of the myxomatosis virus in 1953 the rabbit population was reduced to less than 1 per cent of its former level. Since then they have made a comeback, but their numbers are still not large enough to hold down-land scrub at bay, while at the same time sheep-grazing is declining.

Female rabbits can produce up to thirty young a year, but there are regional variations. In the light warm soils of the southern districts young ones could potentially be found during every month of the year, but in the cold wet ground of the north there is a respite in breeding during the winter months. Even so, 70 per cent of these mammals will die before they are a year old. Myxomatosis still takes its toll on the British population, though nowadays many infected rabbits do not necessarily die directly from the virus, but probably fall prey to predators while incapacitated.

Rabbits feature as an important food-source for several British carnivores and are a much more useful energy-source than the smaller prey, for a carnivore would require fewer rabbits than other rodents. In a balanced food-energy 'pyramid' there should be fewer carnivores than herbivores, each level of such a pyramid providing enough energy to support a smaller level above it. If any level is disturbed significantly or destroyed, the consequences will ripple right through the pyramid. Too many rabbits competing with sheep and other herbivores can cause over-grazing. The lack of vegetable food-supplies severely reduces the populations of less competitive herbivores, and a lack of shelter in the resulting short turf increases the vulnerability of smaller rodents and invertebrates to prey.

When rabbit populations were decimated by myxomatosis some animals suffered and others benefited. All prey species were affected to some degree; but stoats, being less adaptable than weasels and foxes, suffered a steep decline in their population, as did the buzzard in the West Country. One of the im-mediate effects was that other rodent species began to feature largely as alterna-tive food, resulting in a large reduction of their population. But being such rapid breeders they recovered fairly quickly, and the tall thick vegetation that grew in the absence of the rabbit soon provided increased food-supplies and concealment. While the numbers of hole-nesting species, such as the wheatear and stock dove, declined dramatically in some areas, developing scrub provided nesting-sites for other bird species. Two insects which became scarce when the rabbit declined were the large blue butterfly and the brown ant. For a part of the larval stage the butterfly lives in symbiotic existence with the brown ant (a species of the genus *Myrmica*) feeding on ant grubs in return for giving adult ants a sweet secretion exuded only when the larva is stimulated by an ant's stroking foot. The brown ant will actually carry the butterfly larva into its nest, and is only one of two ant species which will tolerate such depredations of its own family. The brown ant does not live in grass taller than 2 inches (about 5 centimetres) high, so without the turf-shortening activity of the rabbit the ant disappeared after myxomatosis. As this ant is essential for the large blue to complete its life-cycle, the large blue also disappeared. Dr Matthews speculates that the two insects did not become a part of the British fauna until after the introduction of the rabbit, and therefore owe their presence indirectly to man.

In some areas the rabbit does appear to be recovering to its pre-1950 population-level, and a conservative estimate of what a full recovery could cost in destruction is in the region of £500 million per year. Brian Lee suggests that as the rabbit is here to stay and it seems there is little man can do about it 'perhaps once again we should turn disaster to advantage and renew the fight with our knives and forks'. He adds that this would help our balance of payments as a large proportion of rabbits for the table are bred in China from previously exported domestic British stock!

In 1880 the Ground Game Act changed the status of the brown hare from sporting animal to pest, allowing farmers, even if not the owners of sporting rights, to destroy the creatures whenever their crops were threatened. It has been suggested that as the remains of the brown hare have never been recovered from any Ice Age deposit, and as dense forest covered Britain after it became separated from the Continent, it is possible that the brown hare is one of man's domesticated introductions to the suitable open habitats he soon created, for the hare is an animal of open country. The species is now most plentiful in extensive arable areas and on rolling downland where it can speed away with ease. Considering that this creature of the open does not even have a burrow to take refuge in, and it does not multiply as rapidly as the rabbit, it holds its own very well. In a shared habitat the rabbit is the more successful competitor, because brown hares were seen to experience an increase in numbers when myxomatosis was first introduced and more food became available to them (hares were immune to the virus). When both species exist together it is difficult to tell which is most responsible for crop damage and debarked trees.

Hares appear to be most numerous in spring, but this is simply because in the breeding season these generally solitary creatures congregate in pairs or small groups. In their solitary disposition during the day they rest in their 'forms', shallow depressions excavated in vegetation or leaf litter, their mottled fur offering excellent camouflage. There may be several forms within their extensive and overlapping territories, but as individuals tend to move along defined routes within this area they do succeed in largely avoiding contact with neighbours when feeding at dusk and sometimes at dawn. When food is scarce individuals may travel long distances to feed away from their territories.

All the rules of solitary life are dispensed with when the March winds begin to blow and the long-eared long-legged 'jacks' can be seen leaping, chasing and sparring in their 'mad March hare' behaviour even at midday! A combat between two jacks may seem charming and comical, the two duellists hopping around on their hind legs while pushing and hitting with their forepaws like boxers. However, such meetings can sometimes result in a serious injury if one hare gets the opportunity to leap over his opponent and deal him a good blow with his powerful heels. More frequently, though, these fights terminate inconclusively, neither duellist any worse off save for the loss of a little fur. And, anyway, being a promiscuous creature the male takes no more than a brief interest in any female, stimulating her by chasing, leaping and squirting urine, and losing interest after mating.

A dam will drop her litter whenever she is ready, making no special preparation of nest or nursery. Her 'leverets', between two and five in a litter, are able to follow her soon after birth, for unlike rabbits they have fur and all faculties, though she will leave them for long periods in the form where they will wait rigid and motionless, their coloration blending so well with the background that they are practically invisible and may even be overlooked by a keen-eyed kestrel hovering overhead. A female that has reared an early litter may be able to have further litters later on in the season but, like rabbits, hares are able to reabsorb their embryos when food is short.

The following rodents are also able to produce large families and are in fact the most abundant mammals of fields, arable land and hedgerows, but one can walk miles and see nothing of them unless by good chance. Clues of their existence can be easier to find if one is prepared to poke and peer for evidence in the tangle of vegetation – such as a cache of gnawed hips and haws, or their ball- or cup-like nests woven of vegetation, minus occupant.

The most successful species among these small rodents are those that are most adaptable. The house mouse and brown rat are universally distributed as they live very successfully in association with man and are found wherever there is human habitation. Both will leave the shelter of barns and farmyards to which they retreat during the winter, for a more carefree life in the adjacent fields and hedgerows in spring and summer. Bank and field voles prefer natural habitats, the former living mostly in scrub, hedgerows and woodland where they will create runs and burrows at ground-level, while the latter prefer rough grassland to scrub and dense cover. A larger vole, the water vole, is a more likely inhabitant of water meadows. However, so versatile are all three species of vole that each may also be found in each of the other habitats. The wood mouse or field mouse can be the most common small rodent of the countryside, for it, too, will adapt to all the above-mentioned natural habitats, but will not visit human habitation frequently. Surprisingly, its less common relative, the yellow-necked mouse, which is only locally common in small pockets in the south of Britain, has been recorded in agricultural buildings, particularly apple-stores. Otherwise it shares the same habitats as those of the wood mouse.

Much rarer in recent times are the harvest mouse and the dormouse. The harvest mouse, the smallest British mouse, is confined to southern and eastern Britain. The first accurate description of this rodent was by Gilbert White in 1767, and even then his records reveal that its distribution was more or less limited to the southern and eastern counties of England, a few localities in Wales and the lowlands of Scotland. While now one is more likely to find its distinctive breeding-nest – a tiny structure of grass-blades slit and woven into a springy ball attached to corn-stalks or grass-stems about a foot above the ground – than the creature itself, there was a time when groups of several individuals would emerge from a disturbed hay-rick, as Mr White witnessed: '. . . a neighbour housed an oatrick lately under the thatch of which were assembled near an hundred . . . two of them in a scale, weighed down just one copper half-penny, which is about the third of an ounce avoirdupois.' The creatures are in fact heavier than so described, but not much more so, for otherwise they could not so easily clamber up stalks of corn and grass, grasping with their prehensile tails for balance, then retreat to their nests or feed on the grain, as artists are so fond of depicting. The breeding-nest is the female's domain, and this limited territory she will firmly defend, but her home range is larger and shared with several neighbours: past records reveal up to 80 mice per acre (0.6 hectare). Breeding several litters of up to eight young could potentially be carried out in quick succession every six weeks or so from early spring to late autumn. Harvest mice live but a few months, and although their rapid breeding cycle is partly the cause of their low life-expectation the extensive use of agricultural machinery and the practice of straw-burning will prove fatal to large numbers. There may be other reasons of a climatic nature or arising from competition with other species or disease, and perhaps more studies of this creature are needed to find out what has led to the disappearance of the harvest mouse from so many English counties.

Recent studies by Paul Bright seem to suggest that climatic effects may partially explain why dormice in Britain are largely restricted to southern England. The overgrown hedgerows of south Devon, Kent, Sussex and Shropshire once accommodated fairly healthy populations of the species. There are stories of lengthmen being so familiar with the nests in their stretch that they laid the hedgerow around these features without causing them much disturbance. Abundant autumn food is vital for their winter survival, and this is more likely in the marginally warmer south where weather conditions are more stable. A lot of natural fruit will not set unless summer temperatures achieve certain levels. Also, like other hibernators, dormice survive best if they can pass winter in a nest that is continually a few degrees above freezing and where low temperatures are consistent. Our recent mild winters punctuated by warm spells are not suitable, and continual arousal from hibernation requires the animal to use up its stored fat more rapidly. However, these creatures have declined so dramatically in the last hundred years that their prime habitats are now deciduous mixed woodlands in nature reserves maintained for their benefit, where there is a multi-layered tangle of both shrubs and mature trees. The severe cutting of hedges, and in many cases their removal, has largely reduced their possibilities as suitable habitats for dormice, for the creatures tend to spend most of their lives in the aerial maze of vegetation and only rarely venture on the ground.

Field and bank voles and wood mice have been relatively little affected by changing farming practices, but their populations wax and wane enormously. Their population (which tends to swell every three or four years, usually due to a succession of favourable seasons giving plenty of food and the absence

The diminutive bank vole may be glimpsed as it scurries between its surface tunnels and its burrows in the hedgebank

of heavy predation) can become a menace of plague proportions. This was the case in 1934 on the hillsides around Lake Vyrnwy in north Wales where the grass and newly planted trees were soon decimated by the munching of a swollen population of rodents. The well-developed and constantly growing incisors of rodents enable them to gnaw efficiently, and they need to keep using these teeth in order to keep them trimmed. Enamel grows on one side only, resulting in sharp teeth. During years of rodent plague populations, predator populations will become healthier. Francis Pitt observed at Lake Vyrnwy that 'it seemed that the abundance of field voles, the most conspicuous culprit, together with the bank vole and wood mouse had caused buzzards, kestrels, ravens and owls to appear in unusual numbers. Weasels, stoats and foxes also flourished.'

There will come a point when such rodent populations will suffer a severe reversal. The increased predators will inevitably take a toll, but a more crucial factor is that the habitat will no longer be able to support the bulging population for lack of resources. When rodent populations are balanced, the juveniles of the previous year will reach maturity and produce several litters during the breeding season – a single summer – and die in the autumn. In turn the overwintering population of immature animals ensures that the species survives and, the youngsters being lighter in weight than their parents, the diminished winter food-supply is able to support more of them than it would adults. By spring the survivors of the overwintering population will establish home ranges and territories vacated by the parent generation of the previous summer. Each year the density of animals a habitat can support will depend on its productivity. While it follows that if there is an abundance of food the creatures will require smaller home ranges, productivity is also affected by the requirements of other species in the same habitat with superimposed ranges. Inter-relationships of territory and social behaviour that can develop within a species and between different species can be very complex. We look at a simplified version of such relationships between the wood mouse, field and bank voles.

Every adult individual in all three species shares the need to defend its private space. But, as the creatures live in close proximity, their home ranges, which are considerably larger than their territories, inevitably overlap and so there is a tolerance, to different degrees, of neighbours. Within each of the three species hierarchies develop. In the case of the bank vole the loose-knit relationship within the species is one of larger animals dominating the smaller ones, with several individuals appearing to use a single system of burrows. P. J. Garson's research on wood mice reveals a hierarchy system of a dominant male, whose home range includes those of his subordinates, and of the females of the colony which have the smallest home ranges. When the population density is low and there is plenty of room for all, while the dominant male will have access to the best feeding-places and more females than his subordinates conflict is avoided if they keep out of his way.

The three species can successfully share a habitat because of their slightly different diets and micro-habitat requirements. Field voles can tolerate a far higher population density than the other two species because they essentially live under the area of grass they feed on. This species can avoid encounters with wood mice in the same area because they are separated by the latter's mainly nocturnal activity, while the bank vole's need for some shrubbery in the habitat extends its feeding-area to the arboreal dimension. Though mainly vegetarian, the wood mice tend to eat more invertebrates and less foliage of woody plants than do bank voles. (Shrews with ranges superimposed on those of the three above-mentioned species are separated by diet, feeding wholly on invertebrates.)

At the height of a plague not only will the creatures have reduced the productivity of their environment, but an overcrowded population also means continuous intrusion of territory, and constant stress and harassment as the owner attempts to drive out the intruder. Females are therefore unable to devote time to their young and may even kill them. Such a state of constant stress seems to affect a female's metabolism, particularly her reproductive metabolism, so that breeding is disrupted. Dr Matthews explains:

... the disruption is due to the malfunctioning of the endocrine system, and is manifested particularly in an increased activity of the adrenal glands followed by their exhaustion, accompanied by the resorption or abortion of the developing foetuses ... breeding stops and the animals die from internal stress caused by disorganisation of the feedback mechanisms of the endocrine system.

The wood mouse has overlapping home ranges, with subordinate males and females living within the range of the dominant male. Subordinates are tolerated so long as the population-density remains moderate

When the pressure of the insatiable rodents is removed the vegetation of the attacked habitat seems to recover surprisingly quickly, or so Francis Pitt's records seem to reveal:

... six months later I revisited the place to find it green and prosperous, and without trace of even one vole. On my previous inspection I had seen mice running about in broad daylight, now they were conspicuously absent, nor could I find any hint anywhere of the presence of voles, which had entirely disappeared. The contrast was startling, indeed almost awe-inspiring.

In fact the hoarding habits of rodents (and birds) can, under normal circumstances, help regenerate their habitat – seed or fruit that is forgotton or accidentally scattered may germinate in due course.

The much larger home ranges of the predators are in turn superimposed on those of their prey and will overlap with those of other predatory species. So, while hundreds of rodent territories may be included in the home range of a weasel, that of a single fox may overlap the ranges of a dozen weasels and thousands of rodents. However, as there is a higher degree of family life compared to insectivores and rodents, which disperse once they are weaned, there is a good deal of territory-sharing and so carnivores will alter the distribution of their home ranges accordingly. Terrestrial mammals do not, as a rule, wander at random over their home ranges, but adopt regular routes within them, so that if disturbed they can rapidly return home or to safety along the familiar trail. Badgers are well known for their well-used long-established ancestral pathways, for where these are traversed by subsequent obstructions, such as rabbit fencing, they will persevere in opening up a hole in the wire. The remedy is to provide a swinging gate which is too heavy for a rabbit to manage, and this is now widely done around Forestry Commission plantations. Where roads now cross these pathways, casualties are high, and in a few places badgers are being persuaded to use drainage culverts or specially constructed badger-passes. The distribution of these particular mammals is not really governed by food, for they are omnivorous, but by suitable geological formations for digging sets, preferably a sloping site and soft stratum below a harder one or under soil-binding features, such as the roots of mature trees or well-established hedgerow shrubs. As badgers prefer cover, an old undisturbed hedgerow bank or sloping deciduous woodland or scrub is most suited for a set. Earthworms form an important part of their diet, so while they use cover for homes and highways they will forage for food in adjacent fields.

The fox also needs a measure of cover of hedgerow, scrub or woodland, and in the treeless expanses of limestone grasslands it will resort to the shelter of rocks and large crevices. It is highly adaptable, demonstrated by the now large urban populations of the creatures, also showing the species' tolerance of man. Yet, considering how numerous the fox is and the interest it excites, it is remarkable how little we see of it, probably owing to its twilight and nocturnal habits. Like most mammals the fox marks its territory with the scent of its urine and the products of its anal glands. While this serves well as a method of communication among individuals, it works to the detriment of the fox, for its scent will lead hunting hounds to it.

Though foxes are born in underground 'earths', in litters of up to five, solitary adults will often lie out in surface lairs among the thick cover of bracken or gorse. Of all the delightful scenes in the countryside, few can surpass young wild mammals at play, and fox cubs are particularly delightful in this activity. The young of most of the aforementioned insectivores and herbivores have to fend for themselves as soon as they are weaned, but, as young carnivores are fed prey by their parents before learning to hunt for themselves, 'play' is more an activity of their group. In foxes play is part of the development of hunting skills and consists of fairly boisterous and even aggressive chasing and biting of each other and pouncing on leaves and other debris blowing in the breeze. As most carnivores are solitary for a large part of their lives, aggression is innate; but, as violent aggression between members of a family would be detrimental, natural selection has presumably transformed this into fairly harmless play. (By contrast, as badgers live in family groups which are hierarchical for much of their lives, their play is more elaborate and suited to their social behaviour. It takes the form of chasing games, shadow fighting, 'king of the castle' and mutual grooming, developing dominance, appeasement and sexual behaviour.) An adolescent fox cub will gradually become more adventurous and make short exploratory sorties within its parents' home range. When the necessity of finding food and fending for itself eventually compels it to do so, it will spread out to develop its own territory and range. Competition with other members of its family will be more severe if the availability of prey is low. However, young carnivores usually take their independence when the prey peak in numbers, and this provides the food-supply while territories and home ranges are sorted out. Fox populations are not governed solely by prey, for when the carnivores swell in numbers they tend to fall victim to epidemic diseases, such as mange, and if earths become infested it spreads rapidly. While fox diseases are not considered to be contagious outside the species, badgers have been implicated in outbreaks of bovine tuberculosis in a small area in the south-west where they have been subject to an extermination campaign by the Ministry of Agriculture. Although badgers enjoy protection from other forms of persecution by man, nonetheless an average of at least 50,000 foxes are killed in Britain each year by hunting and shooting.

Foxes and badgers are adaptable opportunistic feeders and, although the rabbit features large in the diet of the former, after myxomatosis the fox got on perfectly well with other prey, mainly small rodents, while earthworms are also a favourite food. Stoats and weasels are specialist carnivores, concentrating on rodent prey. Weasels feed mainly on voles and mice, being small enough to chase them through their burrows, tracking by scent. Stoats take much larger prey and are in fact quite catholic in their diet, of which rabbits form a large part. The decline in rabbit populations in the 1950s is said to have had a severe effect on stoat populations. Stoats and weasels are able to coexist in the same habitat because of these differences in diet and also in their behaviour. Breeding-nest sites are similar: a niche in a drystone wall, under a hedgerow or in a burrow, which may have been taken over from a victim of a past kill. Rabbit warrens are known to have been taken over by an entire family of stoats. Being a good climber, the larger species' home range could extend into a third dimension if mature trees are present. Research by C. M. Kind and P. J. Moors has revealed that while weasels require an island area of at least 146 square miles (380 square kilometres) to support a population of voles large enough to keep a permanent extended family of weasels, only one-third of that area can support a population of stoats because they take a wider variety of prey. Both species have a high energy requirement, needing to find food at frequent intervals, amounting to at least one-third of their body weight daily. An abundance of prey will lead to overkill and the storage of the surplus. Both species are regarded as vermin, but like other carnivores they play a useful rôle in keeping rodent populations down. Ian Linn's research at Exeter University has revealed that a family of weasels require about 2,000 voles or mice in a single year.

While the weasel is able to breed rapidly to match the multiplying rodent populations, its fairly restricted diet can lead to its population declining with that of voles and mice. Stoats have only one litter a year but may produce as many as thirteen young. The family spend quite a long time together, and this ensures that every young female is pregnant when the litter breaks up. A family

party will forage together, which gives rise to talk of the creatures 'hunting in packs' or 'on the warpath'. Neither of us has had the privilege of ever witnessing this, and once again we quote Francis Pitt who has, and describes it as a 'rather uncanny spectacle . . . the grass squirmed with them, beady eyes appeared first here, then there, white fronts gleamed as their inquisitive owners sat up to get a better look at me, and black tail-tips flicked as the stoats galloped off. I was glad to see them go!'

There are numerous stories of stoats mesmerising their rabbit victims. While rabbit psychology is such that if startled the creatures become so silly with terror that they will sit rigid and await doom, it has been said that the very scent of stoats and weasels has a paralysing effect upon the rodent, even though the predator may not be tracking it. Like other mammals the stoat and weasel mark their ranges and territories with urine, scent from special glands and faeces.

The weasel preys mainly on voles, and a very large territory is needed to support sufficient voles to support their predators in turn

245

246

Centuries of persecution by hunters and farmers largely restricted the red deer to open upland environments, though around Exmoor the animals may still be seen in the fieldscape. Here a fawn sits concealed amongst the herbage while its mother grazes nearby

Previous pages: Fallow deer were introduced by the Normans. Several herds can still be seen in deer parks, and from time to time groups escape and become established in woodland and woodland-edge environments, emerging from cover to feed in the surrounding fields

Now we turn to a group of large mammals that can be plentiful locally and yet remain inconspicuous: the deer. All species prefer woodland habitats with some undergrowth where the animals lie up through the day, but open grasslands and pastures near the trees are frequented for browsing by night. Where locally abundant, deer can do considerable damage to arable crops.

Red deer and roe deer are native species. After a decline in the forest system by the nineteenth century the former were rare outside parks in England, except for Exmoor. Roe deer populations may have suffered even more in England as farmland advanced, for they were not suited to confinement. But being mainly solitary and secretive their survival during this time is difficult to disprove. However, both species have recovered in the last hundred years, and Dr Rackham claims that they are now more abundant in Britain than they were in the heyday of the forest system. Present roe deer populations were partly boosted by deliberate reintroductions in England, but many free-roaming herds of both species are feral, mainly derived from escaped park animals. Introduced species have now also become members of our fauna. The fallow deer is thought to have been introduced to Britain by the Normans for hunting, and the deer were subsequently kept in parks, for ornament, from which they have escaped and become feral. This species occurs widely in England, Wales and Ireland, but being a woodland animal it is found only where there is sufficient woodland cover. Sika deer were introduced to Britain from Japan in 1860 and have become established in small areas in northern central southern England.

We are indebted to Mr Bill Mitchell, former editor of the *Dalesman*, for a delightful afternoon spent tracking wild Sika in the Bowland locality, where the presence of substantial herds of the deer in both field and woodland habitats testifies to the tolerance of most farmers. We were able to watch the activities of several different groups of individuals as they browsed and roamed in the patchwork of fields and woods. An introduced species of deer that has adapted itself to open grassland and meadows is the Chinese water deer. It was first introduced into Woburn Park in 1900 and has established feral herds over large areas of Bedfordshire, Hertfordshire and Buckinghamshire. It prefers areas where there are large expanses of water and marshy conditions. Water meadows near reservoirs are particularly favoured.

Wild cattle have been distinguished from domestic oxen since the twelfth century, but records of these creatures, though few until about the seventeenth century, do reveal some interesting details. Dr Rackham has found on record that the Archbishop of York ate 'six wylde bulls' at his installation feast in 1466; he adds that the creatures 'were treated as a kind of super-deer eaten on festive occasions and possibly the objective of specially thrilling hunts'. Being medieval status symbols, like deer, wild cattle thus survived in semi-captivity. Today four park herds of wild cattle exist as well as smaller herds established by cattle-breeders and farm museums. The best-known herd is at Chillingham in Northumberland, said to be descendants of those driven into the 1,100-acre (445-hectare) park when it was enclosed in the thirteenth century. However, there is little documentary evidence before 1600 to reveal whether the park herds were derived from the original free living cattle or whether they have at some stage been crossed with domestic cattle; a study of the skull anatomy of Chillingham cattle shows a resemblance to that of domestic cattle. Also, the herds in other parks differ from the Chillingham strain and from each other, suggesting that they may not have a common origin. It seems that the history of Britain's surviving wild cattle is controversial, but in the case of its free-roaming goats and sheep there is little argument that these are not truly wild, but feral.

In Dr Matthews's opinion, 'much of our mammalian fauna is as artificial as the rest of the environment of which it makes a part'; and, on the whole, we tend to agree with this, as the distribution and changes in the populations of British mammals have been caused by man's deliberate action or by the side-effects of his agricultural and industrial activities. But the resistance of our mammalian fauna to these changes contrasts sharply with the losses suffered by other forms of wildlife, for apart from four species (the brown bear, wolf, wild boar and beaver) all the other indigenous post-glacial ones are still with us. Some rarities, like the wild cat and pine marten, which would occasionally be glimpsed in the fieldscape, are now localised in remote desolate places. Most have adapted to coexist with man, and some have even taken advantage of the changed conditions; the recent explosion in the deer population may reflect the reduction in human disturbance caused by the mechanisation of farming. Although many of our native mammals are regarded as vermin, particularly the carnivores, ironically the most serious damage has been done by those species like mink and rabbit that have been introduced and that have become so successfully established that they are resistant to all human efforts to get rid of them.

CHAPTER 14

THE CHANGING BIRD LIFE

'It is one of the great pleasures in life to lie amongst the tiny flowers and bruised thyme and listen to the incessant almost birdless hum of the August afternoon on the Downs,' writes Eric Simms. And indeed, where large, seemingly endless fields are still maintained, as they have been for centuries by grazing, only a few bird species are able to adapt to the lack of cover.

The traditional haunts of the now rare stone curlew were on downland or heathland turf cropped short by sheep and rabbits. Since the war many of these grazings have changed to arable farmland. Some stone curlews have adapted to nesting on arable fields in East Anglia, and in Wiltshire, Hampshire, Dorset and Bedfordshire. While 2,000 pairs were known to breed in England in the 1930s, today there are fewer than 200, and half this breeding population now nests on farmland. Their dark-streaked sandy-brown plumage and eggs are well camouflaged against a background of bare, flinty or stony ground where they choose to nest. Their nest is nothing more than a shallow, virtually unlined depression save for a few bits of debris, rabbit or hare droppings or small pebbles for decoration or, more likely, to mark the site. Each spring the birds re-turn from Spain and Africa to breed on farmland, where the eggs and chicks are vulnerable to the maintenance of spring-sown crops on arable land and the practices of rolling and harrowing on grassland. However, the Royal Society for the Protection of Birds is now working with farmers to save as many birds as possible, and when nests are found on farmland their sites are marked to avoid damaging them. Eggs are also lost through predation and theft by collectors, an illegal activity. The birds are most active at night, and in the breeding season may be heard communicating with one another across arable fields or down-land pastures with their plaintive *coor-lee* calls. The stone curlew is insectivor-ous, feeding on soil fauna and on farmland pastures treated with farmyard manure, which are especially rich in invertebrates.

In spring skylarks, lapwings and meadow pipits sing in display flights while hovering, gliding and thrusting above their territories in open downland pas-ture, for they do not require song-posts or woody cover for nesting. The corn bunting will happily nest in a natural hollow in the ground, where it will build a structure out of bents and other fine grasses, lining it with feathery plant mate-rial and animal fur. In a shrubless environment it may use no more than a hum-mock in the ground, such as a mole or ant hill, or a fence-post as a song-post. On areas of downland which are no longer heavily grazed scrub has developed,

and this has provided niches for a range of other birds. Yellowhammers, thrushes, stonechats, hedge sparrows, finches and wrens favour a measure of woody cover for song-posts, roosting and nesting, and little more than a clump of thorns and occasional elder may be sufficient to attract them, for food is plentiful in the rich pickings of wild grains, seeds and invertebrates of the chalky grasslands.

Many birds feed in the downland pastures but do not nest there. A green woodpecker's home range (see p. 232) may include an area of ant-hills on down-land. The hobby hunts over these pastures and, if fortunate, this uncommon migrant may be seen taking its prey – ranging from the skylark to large moths – direct from the air. One is extremely fortunate to witness the drama of the dis-play flights of this bird of prey: the pair soar, hover, dip and loop, seeming to perform their dazzling feats for pure joy. Away from the rivers, water is another scarce factor in the chalky grasslands of the south. However, there exist 'dewponds' or sheep-ponds scattered along the crest of the downs. These circu-lar artificial basins were cut out of chalk, lined with rubble and flints, and layered with thatched straw and clay brought up from the Weald to provide water-sources for sheep. Only rainwater kept them filled, and they are said to

Half of Britain's population of just 200 pairs of stone curlew nest on farmland, often adopting sites on arable land following the ploughing-up of their downland nesting-places

251

have rarely dried out. No longer used or maintained, many have been colonised and even choked with aquatic vegetation. Acquatic animals have found their way here; and bird visitors, such as warblers, search for insects in the vegetation. Swallows and swifts come swooping over the water-surface to collect the emerging insects, while other bird species come to drink and bathe.

In winter when snow blankets the fieldscape many birds are unable to feed and will perish if the snow-cover persists. In this scene, near Askrigg in the Yorkshire Dales, even the walls and verges are obscured by the drifts

Birds undergo all sorts of changes in their distribution in winter, when they will move in response to changing weather and food-supply. While some species, such as swallows, yellow wagtails and whitethroats, avoid the British winters by migrating south, massive numbers of redwings and fieldfares will migrate to Britain from their breeding-grounds in northern Europe. In autumn

Several bird species flock in winter to exploit 'clumped' food-sources. Extra pairs of eyes are available for the detection of predators, but in the case of starlings time which could usefully be devoted to feeding is often invested in squabbling, though the periods spent spying for hunters is reduced by four-fifths

large flocks travel widely between the open grasslands of the downs and the adjacent farmland, scrub and copses to feed on the variety of food that is available, including wild fruits, seeds and invertebrates. Some resident species will also gather in flocks as winter approaches, making local movements in search of food. Chaffinches may join into mixed flock with visiting bramblings and forage near clumps of beech trees, such as those at Chanctonbury Ring on the South Downs, where they will devour beech mast.

In general it is birds that live on 'clumped' food, such as seeds, fruits and swarms of invertebrates, that group in flocks. There are two main advantages in living in groups: food is easier to find and there is less chance of being singled out by a predator in a crowd of fast-moving birds. Also, when many pairs of eyes are on the look-out it is harder for a predator to make a surprise attack. Group vigilance of this sort allows more time to be spent on feeding. Starlings spend a lot of time with their beaks in the ground prising out soil and litter invertebrates, and experiments have shown that a lone starling spends half its time looking around, compared with only one-tenth of its time while in a flock. The shorter daylight hours reduce the time that can be spent searching for food, so birds must spend most of the day feeding to maintain a fat reserve

which serves as insulation from cold and which can also be drawn upon when feeding is impossible. A heavy snowfall makes it hard for ground-feeding birds to find food, so instead of wasting energy in fruitless search they may not even attempt to do so, but instead continue roosting with feathers fluffed up for extra insulation. Flocking also enables young birds to learn from others where the best food-sources are to be found in winter. Usually solitary birds, wrens change their behaviour remarkably in winter to congregate in roosting flocks huddled together for warmth.

In the stone-walled limestone grasslands of the north the bird life is largely much the same as in the southern chalk pastures in spring and summer, skylarks, lapwings and meadow pipits being typical. Wheatears, summer migrants, can be seen where rabbits and sheep keep the turf suitably short and where there are rabbit holes, pavement crevices or stone walls available for nesting. Adaptable birds that they are, wrens will take up residence in stone walls, as will dippers and grey wagtails. In winter merlins may become seasonal fugitives hunting in grasslands on lower ground. A few British merlins fly across the Channel to overwinter, while others come from Iceland to spend the winter here. A serious problem in their wintering-areas is the risk of eating

Some British robins migrate in winter, when they become terribly vulnerable to the thousands of Mediterranean huntsmen who regard blasting tiny birds with shotguns as 'sport'

contaminated prey. Colin Bibby writes: '... residues of toxic chemicals continue to occur in merlins' eggs at levels that leave no room for complacency ... the problems caused by toxic chemicals may be enough to tip the balance for a species already beset with problems.' Like the merlin, golden plover and curlew will return from lower pastures and fields to their breeding-places in the hills in spring. Few pairs remain in the lower grasslands, and by the end of March their breeding activity is well under way and confirmed by their territorial flight displays. When incubating eggs or rearing young their alarm-calls, *curleek-curleek* (curlew) and *tee-tee* (golden plover), will ring eerily through the air, and because they can be heard over a considerable distance it can prove difficult to spot a calling bird.

'If new farming methods, and not climatic changes have forced lapwings to change their breeding range it is ironical that lapwings are one of the most useful birds to farmers,' remarks Brian Lee. He has found that 60 per cent of their diet consists of insects harmful to agriculture, while the other 40 per cent is of molluscs, agriculturally neutral insects and vegetative material. This bird species illustrates several effects of changing farm management. While their population, as revealed by the Common Bird Census, is shown to be fairly stable over the last ten years, it hides the fact that lapwing numbers have increased in upland pastures of northern and western Britain and decreased in the south and east. Their numbers may seem large in the south when they feed in large mixed flocks of waders in newly ploughed fields in autumn and winter, but these are largely visitors which by March will have returned to their breeding-grounds in the Netherlands, north Germany or Scandinavia. Those that breed in Britain will have wintered in Ireland, France or Spain and return to nest by mid-February.

Highest numbers of lapwing occur where there is pasture and arable land rather than areas of pure pasture. Their streaked and blotched eggs are well camouflaged on stony arable ground (though vulnerable to farm machinery), while the chicks are better-hidden in the cover of grass, and so the birds tend to move their young. Only twenty-five years ago their traditional breeding-sites were in the south and east where half the fields were under grass. Now two-thirds of all fields here are under crops, mainly cereals, and specialisation and intensification are favoured. Within this same time there has been a swing towards the autumn sowing of cereals. By the breeding season in early spring the crop is too tall and dense; the birds avoid vegetation over 3½ inches (*c*.9 centimetres) high. While spring sowing breaks up the soil, making prey more accessible when young are being raised, with autumn sowing the soil remains untouched until after the harvest. The ploughing in autumn does, of course, turn over invertebrates, but this is at a time when there is plenty of food anyway. Lapwings are said to entice worms to the surface by pattering about imitating the sound of falling raindrops; these vibrations induce the worms to emerge. Their food, and that of other insectivores, is reduced when surface-living invertebrates are destroyed by pesticides and plants which shelter and feed other insects are destroyed by herbicides.

In the north and west, where modern trends in farming have made less of an impact, a mixture of permanent pasture and scattered arable fields of winter fodder form suitable breeding-environments. The grazing animals keep the

grass short, while their manure enriches the soil and dung fauna. However, even upland havens are not entirely safe. Where hay fields are rolled, eggs may be crushed. A correspondent to the RSPB magazine tells of his boyhood days when hay fields were rolled with horse-drawn rollers and eggs were lifted from nests and returned behind the rollers: 'It was quite easy to see the nests as the birds sat on these until the last minute. Skylarks' nests were unharmed as they were always in a small depression.' In many places grass is being cut earlier for silage rather than hay. Also, the silage sward is sown densely and receives fertiliser, and so is much taller by April. Both practices are unsuitable for lapwing chicks. If livestock densities are increased where the birds nest, then more eggs are trampled. Rhys Green of the RSPB has shown that at a level of two cows per acre (0.4 hectare) 60 per cent of lapwings eggs are likely to be trampled by the animals.

The corncrake is another rather specialised grassland bird which has suffered

After they have hatched their young, lapwing parents move their chicks from arable land to pasture. The young then rely upon freezing close to the ground as protection against predators

257

as a result of changes in farming methods. The birds were common half a century ago, being particularly associated with hay meadows. Now they are largely confined to the north and west of Scotland, particularly the Hebridean islands where traditional methods of cultivation still occur, and are also said to be widespread in Ireland. The reasons for their decline in number and range is not properly understood, and in 1985 the RSPB in conjunction with the Nature Conservancy Council initiated a research project in the Machair of the Hebridean islands of North and South Uist. Mechanisation and earlier mowing of the hay harvest are suspected to be the factors largely responsible for the disappearance of the corncrake in other regions, for nests and young may inadvertently be destroyed by these practices, but there is a suggestion that variety in the habitat is also a necessary requirement. In the Uists farming methods are still traditional: cultivated strips are left fallow every two or three years, hay meadows are unintensively cropped, drainage is poor and there is comparatively little use of fertilisers. The habitat is thus suitably varied with wetter areas of marsh, large iris beds and uncultivated land in the fallow strips and at the edge of hay meadows. The Uist corncrake populations were seen to use all these niches at different times for different purposes. Strangely, although the birds seldom fly while on their breeding-grounds, each autumn they migrate 6,000 miles (9,650 kilometres) to south-eastern Africa to overwinter in drier grasslands or close to marshes and rivers anywhere between 3,000 and 6,000 feet (900 and 1,800 metres) above sea-level. While in Africa their habitat itself is under no threat, safely reaching their wintering- and breeding-grounds may be proving hazardous, for *en route* they have to cross large deserts and their routes also take them through Egypt, Sudan and East Africa where recent drought and poor farming practices may no longer offer sufficient food for 'refuelling'. The research team are attempting to determine whether our remaining populations are rearing enough young to sustain their numbers in their last few strongholds and remark: '. . . conserving some endangered species is relatively easy but for the corncrake – dependent on the traditional farming methods of cultivation – it may be necessary to conserve the crofter and his farming methods as well.' Regrettably the area is under threat. Agricultural subsidy programmes aim to increase the productivity of the land so that more fodder can be produced for wintering cattle. In 1982, 59,000 acres (24,000 hectares) of meadows and grazing land were earmarked for 'improvement' by reseeding and fertilising with Common Market grants of up to 85 per cent. Conservationists were of the opinion that it would be better if environmental funding were provided to continue the traditional systems of land-use which have produced such a delightful landscape.

Seasonally wet pastures where the traditional system of grazing management is in operation – the Ouse Washes reserve being one of the best examples (see p. 177) – will support breeding populations of sedge and reed warbler, reed bunting, yellow wagtail as well as waders such as redshank, snipe, black-tailed godwit, curlew, ruff and dunlin. Ducks, such as mallard and shoveller, may also breed here, but many more duck, geese and other wildfowl species winter in these habitats. In the Washes grazing takes place in summer only, and stock densities in each field change annually. This ensures diversity of the sward to meet the birds' different needs for feeding and nesting. Where the washfields are closely cropped by sheep in summer, softer, more palatable autumn meadow grasses, like marsh foxtail and white bent, grow. This sward best provides feeding-grounds for two vegetarian species of wildfowl, Bewick's swan and widgeon. In November, when the livestock grazing season ends, the water-level is carefully raised. By diversifying the habitat in this way, for the pasture is now under shallow water, dabbling ducks appear. Pintail, teal and gadwell can feed on the invertebrates and molluscs shifted from the grass and suspended in water by the turbulence created when the ducks move through the water. Where cattle are grazed, because of their selectivity the sward develops a more tussocky character. Under flood the tussocks are not covered by water, providing vegetable matter for the grazing wildfowl species as well as a profusion of floating seeds for the dabbling species. When the floods recede in spring the exposed and now muddy pastures are teeming with aquatic life, providing feeding-grounds for passage and resident breeding waders. In spring the clumps of taller, tussock-forming vegetation untouched by grazing cattle, such as tufted hair grass, reed grass and sedges, provide nesting-sites. Although the fields are not under water at this time of year the high water-table keeps the invertebrates from burrowing deep in the soil, and so plenty of food for insectivores is available in the breeding season and right through the summer. While considerable skill is involved in the management of the Ouse pastures, the weather may disrupt the balance now and then: in 1981, for instance, the Washes were frozen for long periods, and in summer nests were lost as a result of late flooding. While visiting wintering birds may move elsewhere in search of food, a severe toll is taken of breeding populations in such times.

When natural foods are not adequate, some bird species show a readiness to forage for 'unnatural' food. Flocks of the dark-bellied brent goose winter in a string of haunts spread around the south-east coast from The Wash to south Devon. Owing to an increase in their population – the combined result of good breeding seasons and a ban on shooting them – and a decline in their almost exclusive natural food, eelgrass, as a result of the invasion and dominance of salt marshes by a hybrid cord grass, small numbers of brent geese began to move inland to try the farmland pastures and high-protein winter cereals. 'In a matter of a few winters in the mid 1970s the food of cattle or man had quickly become that of the geese, and the conflict was born,' writes Richard Porter. While the barnacle goose has traditionally grazed cattle-pastures, the brent goose's recent liking for grass and cereals has become a new problem for farmers. On pasture the geese are accused of taking 'the early bite' intended for cattle, while the loss-yield in cereal damaged by the goose is said to be between 10 and 50 per cent 'depending on weather conditions and what might loosely be determined the "hatred factor"'. Some damage is also said to be done when their large feet cause 'puddling', while caking of the soil deters seed germination. Since the early 1980s licences have been granted to farmers in East Anglia, Sussex and Hampshire to kill a limited number of brent geese to control crop damage, while farmers are also encouraged by the Ministry of Agriculture to ensure that vigorous and efficient scaring techniques are used as soon as the geese arrive in autumn. Between 1982 and 1984, 0.7 per cent of the wintering brent geese and 7 per cent of the rarer barnacles were killed under licence. While this is particularly tragic for the latter species with a total world population of 75,000, there is hope for

Overleaf: Bewicks and whooper swans flocking in February amongst the commoner coots, pochard and mallard on the flooded pastures of the Ouse Washes

the brent goose. Richard Porter explains that the National Farmers Union agrees with conservationists that systematic scaring and limited shooting are solutions to the problem as well as 'establishing grass refuges where brent will be tolerated and payment through management agreements to farmers for their loss of yield in these areas. The problem then is how much does one pay and who pays it? Research into loss of yield is essential in determining the former.'

Farmland that embraces many kinds of habitat – small fields, pockets of woodland or hedgerows with mature trees, strips of uncultivated ground at the edges of fields, a diverse cropping programme, water-bodies, orchard, garden and outbuildings – can harbour anything up to forty different bird species of grassland and woodland. The recent agricultural trends towards greater uniformity and continuity of crops grown on larger, better-drained fields without hedgerows may seem at first to have less of an impact on birds of the open field, but intensification and reduction of wild flowers ('weeds') and invertebrates ('pests') brought about by the use of herbicides and insecticides is having a deleterious effect on both the density and variety of the farmland bird populations.

The most bare and open of fields seem to spring to life when rooks descend in their black regiments to swagger to pasture or ploughland in search of invertebrates. These and other members of the crow family are often regarded as pests by farmers and gamekeepers when the good they do in devouring leatherjackets, wireworms and other noxious insects is claimed to be offset by the damage they do to agriculture. The rook is a characteristic bird of most tree-clad farmland. Breeding rookeries may be a collection of several nests of a single colony, but a winter roost is often a focal gathering-point for many colonies in a district. Cereals and legumes form a major part of their diet in arable areas and, while bird-scarers are used to deter them by some farmers, others resort to more drastic methods such as letting off a few rounds from a twelve-bore into the nests in an attempt to arrest new additions to the population. Hatred of these birds goes back a long time: in 1424, James I of Scotland decreed the extermination of the rooks in his kingdom because they were feeding on the corn. The British rook population has fallen for several reasons. In the early 1960s rook numbers declined from the effects of organochlorides. While Dutch elm disease destroyed their favoured nesting-trees, they readily took to nesting in ash and other tall trees, but the complete removal of trees as farmland is opened up destroys nesting- and roosting-sites. Where permanent pasture is ploughed up and replaced with temporary crops of grass and clover the soil fauna is much reduced.

Rooks are not only sociable towards their own kind but also seem to tolerate the company of other birds when feeding – starlings, seagulls, thrushes and jackdaws often joining their throng. While the jackdaw is well known for its thieving habits, its cunning intelligence endears it to human beings, for it is far less persecuted than the rook and the magpie. This may also be so because jackdaws do much less damage than rooks and magpies, for their diet largely consists of animal matter. While they nest in holes in trees, they will also use crevices in buildings and are often a familiar feature of unused chimneys and derelict buildings in villages and towns; they are less tied to farmland than other crows. Jackdaw nests are lined with a variety of materials, and they will even pluck wool directly from sheep.

Magpies will, more usefully, remove parasitic larvae and flies from the backs of livestock, but this bird has suffered severe persecution for its menace of stealing eggs and nestlings of game birds. It is in fact omnivorous in diet for much of the year, depending on soil invertebrates in pasture and arable land, turning to fruit and cereals when available, but also taking advantage of any carrion it comes across. Magpies are well known for hoarding surplus food, and Eric Simms reports an individual which was seen to dig up and hide elsewhere a newly planted row of shallots on an allotment! Since the 1940s their populations have declined in some parts of the countryside but, being opportunists, large numbers have invaded the gardens and green spaces of towns and suburbs. Here in the Nidderdale we have an apparently healthy population and they are particularly noticeable in spring when small flocks come together chasing each other in short excited flights accompanied by calls that sound like hoarse laughing chatter. In the 1986 report of the Harrogate and District Naturalists' Society they were reported as locally 'becoming very numerous, even common on well-kept estates. Several flocks of 20 were reported in the spring, but in the first week of October larger flocks were seen at three separate sites where the numbers counted were 43, 35 and 53.' In the countryside they are seen to forage in the open but will spend a great deal of time in hedges and scrub at the edge of fields where they roost and nest, so their absence from southern and eastern farmland is no doubt partly due to lack of cover.

Its scavenging habit and harsh croaking call have never endeared the carrion crow to man. This species has been regarded as vermin for centuries and has long since been persecuted, but because it is a highly adaptable and versatile species it still breeds in all parts of the British Isles, and Ian Prestt regards the carrion crow as the 'second most widespread [widely distributed] bird, exceeded only by the skylark'. Being less sociable, and usually seen singly or in pairs, it is difficult to decide which is a favoured habitat, and in many areas they are absent from the fieldscape because of the continuing and often harsh persecution to which they are subjected. They feed on a wide variety of foods, including birds' eggs and any sort of carrion, but contrary to folklore rarely (if ever) peck out the eyes of living young lambs, though they may when scavenging on the carrion of a dead lamb. Being opportunists, high densities can build up in wooded areas in the vicinity of sheep-farms. They usually nest high in the fork of a tree, but where trees are scarce and there is little disturbance, as on the peninsula of Dungeness in Kent, they are known to establish territories in elder bushes just a few feet from the ground.

While the members of the crow family have been persecuted at the expense of game birds, the existence of the latter is apparently justified purely for the sake of 'sport', for the losses in cereal crops due to them – grain can constitute about a quarter of their diet – are quite considerable. Game birds in the fieldscape are represented by the grey partridge, the red-legged partridge and the diminutive quail (the last being rare since Victorian times when they were a much prized item on the menu). Pheasants, although birds of woodland habitats, are often seen feeding in open fields adjacent to hedgerows and woodland. In fact the partridges also require cover for breeding and retreat, hence the

263

The blackbird is one of the commonest of field and hedgerow birds, the hedgerows providing it with food, shelter and nesting-sites: the taller the hedge, the greater the number of blackbirds to be seen in the adjacent fields

decline in the populations of the native species in some areas since the 1950s. Apart from hedgerow removal and the lack of uncultivated land at the edge of fields, the grey partridge has suffered, like other birds of the field, from the effects of the increased use of pesticides, autumn ploughing, stubble-burning, and natural factors such as cold wet spring weather. The young, like chicks, remain in the safety of a brood but fend for themselves from hatching. Initially they are completely dependent on a diet of invertebrates, so at this time are very vulnerable to cold, wet and a shortage of food. Adult partridges extend their diet to include leaves, fruits and seeds of a variety of wild plants, chickweed being a favourite in late spring and summer, and at this stage the birds are vulnerable to herbicides. The introduced red-legged partridge has similar diet and nesting requirements, but its populations are boosted by regular new introductions.

In 1983 the Game Conservancy's Cereal and Game Research project, funded entirely by farmers, was set up to investigate the effects of pesticides, and the benefits from leaving small areas of cereal fields unsprayed. In control areas

20-foot (6-metre) strips around the edge of crops were left unsprayed with pesticides while the rest of the cereal field was treated with chemicals in the usual manner: about 2 per cent of the crop remained untreated. Within the first year, as one might expect, wild-flower species appeared in the strips, including some species, such as pheasant's eye, which had not been seen on the farm for decades! The combination of no pesticides and the flourishing wild flowers increased the invertebrate populations threefold. But more to the point of the research the grey-partridge chick survival rate increased from 19 per cent to 48 per cent and average brood size increased by two chicks per brood. The red-legged partridge and pheasant were also seen to benefit with increased brood size. While the British Trust for Ornithology, the World Wildlife Fund and the British Butterfly Conservation organisations could take advantage of such a project to study the effects of such unsprayed areas on a wider range of farm-land wildlife, it should be stressed that the aims of the project 'are to investigate the implications of such techniques to farm profits and crop yields and, where possible, to keep any losses to a minimum'!

Peter Lack writes: 'A characteristic feature of winter arable land used to be flocks of tree sparrows, finches and buntings sometimes more than a thousand strong . . . [but now] . . . a flock of more than a few tens is worth recording in southern England.' Indeed, in spring and summer farmland with hedge-lines, trees and woodland fragments could be rich in small arboreal birds. A range of factors govern the attraction of a hedgerow to birds, and different types of bird have different ideas of what constitutes the ideal hedgerow abode. For example, the ecologist G. W. Arnold has described how blackbirds and song thrushes favoured similar hedges – bushy ones which are at least 4½ feet (1.4 metres) tall to provide cover above a nest built at a height of about 3 feet (1 metre). Dr Arnold also found that

. . . whilst numbers of blackbirds, tits and dunnocks increased with hedge height, those of skylarks decreased. Increasing numbers of species of shrubs and herbaceous plants favoured gamebirds, finches and dunnocks, but had an adverse effect on numbers of doves, song thrushes, blackbirds, starlings and house sparrows. . . . The number of song thrush and blackbird territories . . . was more strongly influenced by ditch volume and cover than by other characteristics. When it came to nesting, numbers of thrush nests increased with hedge cover, but declined in the presence of trees.

The general setting of a hedge also has an effect: if woodland is part of the local environment, some birds prefer to exploit the alternative woodland nesting-sites; adjacent gardens and orchards will supplement the critical winter food-supply, though proximity to habitation and popular tracks and footpaths causes greater human disturbance. While mechanical cutting of hedges affects birds, it is not yet known how birds react to different cutting régimes. A study carried out in an area where drastic cutting was sporadic rather than annual, with little attention in between, found there was a reduction in the numbers of certain species but others maintained their total numbers by redistributing to adjacent hedges and gradually returning as the hedges regrew over the following two years. The effects of hedgerow removal are irreversible and, in our opinion, tragic when farmers received government aid to do it where rare species were nesting. In 1985 the RSPB's south-west office reported a case of a

Opposite above: The swifts
swooping above the fieldscape
are an essential ingredient of
the British summer. The legs
of the birds are so short that, if
grounded, the swift is unable to
take off again and so it chooses
nest- and roosting-sites from
which it can launch itself
directly into the air

south Devon hedgebank used as a nest site for cirl buntings grubbed out and replaced by a wire fence. In Britain there are fewer than 200 pairs of this species,
most of them concentrated in the still thickly hedged countryside of south Devon. The RSPB is strongly supporting the Hedgerow Protection Bill introduced
into Parliament by Robert B. Jones at the time of writing. The bill would prop-
ose the current Tree Preservation Order to extend to include hedgerows. Protection and the encouragement to plant new hedgerows will also exist under
schemes in ESAs (see p. 194).

One of the long-term effects of herbicides to control weeds is to deplete the
seedbank, and this has steadily decreased the numbers of birds, such as the
linnet, dependent on wild-flower seed for its food. Some species learn to adapt
to other food-sources over time with the possibility of recovering their numbers. It is emerging that some seed-eaters will readily feed on seeds of oilseed
rape, a crop that is rapidly increasing in acreage. While this phenomenon is encouraging, as yet it is too soon to evaluate the effect of this crop on the recovery
of bird populations.

By late spring our skies will be the feeding-place for swallows, martins and
swifts. While in dry conditions their prey is found high in the air, on warm
humid days the insects of pasture and hedge seem to leave their cover in gay
abandon, and swallows and martins will fly low over fields and farms catching
their prey in wide-gaped mouths. Like all migrants their numbers are declining:
swallows are said not to be badly affected yet, but for every hundred sand martins one could see twenty years ago there are now only seven. While some of the
problems lie in the United Kingdom, most of their troubles occur when they are
migrating to and from Africa. Natural hazards, such as adverse weather conditions, take an irregular toll, but in the annual annihilation by shooting and trapping no less than one in seven of all migrants passing through the Mediterranean is killed (around 900 million individuals!). The remaining birds must then
cross the ever expanding Sahara. Once over these obstacles the safety of their
rich habitats in the southern hemisphere is no longer guaranteed: wetlands are
being drained, forests felled, and pesticides are destroying their food. 'Our'
birds are in fact not ours most of the time. Alistair Gammel, RSPB international affairs officer, explains: 'The robins you so carefully protect in your garden in
spring may well end up on a Portuguese barbecue in the autumn. So while "our"
birds may benefit from our protection, they do not confine themselves to
national boundaries. To be effective [in protecting them], we ... must act
internationally.'

A variety of raptors may be seen from time to time in the fieldscape. The
story of the effects of organochlorines and DDT on populations of birds of prey
is well known, but we repeat it here because the repercussions are still felt. In
the 1950s DDT, Aldrin, Dieldrin and Heptachlor were widely used in arable
areas of eastern England, mainly to treat seeds, protecting them from insect
attack after sowing. The seeds spilled on the soil surface, and were eaten by
birds and small animals. The poisons are stored in the tissue and body fat,
which is absorbed in times of food shortage, weakening the creature, making it
vulnerable to predators or eventually killing it. Lethal amounts can grow cumu-
latively through the food-chain. Predators eating infected animals in turn concentrate these substances into their own bodies. Even if the pesticides are not

Wheatears can be common in
limestone grasslands where
rabbits and sheep keep the turf
suitably short, and where there
are rabbit-holes, pavement
crevices or stone walls available
for nesting

taken in sufficient quantities to kill the predators, these chemicals can reduce populations by causing breeding failure. Infertility, less fertile eggs, or eggs with thin shells which collapse when incubated have been the sorts of problem experienced by the infected birds. If fledglings hatched, they were vulnerable from being fed with infected prey. A series of 'voluntary' restrictions on the use of these chemicals has enabled the birds to make some recovery. The kestrel has probably seen one of the best recoveries, possibly helped by its ability to exploit the developing undisturbed roadside verge habitats where voles and other small mammals thrive: a hovering kestrel over a highway is always a spectacular, but now fairly common, sight. Sparrow-hawk populations have not fully recovered, although, apparently, 90 per cent of their potential range is now said to be occupied once again. The population is expanding slowly because breeding success is low: DDT and organochlorines are still widespread in the environment because of their persistency. The current illegal use of alpha-chloralose, mevinphos and strychnine can be added to the list of chemicals harmful to wildlife. Every single sparrow-hawk body or egg analysed since 1963 has been found to be contaminated! A shortage of food may also be a limiting factor. Although formidable hunters of the avian world, the fact that a large part of their prey is songbirds appears to be why sparrow-hawks often go hungry. Ian Newton explains:

Only a fraction of the birds that a hunting hawk encounters can be attacked with any chance of success and even then they usually detect the hawk in time to escape. A warning call from just one individual is enough to send all the small birds in the vicinity scuttling for cover . . . its passage is marked by a succession of alarm calls; and as it crosses fields flock after flock rises before it, safely out of range . . . after detection the hawk has no more than three seconds to grab the prey before it escapes.

The buzzard may formerly have bred in every British county, but intensive persecution from game interests much reduced its population to its lowest level at the turn of the century. A recovery, due to legislative protection, was dramatically hampered by myxomatosis, as rabbits formed a principal item of diet for many populations. Their versatility at finding and capturing their prey and now a more catholic diet – ranging from rabbits and leverets to adders and beetles – account for the increased population to over 10,000 pairs. The densest populations are now in the lowlands, particularly Devon and Wales, in areas of lightly wooded valleys with well-hedged meadows, though they are more easily spotted when their hunting excursions take them to open hillsides.

Much rarer are the marsh and Montagu's harriers. Though never exactly thriving in Britain, both suffered heavy persecution and loss to egg collectors, but with the passing of the 1954 Protection of Birds Act they reached a peak in the late fifties. Fenland drainage has since had a severe effect on the marsh harrier, but the crash in the population of both species by the 1970s was attributed to pesticides. By then only a single pair of marsh harriers was recorded, and for years only the odd Montagu's harrier was occasionally glimpsed, and it was thought that these summer visitors had stopped breeding in Britain altogether. Things have improved recently, for the marsh harriers have presently increased to twenty breeding pairs, and in 1986 seven nests of Montagu's harrier were reported. The resident population of the former is boosted by a small number of

Opposite. Young kestrels like these now enjoy better prospects for survival following reductions in the use of organochlorines on British farms

summer visitors, and the majority nest in the small reed beds surrounded by arable agriculture in the East Anglian Fens. The latter, however, breed *in* arable crops. It seems both are succeeding in this habitat because of the availability of prey – rabbits, rats and mice thrive in cornfields. As the harriers are the only large birds of prey to breed in lowland England, and it seems that their future is linked with farmland, it is becoming essential that farmers and landowners work with the RSPB to do what they can to protect the birds, particularly the Montagu's harrier, from the hazards of modern farming. So far their close co-operation and sympathy are said to have been unstintingly given everywhere.

Like those of the stone curlew, the eggs of the Montagu's harrier are removed and replaced behind the farm machinery to prevent them from being crushed. At this stage spraying is tolerated by the birds, for the female flies up from the nest just before the spray-boom passes and returns a few minutes later. However, the real commitment begins when the young are hatched: spraying must be carried out with care – the chicks either covered, or temporarily removed; fledglings must also be removed during harvesting or the farmer be prepared to lose a small area of his crop around the nest by leaving this uncut; and care *par excellence*, by subsidising with prey if one parent is killed and actually feeding the young if both adults are lost. The last is a heavy commitment when it is appreciated that as many as twenty items of prey are brought to the nest during the course of the day! In 1986 six pairs of Montagu's harrier raised a total of thirteen young. The seventh pair was, unfortunately, not discovered until after the nest had been destroyed by a combine harvester.

A buzzard scouring the countryside for prey, which ranges from hares to snakes and beetles

Owls are mainly denizens of the night, taking over from the diurnal birds of prey from dusk onwards. Five of the six species found in Britain may be located in the fieldscape. The short-eared owl favours grasslands such as moors, marshes and open tracts of rough farmland, their main breeding distribution lying north of an imaginary line drawn from southern central Wales to the Humber. The British population is boosted in winter by migrant birds from the Continent. Being a mainly diurnal species, it may, at this time of year, be the most frequently observed species in some parts of the north. The little owl is another diurnal species and can frequently be observed on a fence-post, tele-graph-pole or low branch of a tree. After it was introduced from the Continent during the nineteenth century this species colonised widely in the lowland areas, preferring the farmland habitat, but now is often locally scarce. While populations that suffered a decline because of persecution – as they were thought to take large numbers of chicks of game and domestic fowl – may not have fully recovered, in the last decade little owls have suffered more directly from insecticides and other effects of modern farming, for a large proportion of their prey consists of earthworms and beetles (see Chapter 12). Long-eared owls are probably the least common in the fieldscape, being very localised, and as they are nocturnal and nest and roost mainly in coniferous woodland and plantations they are not easily observed. Long-winged owls generally hunt in open country, and short-winged species are able to operate in woodland. The rather short-winged tawny is really a woodland bird but has proved so adapt-able that it is even seen in urban areas. Here in our Nidderdale patchwork of hedgerows, woods and pasture it is a very common bird of prey, and during our evening walks in autumn rarely does one not enjoy one or more individuals revealing their presence by a sharp insistent *kewick* alarm call, or several individuals hooting and echoing across the valley.

'Our islands are the northern limits of the barn owl's range, and the species would probably never have been very successful here if humans had not opened up woodlands to create fields and farmsteads,' writes Colin Shawyer. On behalf of the Hawk Trust, Mr Shawyer has recently completed the first barn owl sur-vey in Britain and Ireland for more than fifty years. His conclusions are enlight-ening. The total population in the British Isles is now 5,000 pairs, of which there are 3,800 in England and Wales, a decline of nearly 70 per cent since George B. Blaker's pioneering census in 1932. Barn conversions and lack of other nesting-sites, the usual reasons given for their decline, are in fact not a primary cause. Mr Shawyer gives the example of Hertfordshire where tradi-tional sites are intact but the population has been reduced from 210 to ten. Neither is the cause the disappearance of vole-rich meadowland, for in the in-tensive agricultural areas of the Lincolnshire fenlands barn owl numbers were 'the same as, or higher than, those in much of the traditionally farmed areas in south-western counties such as Devon'. Though it has to be said that in hay fields mammal numbers can build to coincide with the time when food is most needed to feed growing owl chicks, mammal numbers are low in fields cut much earlier for silage.

Instead the reason for their decline seems to lie in a complex combination of factors. Being an essentially tropical species and therefore unable to accumulate sufficient fat reserves, populations crash following winters when snow-cover

Above: The kitten-sized little owl is a diurnal hunter which may be seen perched on a hedgerow tree or fence lookout-post. Beetles form a large part of its diet

Opposite: The barn owl is our most beautiful predator of the fieldscape, swooping along the hedgerows on silent wings in search of voles and other rodents. Various groups are currently working to re-establish breeding pairs of barn owls in their traditional habitats

exceeds twenty days. From 1940 to 1986, twenty-one winters experienced this level of snow cover. Small rodent populations experience a three-to-four-year cycle of dramatic population-decline (see Chapter 13), and under a blanket of snow the fewer rodents are even harder to find, so rhythmical declines were seen to coincide with those of their main prey, the short-tailed vole. While the owls may have coped with climatic severity, the advent of the tractor and com-bine harvester along with improved grain storage reduced the owls' alternative food in the fields and stackyards; with the disappearance of corn-ricks went the enormous populations of mice and rats which, although a menace for farmers, were an important food-source to tide barn owls over a severe winter. Also, these days the problem of farmyard rodents is being treated with poisonous chemicals, so this prey can now be hazardous. Mr Shawyer reports that the barn owl has essentially disappeared from land higher than 300 feet (100 metres) in the north and east, where snow covers the ground for longer periods than else-where in Britain. Dr Iain Taylor reveals that, while they do nest above 300 feet in Dumfries, 'the problem with these areas is that mortality can also be

extremely high . . . the death rate of birds nesting higher than 150 m [500 feet] above sea level could not be offset by their breeding input'.

In lowland areas, however, healthy communities are threatened by being cut off in isolated pockets amongst expanses of urban land and intensive cultivation, the corridors of grassland, hedges and river meadows having been eroded, drained or lost where fields have been enlarged. Where some kind of continuity exists barn owls are seen to survive alongside modern farming. Populations have remained viable in the Lincolnshire fenlands because of a network of grassland corridors, many being roadside verges. But mortality can be high in these habitats because of the low-flying hunting techniques and dazzling by vehicle headlights: losses are enormous on roads, between 3,000 to 5,000 every year.

Where the habitat is varied, such as in Dr Taylor's study area in Dumfries – dairy farmland and well-trimmed hedges, pastures, wetland areas, ditches and numerous small areas of woodland – up to twenty-two pairs could be accommodated in an area of 225 square miles (600 square kilometres). The ideal habitat here was woodland edge, the essential requirement being a strip of rough grassland between the field-boundary and trees which supported a population of rodents. According to where they nested, Dr Taylor calculated that the best-selected sites were 'where there was at least a total of four kilometres [2 miles] of woodland edge within one kilometre [0.6 mile] radius of the nest'. However, to maintain a stable population about 5–6 miles (8–10 kilometres) of woodland-edge hunting-ground was needed per pair. Dr Taylor concludes: '. . . with more emphasis being placed on tree planting as an alternative to current overproduction of food crops more areas may become suitable, particularly if farmers are encouraged to leave grassland strips around the edges of their fields, especially next to woodland.'

Fields are not 'natural' to the British environment. Therefore the birds of the field are ones which have exploited the man-made habitats of the field, either by adapting to make use of the niches and resources that farming activities have created or by moving into the British fieldscape from natural open environments – like tundra or steppe – which exist overseas. Recent decades of far-reaching changes in the nature and management of fields have led to a general impoverishment of our fields as habitats for wildlife, and only a few species have been able successfully to exploit the new conditions without severe alterations in their populations. It remains to be seen how far the localised conservation of habitats, in contrast to the more sweeping changes, like afforestation with conifers or recreation, will affect bird populations in the years to come. But the sad fact remains that the bird life of fields that we see today is far poorer than that which our grandparents once enjoyed.

SOME PLACES OF INTEREST

The ecosystem of each location is influenced by many complex physical and management factors, and some knowledge of an area may guide one to the possible presence of the birds (and other wildlife) that may be seen there. The following locations have been suggested because they reflect a range of birds (and other wildlife) in relation to the fieldscape.

Arundel Park and Wildfowl Trust (TQ 0208). A visit to this refuge set in down-land offers the opportunity to study both the natural fauna and flora of chalky grassland and the many passage migrant and visiting birds that are attracted to the lake, reedbed and marshy fields. Information from centre on site. North of Arundel (West Sussex) along minor road to Offham.

Croxteth Country Park (SJ 4394). An area of parkland and farmland on the outskirts of Liverpool. In the varying habitats of pond, pasture and woodland, over a hundred bird species have been recorded. Information leaflet available from Merseyside Metropolitan Borough Council (Metropolitan House, PO Box 95, Old Hall Street, Liverpool L69 3EL). Junction 3 off the M57, minor roads off the A580.

Cwm Clydach. This RSPB reserve in Gwent is set in a location which is said to have the greatest concentration of unimproved meadows in southern Britain. The flora includes rarities such as dyer's green weed and whorled caraway. Birds such as buzzard, red kite and raven roam the higher slopes, and in the farmland mosaic of woods, hedges, walls, meadows and streams sparrowhawk, wood and grasshopper warbler, tree pipits, pied flycatcher and redstart are regularly recorded in summer as are large numbers of more common species. Derelict farm buildings in the area are used by a small population of barn owls. In winter fieldfare roam in hordes feeding on the berry harvests of the hedge-rows and bushes. Insects include marbled white, marsh fritillary and green hair-streak butterflies and the golden ringed dragonfly, while the scarce blue-tailed damselfly has been known to turn up irregularly in the wetter areas. Permission to visit the reserve and details of location from RSPB Wales Office (Bryn Aderyn, The Bank, Newtown, Powys SY16 2AB).

East Park (NY0565). Most of the farmland around this Wildfowl Trust Nature Conservancy Council reserve was purchased to ensure undisturbed feeding-grounds for the Solway's wintering geese and other wildfowl, but also provides attractive wintering-grounds for birds of prey such as peregrine, merlin, hen harrier and sparrowhawk. Excellent observation facilities are provided for bird-watchers when the site is open between September and April, but visitors to hides must be escorted. The most spectacular are the large flocks of geese, and on the grassland flocks of widgeon and teal congregate joined by small numbers of waders such as curlew, golden plover and lapwing. Off the B725 at Bankend and then approach on minor roads via Blackshaw.

Ouse Washes. A joint Cambient, RSPB and Wildfowl Trust reserve in Cambridgeshire and Norfolk. Although it is the birds that the Washes are visited for, particularly the winter wildfowl, the pastures are also rich in plant and insect life including some uncommon species such as the large tortoiseshell butterfly and obscure wainscot and cream-bordered green pea moths. Many mammals also inhabit the meadows, including bank vole, short-tailed vole and common and pygmy shrews, harvest mouse and wood mouse which are hunted by stoat, weasel and fox. Mammals such as water vole, mink and coypu inhabit the dikes. Access to the Ouse Washes is obtained at all times from Manea village (TL 4786). Information centre and toilets.

Rutland Water (SK 8904). The fields surrounding the second-largest man-made lake in England add to the varied habitats of the reservoir shores and lagoons, resulting in a reserve rich in wildlife. Although the reserve is important for the wildfowl and waders it attracts because it lies close to the bird migration routes along the Welland and Nere rivers, the fields around the foreshore are managed to accommodate a wider range of wildlife. Fields range from herb-rich old meadows to reseeded grassland. Some are hedgebound and others fenced but with wide headlands. The damp meadows have quite a few species of orchid in early summer as well as other more common flora. Birds recorded as breeding in the pastures and hedgerows include lapwing, both species of partridge, pheasant, meadow pipit, skylark, members of the crow and pigeon families, spotted flycatcher, greenfinch, goldfinch, linnet, bullfinch, redpoll and yellowhammer. Migrants include blackcap, chiffchaff, whitethroat and warblers which mark their territories in the reedbeds. The northern and middle sections of the reserve are restricted to permit-holders only, but the southern section is open to anyone. Carpark near Lyndon. Minor roads off the A6003 and the A6121.

Stocking Pelham (TL 4528). Although access in this Central Electricity Generating Board reserve is restricted mainly to a nature trail in spring and early summer, chalk grassland, spinneys, ponds and a particular feature, an ancient hedge, are all included. Over sixty species of bird have been recorded here, including blackcap, greenfinch, tree creeper, willow warbler and woodpeckers. North of Bishop Stortford (Essex). Off the B1383 or the B1368.

Vane Farm Nature Centre (NT 1699). An RSPB reserve in Tayside which is part of the Loch Levan wildfowl site of international importance. An excellent vantage-point on the centre's upper floor provides comfortable viewing of the loch's vast flocks of geese and other bird life. Much of the arable land is managed for the birds to provide autumn gleanings from barley and potatoes for the geese. The farm has other features which attract a variety of other birds and wildlife. A man-made lagoon offers feeding- and nesting-grounds for ducks and waders, and a small woodland attracts many of the common arboreal birds. A series of small farm streams attract a range of aquatic life. A couple of miles east of junction 5 on the M90 off the B9097.

BIBLIOGRAPHY

Many of the books that are out of print, and xerox copies of the articles listed, are generally available for a small fee through the inter-library loan services offered by local and county libraries.

ALCOCK, M. R. *Yorkshire Grasslands: a Botanical Survey of Hay Meadows within the Yorkshire Dales National Park*, Nature Conservancy Council, England Field Unit, Project No. 10, 1982.

BAKER, A. R. H., AND BUTLIN, R. A. (eds), *Studies of Field Systems in the British Isles*, Cambridge University Press, 1973.

BALAAM, N. D., SMITH, K., AND WAINWRIGHT, G. J., 'The Shaugh Moor Project: Fourth report – Environment Context and Conclusion', *Proceedings of the Prehistoric Society*, *48*, 1982, pp.203–78.

BIBBY, C., 'Making Room for Merlins', *Birds*, *11*, No. 1, 1986, pp.40–2.

BLUNDEN, J., AND CURRY, N. (eds), *The Changing Countryside*, Open University/Croom Helm, 1985.

BOARDMAN, J., 'A land farmed into the ground', *Guardian*, 18 December 1987, p.22.

BOWEN, H. C., AND FOWLER, P. J. (eds), 'Early Land Allotment', *BAR*, Series 48, 1978.

BRIGHT, P., 'To Let: Small Des. Res. for Dormouse', *Natural World*, No. 20, 1987, pp.12–15.

BROOKS, S. D., *A History of Grassington*, Dalesman, 1979.

BUNCE, R. G. H., CRAWLEY, R. V., GIBSON, R. A., AND PILLING, R., *Composition of Enclosed Grasslands*, Yorkshire Dales National Park Committee, 1985.

CANTOR, L. (ed.), *The English Medieval Landscape*, Croom Helm, 1982.

CLAPHAM, A. R., TUTIN, T. G., AND WARBURG, E. F., *Excursion Flora of the British Isles* (3rd edn), Cambridge University Press, 1981.

COUNTRYSIDE COMMISSION, *Agricultural Landscapes: Demonstration Farms*, 1984.

COUNTRYSIDE COMMISSION, *Monitoring Landscape Change*, 1986. Full report in ten volumes (each available separately) of detailed tables is available from Hunting Technical Services Ltd, Elstree Way, Borehamwood, Herts.

CROSS, E. J., 'An investigation into the factors influencing the plant communities in a Yorkshire Dales haymeadow and their implications for a management programme aimed at conserving species-rich flora', unpublished BSc thesis, University of Newcastle-upon-Tyne, 1984.

DAVIS, N. B. K., 'The Hemiptera and Coleoptera of sting nettle (*Urtica dioica*) in East Anglia', *Journal of Applied Ecology, 10,* 1973, pp.213–38.

DREWETT, P., 'Later Bronze Age Downland Economy and Excavations at Black Patch, East Sussex', *Proceedings of the Prehistoric Society, 48,* 1982, pp.321–400.

DRURY, P. J., AND RODWELL, W., 'Settlement in the later Iron Age and Roman Periods', in D. Buckley (ed.), *The Archaeology of Essex AD 1500, CBA Res Report No. 34,* 1980, pp.59–64.

DUFFEY, E., *Grassland Ecology and Wildlife Management,* Clapham and Hall, 1974, pp.201–6.

FOWLER, P. J., *The Farming of Prehistoric Britain,* Cambridge University Press, 1983.

FRAZER, D., *Reptiles and Amphibians in Britain,* Collins New Naturalist, 1983.

GAMMELL, A., 'Whose birds are they anyway?', *Birds, 11,* No. 5, 1987, pp.14–17.

GARSON, P. J., 'Social Interactions of Woodmice (*Apodemus sylvaticus*) studied by direct observation in the wild', *Journal of Zoology, 177,* 1975, p.496.

GIBBONS, R., 'Pavements in the Countryside', *Natural World,* No. 20, 1987, pp.22–4.

HALL, D., *Medieval Fields,* Shire Archaeology, 1982.

HUSTON, T., 'Batwatching', *Birds, 11,* No. 2, 1986, pp.35–7.

JENNINGS SMITH, D., *Essex Landscape No. 1: Historic Features,* Essex County Council, 1972.

KIND, C. M., 'The homerange of the Weasel (*Mustela nivalis*) in an English Woodland', *Journal of Animal Ecology, 44,* 1975, p.639.

KIND, C. M., AND MOORS, P. J., 'On co-existence, foraging strategy and bio-geography of weasels and stoats (*Mustela Nivalis and M. erminea*) in Britain', *Oecologia (Berl.) 39,* 1979, p.129.

KNEALE, W. A., AND JOHNSON, J., 'Manuring of permanent meadows 1962–70', *Expl. Husb. 22,* 1975, pp.15–24.

LACK, P., 'Birds of the Field', *Natural World,* No. 17, 1986, pp.12–16.

LARS Technical Report 96, 'Studies of the flora in arable field margins'. Available from Scientific Liaison Officer, Long Ashton Research Station, Long Ashton, Bristol BS18 9AF.

LEAN, G., AND OSMAN, A., *The Observer,* 19 August 1984, p.3.

LEE, B., *Fields, Farms and Hedgerows,* Crowwood Press, 1985.

LUFF, M. L., AND MOORE, R. J., 'Preliminary survey of insects in herb-rich meadows in the Yorkshire Dales', *British Ecological Society Bulletin XIV,* No. 2, 1983, pp.46–50.

Marston, M., 'Down the Farm', *Birds*, *11*, No. 6, 1987, pp.15–20.

Matthews, L. H., *Mammals in the British Isles*, Collins New Naturalist Series, 1982.

Matthews, R. (ed.), *Conservation Monitoring and Management*, Countryside Commission, 1987.

Muir, R., and Muir, N., *Hedgerows: Their History and Wildlife*, Michael Joseph, 1987.

Nature Conservancy Council, *The Management of Chalk Grasslands for Butterflies*, 1987.

Nature Conservancy Council, *Nature Conservation in Britain*, 1984.

Newton, I., 'A streak of lethal lightening', *Natural World*, No. 19, 1987, pp.8–10.

O'Connor, R. J., and Shrubb, M., *Farming and Birds*, Cambridge University Press, 1986.

O'Riordan, T., 'Managing Broadland', *Natural World*, No. 14, 1985, p.11.

Perring, F. H., and Mellanby, K. (eds), *Ecological Effects of Pesticides*, Academic Press (*Linnean Society Symposium No. 5*), 1977.

Pollard, E., 'Biological Effects of Shelter-Interrelations between Hedge and Crop Invertebrate Faunas', *Proceedings of Monkswood Symposium 4*, Nature Conservancy Council, 1968.

Porter, R., 'Black geese green fields?', *Natural World*, No. 13, 1985, p.28.

Prestt, I., *British Birds: Lifestyles and Habitats*, Batsford, 1982.

Probert, C., 'A New Approach', *Environment Now*, No. 4, 1987, pp.47–9.

Pryor, F., *Fengate*, Shire Archaeology, 1982.

Rackham, O., *The History of the Countryside*, Dent, 1986.

Ratcliffe, D. A. (ed.), *A Nature Conservation Review, Vol. 1*, Cambridge University Press, 1977.

Reed, M., *The Making of Britain: The Georgian Triumph 1700–1830*, Routledge, 1983.

Rees, J., 'Keep Off the Grass', *Guardian*, 22 July 1982.

Reynolds, P. J., *Iron Age Farm: The Butser Experiment*, British Museum, 1979.

Reynolds, P. J., *Ancient Farming*, Shire Archaeology, 1987.

Riley, D. N., *Early Landscape from the Air*, University of Sheffield, 1980.

Rollinson, W., *Lakeland Walls*, Dalesman, 1978.

Rowley, T. (ed.), *The Origins of Open Field Agriculture*, Croom Helm, 1981.

Royal Society for Nature Conservation, *Commons: Their Management for Wildlife*. Free leaflet available from the RSNC.

Shawyer, C., *The Barn Owl in the British Isles: Its Past, Present and Future*, The Hawk Trust, 1987.

Simms, E., *A Natural History of British Birds*, Dent, 1983.

Skinner, B., *Colour Identification Guide to Moths in the British Isles*, Viking, 1984.

SMITH, M., 'Dung Roamin', *Guardian*, 7 August, 1987, p.9.

SMITH, R. S., *Conservation of Northern Upland Meadows*, Yorkshire Dales National Park Committee, 1985.

SMITH, R. W., 'The Ecology of Neolithic Farming Systems as Exemplified by the Avebury Region of Wiltshire', *Proceedings of the Prehistoric Society*, 50, 1984, pp.99–120.

SOUTH, R., *The Moths of the British Isles*, (2 vols), Warne, 1961.

STOTT, M., 'Levels of Control', *Birds*, 9, No. 4, 1982, pp.53–5.

TAYLOR, C. C., *Fields in the English Landscape*, Dent, 1975.

TAYLOR, I., 'Ghost Bird', *Birds*, 11, No. 8, 1987, pp.9–13.

THIRSK, J., 'Origins of Common Fields', *Past and Present*, 33, 1966, pp.142–7.

THOMAS, J., 'Butterfly Countdown', *Natural World*, No. 5, 1982, pp.30–2.

THOMAS, J., *The RSNC Guide to Butterflies of the British Isles*, Countrylife Books, 1986.

WEAVER, P., 'Where have all the peewits gone?', *Birds*, 11, No. 6, 1987, pp.22–4.

WILDGOOSE, M., 'Royston Grange', *Current Archaeology*, 105, 1987, pp.303–7.

WILLIAMSON, T., 'Early Co-Axial Field Systems on the East Anglian Bouldar Clays', *Proceedings of the Prehistoric Society*, 53, 1987, pp.419–32.

WELSH, P., *A Vegetation Survey of Selected Haymeadows in Cumbria*, Nature Conservancy Council, England Field Unit, Project No. 4, 1980.

YOUNG, G., AND JACKMAN, B., *The Sunday Times Countryside Companion*, Country Life Books, 1985.

Index

Page numbers in italic refer to illustrations or figures.

Picture Acknowledgements

All the photographs were taken by the author with the exception of the following: University of Cambridge, Committee for Aerial Photography: pages 18, 65, 94, 101, 105, 113, 123. The illustration on page 76 is from the *Illustrated London News*, 15 May 1880, and on page 140 by Robin Tanner from *Wiltshire Village*, 1939. For permission to reproduce line artwork the author thanks the following: Dr Richard Hodges and Martin Wildgoose, University of Sheffield, Department of Archaeology and Prehistory – Roystone Grange Project: page 142; National Archives and Records Administration, Washington: page 33; University of Sheffield, Department of Archaeology and Prehistory, *Early Landscape from the Air*, 1980, by D. N. Riley: page 28; Warden and Scholars, Merton College, Oxford 66–7, 70, 116; Tom Williamson, *Early Co-axial Field Systems in East Anglia*, from the *Proceedings of the Prehistoric Society*, Volume 53, 1987, page 31.